PRAISE FOR *PEOPLE AS*

"A catchy name. An engagi ___ ___ ___ Attractive credibility. The list goes on and on. People as Merchandise is not another vague guide, rather a piece of art among recruitment manuals. Definitely a no-brainer for all recruiters."

Jeanne E. Branthover, Managing Director at Boyden and the World's Most Influential Headhunter by BusinessWeek

"The technological sector is probably the most demanding market when speaking about hiring experienced professionals. There will be 900,000 ICT job vacancies unfilled just in the EU, by 2015! Such a tremendous number generates enormous pressure on staffing managers who are looking for any new or improved candidate pipeline. People as Merchandise excels where others fail. I highly recommend Josef's book to any HR and staffing manager."

Horst Gallo, Director HR at IBM

"People as Merchandise is not only a social recruitment bible but also an ultimate networking guide. Being a manager at a world-leading employment agency places high demands on providing complex services. We need to recruit, network and acquire information about our prospects as well. And these subjects are exactly where Josef's book delivers."

Agnieszka Nordbo, General Manager at Randstad

"Founding and managing a 1000-employee software house is one hell of a job when speaking about talent acquisition. Our HR department is under pressure to gather suitable employees and in increasing amounts. I know Josef as a graduate of software engineering so I was a little bit doubtful about what he can bring to the table related to human resources. But I was wrong! The book People as Merchandise shows Josef's superb cross-field talent."

Vladimir Kovar, CEO at Unicorn and the Entrepreneur of the year 2008

"Recruitment work has changed a lot over the past few years and People as Merchandise opens a brand new dimension of this inevitable development. There are far more options on LinkedIn than I had been aware of, before reading this book. I will make sure that our recruitment team gets this book and benefits from it."

Hana Willett Smidlova, HR Director at Hewlett-Packard

"As a technology recruiter, I am always looking for the most effective method to search for the most qualified technology candidates. My go-to search tool is LinkedIn and it has proven to be a major key to my continued success. Once I read 'People as Merchandise: Crack the Code to LinkedIn Recruitment' I was able to hone my LinkedIn search skills to an entirely new level. With my sharpened LinkedIn skill set I am on track to grow my book of business by an additional 20% this year."

Joseph Price, Recruiting Manager at Robert Half Technology

"I have read many HR books in my life but this one definitely steps out of the crowd. In a good way of course. To be crystal clear, Josef did an awesome job! He is not afraid to reveal his secrets to success in recruitment with LinkedIn, which I really appreciate. On top of that, it is very well organized, nicely designed and original."

Stepan Marzini, Vice President HR Management at T-Mobile

"As an author, I am aware of what it takes to structure a catchy and meaningful book at the same time. I especially like the fact that People as Merchandise is revealing information considered a public secret amongst the recruiting community. That's where Josef's book is delivering its value. All entrepreneurs dealing with staffing should read this book cover to cover."

John Vanhara, CEO at Shipito, America's Fastest-growing logistics company

"My colleagues and I appreciate every new source of high-quality candidates which LinkedIn definitely provides. However, we found out that without the proper knowledge of how to use LinkedIn for recruitment, you are not able to beat your competition. People as Merchandise is the ultimate driving license for every HR professional. Feel free to contact Josef if you need to utilize LinkedIn to the highest degree. He is kind and helpful."

Daniela Souckova, Head of HR at Barclays

"Josef - you have no idea how much your book has helped me and how much time you've saved me. The description of how to source candidates from LinkedIn is covering all major aspects including the small details. I have never realized that some of the methods are even possible. People as Merchandise is definitely a must-read for all recruiters."

Martin Schneider, Head of Permanent Placement at Adecco

"As a VC, you know that it is all about people. To make a successful investment means to invest into the right people, and right after the investment to help them to get other stars on board as well. One of the most common advisory role of an investor is related to people. The book People as Merchandise makes networking and recruitment so clear and easy to understand. Josef did a great job, and I will be happy to recommend the book to the companies we invest in."

Ondrej Bartos, Partner & Chairman of the Board at Credo Ventures

"Being a tier-1 recruiter means going beyond your profession into areas, such as psychology. Do not expect that People as Merchandise is yet another superficial recruitment manual. For example, when Josef advises you to send a job proposal, he will also show you the example of such a proposal, analyze all its parts, explain their purpose and suggest other options too."

Nathan Peirson, VP Talent Acquisition and HR Operations at Vantiv

"A bit provocative, but mainly a very honest and genuine reading. Employee acquisition at an international IT company is connected with LinkedIn even more tightly than other industries. So I needed a reference guide covering this topic from scratch. The minute I started reading it, I knew it was exactly what I was looking for."

Petra Vahalova, HR Director at AVG

"When I got this book into my hands my first impression was: What a cover! People as Merchandise can definitely be judged by its cover because the book's content is equally catchy. It starts with general polemics about recruitment using social media, LinkedIn preferably, and pretty quickly goes deeper into the hands-on recruitment techniques which can be incorporated into daily operations immediately."

Tomas Brozek, Operation Manager at Manpower

"I have always considered myself a LinkedIn power user and over the years I have grown my network to more than 19,000 first line connections. However, after going through 'People as Merchandise' I realized that I have only been using a small portion of what LinkedIn offers. In my opinion, 'People as Merchandise' is the definitive book on getting the maximum value from LinkedIn -- this book is definitely about working smarter, not harder!"

Tom Bartridge, HR Director at Future Pipe Industries

PEOPLE
AS
MERCHANDISE

Crack the Code to LinkedIn® Recruitment

Josef Kadlec

ISBN 978-80-260-4174-0

1st edition

Language edit and corrections by Paul Coupland and Brian Mattison.
Cover, interior design and type set by Lenka Vansurova.

Jobs Consulting, s.r.o.
Taboritska 1083/13
Prague
ZIP 130 00
Czech Republic

www.PeopleAsMerchandise.com

To my father who died of brain cancer when I was 4 years old.

Based on that, 10% of author royalties and profits from all LINREA.com products and services go to the internationally respected research on brain cancer at the Institute of Molecular and Translational Medicine (www.IMTM.cz) in the Czech Republic.

TABLE OF CONTENTS

Foreword by David E. Perry

David Perry is a recruiting black-belt who builds executive teams for explosive growth. Nicknamed the "Rogue Recruiter" by The Wall Street Journal, Perry is a veteran of more than 1,000 search projects. He has negotiated more than $200 million in salaries and has a verified success rate of 99.7% over 25 years in the business. He is a co-author of the famous book Guerrilla Marketing for Job Hunters 3.0.

During my 25 years as managing partner of my executive search firm Perry-Martel International Inc., hardly a week has gone by when somebody hasn't launched a new 'thing' designed to eliminate recruiter's fees. People "in the know" gleefully proclaimed that job boards would stomp out the recruiters once and for all. Like most self-proclaimed prophets, thankfully, they were wrong.

The recruitment industry today is closing in on $500 billion annually in revenue while job boards fight for relevance. How can that be? The simple answer: recruiting is a people business, it always has been and always will be. But the industry has changed – for the better in my mind – and it will continue to evolve, albeit at a faster pace. Will you keep up?

In the fall of 2008 *The Wall Street Journal* nicknamed me the *"Rogue Recruiter"*. We all had a good laugh at the office, but the label fit and not solely because of the unconventional approach I took to hunting down the best people for my clients or my unapologetic take-no-prisoners attitude. It fit because my book, *Guerrilla Marketing for Job Hunters*, had ripped the lid off of job search secrets and recruiting tactics that were previously known by only a handful of America's wealthiest recruiters.

Many people will also be angry when they finish this book. You shouldn't be one of them – but I'll get to that.

When I wrote *Guerrilla Marketing for Job Hunters: 400 Unconventional Tips, Tricks and Tactics for Landing Your Dream Job*, it was for the express purpose of teaching the unemployed how to find their own job and not rely on recruiters. At the time I singled out a little known social networking site called LinkedIn. I remember thinking to myself, "Here's the Monster killer". As the 113,709[th] member I saw its potential early, singling out LinkedIn in the book as my social networking platform of choice for recruiters AND job hunters.

Today LinkedIn is an 800 Pound Gorilla: job boards are a mere afterthought.

Today, scarcely a week passes when a new book on LinkedIn doesn't cross my desk with a request for an endorsement. I always decline. While these books may all be written with the best of intentions, many of them lack any practical ideas, strategies or techniques proven to help recruiters uncover top talent. It's with that bias that I agreed to read *People as Merchandise: Crack the Code to LinkedIn Recruitment*. By page 19, I was hooked, highlighting complete pages and writing notes. Josef Kadlec really gets it!

One of the reasons I'm so impressed by what Josef has written is that his focus never veers off course. Every page, every idea, every example is written with a singular purpose: to educate recruiters on how to use LinkedIn to drive their business forward. Not only does he cover the topic in terms of the critical issues that need addressing, he presents it in clear, logical steps that you can apply immediately and that can put money in your pocket today, all the while helping you build a prosperous business.

This is not a book written by another would-be 'LinkedIn Guru' trying to establish a speaking career. Nor is Josef someone who's been observing the action on the frontlines from the safety of the sidelines. No, Josef's an unrepentant *head-hunter*. He grew up on the mean streets of contingency recruiting where you eat what you kill - where you learn to hunt aggressively - and where "personal production" is the key to your personal success. This is an environment where people are too often treated like merchandise to be bought, sold and traded to the highest bidder.

The wisdom gained from his time as a contingency recruiter has enabled him to break out on his own. Josef has ascended the noisy marketplace of the common recruiter and established a trusted advisor role with both his clients and prospective candidates, at a time when LinkedIn has disintermediated the recruiter's role as middleman, enabling employers and candidates to meet directly.

In the old days (5 years ago) recruiting was akin to a two dimensional board game. It allowed a recruiter a leisurely amount of time to send out requests for resumes, which could then be judged along a price/

performance axis. It allowed for a precise, two dimensional axis and a recruiting process so structured and simple that judgments could be handled by a corporate human resource department's less skilled staff. Now the world moves in three dimensions, at a speed more resembling a video game. It's zap or get zapped, in real time. In such a fast paced dogfight you need to define your missions very carefully: no wasted energy, no blurred vision. Today employers will only pay a fee for 'passive candidates', so it's even more important to find the best people. Ironically, the candidates you're looking for are not looking for you. They already have a job - almost certainly a good one. So how do you find someone who doesn't raise a hand and say "Here I am?"

Employment agencies which use advertising to recruit candidates typically yield the "Best of the Unemployed", the "Best of the Unhappy" and the "Best of the Unqualified". Truth is the winners and achievers you want are busy winning and not surfing the job boards or registering with employment agencies. They may have a LinkedIn profile, but if they do, it'll be light on specifics.

We're all familiar with the recruiting call that starts "… who do you know…", it's the hallmark of an inexperienced recruiter, hoping you'll say: "why that person you described is Me". The over-used ploy today nets the response: "I don't know anyone…" and a prompt hang-up. This conventional and unimaginative approach ends quickly and doesn't garner the recruiter an opportunity to present the career opportunity, pique their interest, or qualify their background. Prospects hang up quickly because the caller is deemed to be unimpressive.

Candidates today are more sophisticated than ever and expect recruiters to be professional and knowledgeable. So many people are now aggressively managing their own careers, that if they are going to talk to a recruiter, they want someone who can speak with them, about their industry and their challenges. As a recruiter you need instant credibility, spontaneous bonding and respect – in less than 5 seconds – on your first phone call. Winners recognize winners and they're not going to waste time telling you something obvious.

Traditional recruiters are human resource amateurs, and that is why the placement industry has such high turnover. These unprepared people get shot down in flames by yet another prospect before they even get a chance to tell the story of the opportunity.

How you attract and land the star candidate you want requires rethinking your approach. How do you meet the needs of the human being you're dealing with and the performance expectations of your client, while still putting food on the table every day?

I'm not going to spoil the ending… suffice it to say, *People as Merchandise* provides the strategies and tactics needed to create relationships that transcend the current transaction mentality in the industry. You will be viewed as resourceful and relevant to the people you serve, be they clients or candidates, and you'll do it by leveraging LinkedIn and you'll NEVER have to pay to upgrade your account.

Many people will be upset after *People as Merchandise: Crack the Code* to LinkedIn Recruitment is published. You won't be one of them. You will be the 'career advisor' candidates trust and the headhunter who always delivers the 'right stuff' for employers.

In the immortal words of Mr. Spock, "Live long and prosper".

The future is in your hands,

DAVID E. PERRY
www.linkedin.com/in/davidperry

Ottawa, Canada
April 20 2013

The Target Audience

This book is for anybody who is dealing with recruitment activities regardless of their level of LinkedIn® knowledge. No matter if you are a LinkedIn® beginner, maybe even without a LinkedIn account yet, or you use LinkedIn for recruitment purposes on a daily basis, you are going to benefit from this book considerably.

Just having a LinkedIn account and using basic features is not rocket science, nor does it make you an expert. The science starts when you go after lasting positive results, utilizing LinkedIn for recruitment on a daily basis and a lot more. Then you hit a wall if you do not know how to use LinkedIn® properly, and your competition will squeeze you like a lemon.

This book is intended for:

- Internal, Agency and Freelance Recruiters
- Headhunters
- Recruitment Consultants
- Executive Search Consultants
- Hiring and HR Managers
- People Sourcers
- HR generalists
- Researchers
- Talent Miners
- Corporate and Agency Recruiting Teams
- Entrepreneurs and Startupreneurs
- Anybody else involved in hiring people.

This book is not industry dependent. You can be in the Information Technology, Pharmaceutical, Finance, Automotive, Health or Construction business and benefit from this book equally.

My Success Story and Why You Need This Book

My Success Story and Why You Need This Book

Every day for a year and a half after graduating from university I was going to my regular full-time job as a software engineer. All of sudden I had a "side" income that multiplied my salary more than five times over. I was 25. From nothing I purchased my very first car, a new Audi A6 sedan, a luxurious flat with some nice pieces of art and a couple of LVs for my girlfriend. I had cash, money. End of story.

Not bad for a software engineer with 1 year of experience, right? The dark side of the story is that I basically lived by my computer screen. You have to do what it takes.

How did I do it?

I saw a gap in the market with IT specialist recruitment which I tried to take advantage of. IT professionals were, and still are, simply in high demand. I established a personnel agency providing corporations with IT specialists. As a hardcore techie I had never planned to have a recruitment business at all. But it fulfilled all my needs including creativity, being motivated by results and communication with people. All of this I lacked at my regular job, which was the initiator in changing my life avenue.

I believe that having a background OUTSIDE of the human resources industry provided me with the necessary point of view to be successful at the beginning. I was not inspired by the competition at all. As a software engineer I was hired by one recruitment agency, a big one, and I wondered how their business could run with such ineffective procedures. Arranging a personal interview at the personnel agency took such a long time, and I still didn't know the company I was applying to until the end of the interview!

It was unbelievable from a current perspective.

I looked at the problem from the perspective of a potential candidate and decided to set new standards, including naming the targeted company, providing instant feedback to all candidates and working with them even if they were unsuccessful the first time. These were the weapons I used to penetrate the competitive recruitment industry.

Did I piss off some of the big players in the recruitment world?

You bet I did! Some of them were calling my company clients to cancel contract agreements with my agency, unsuccessfully. There was no reason to do this. I was delivering desperately needed merchandise, where others had failed. After some time the majority of agencies were forced to accept my new standards and implement them into their own procedures to stop losing money.

I was not satisfied with the number of incoming resumes from my own recruitment website, so I was looking for other sources which I could actively use. At the beginning, I had no idea that there was something like LinkedIn®. At that time LinkedIn was far less popular than it is now and had only a small number of users.

Without any previous knowledge, I tried LinkedIn® and it worked, more or less, even if there were a fraction of the current number of users. On the other hand, there were no other similar recruitment websites so LinkedIn became my main resource for finding successful candidates.

Nowadays you **avoid LinkedIn at your peril!** LinkedIn is saturated with potential candidates, but also with many recruiters, so you have to be really skilled at using LinkedIn to be a successful recruiter.

Currently, I focus on only a few pre-selected company clients where I provide potential candidates. I am hiring only senior and key employees, usually for above standard commission. For some IT professionals, my agency is the only one which can deliver results, therefore my clients can easily pay me 30% of a candidate's annual salary.

However, I have to decline other recruitment offers. Unfortunately, I cannot represent many market players because I need to have them as a resource for my headhunting. My agency and I are the tools of the hidden war in search of obtaining in-demand employees.

Even if there are many books about LinkedIn, there is no solid book about LinkedIn for recruiters, which is a completely different ball game. This is why I decided to write this book and to create a LinkedIn recruitment academy called LINREA.com, which have become the major resources of LinkedIn knowledge for recruiters and other HR people.

My motivation for doing all of these things is that I like to positively influence people. If my candidate is successfully hired, with my assistance, and tells me that their new job is the best change in his life, there is nothing more satisfying. It gives my work purpose and empowers me to continue pushing the flywheel. I would like this book to have a similar positive effect on others and I hope it will help many of you to move forward.

On top of all this, I hate the average, often poor quality, not to mention, lousy approach to work. This is why you can expect that **this book will be extraordinary.**

There are three main reasons to read this book:

1) Become a world class LinkedIn recruiter. This is not a guide where you can expect descriptions of how to set up a LinkedIn® account or any other such basic features, unless they are important. I expect that you are PC literate, so I will get straight to the important points.

2) Learn from the best or die like the rest. This book is written by a recruiter for recruiters. So do not expect any copy & paste from Wikipedia. Get the relevant knowledge from top world recruiters and become one yourself.

3) Benefit from many revealed shortcuts. As a former ethical hacker I cannot break my habits. Therefore, you can expect that some helpful hacks will be unveiled including:

- How to uncover a full view of LinkedIn profiles of potential candidates without upgrading to premium

- How to override the limit of the number of invitations

- How to search through groups you cannot join

- How to use search engines to scan LinkedIn for candidates

- How to automate candidate searches

- How to track the steps of your competition on LinkedIn

- And many others…

How This Book is Organized

Each chapter starts with a summary of important facts and issues we are going to solve in that chapter. In addition, each chapter also has a conclusion with a summary of strategies and hacks revealed in that chapter.

Some of the topics covered in this book might be a bit modified due to LinkedIn development. Therefore, do not forget to check LINREA.com for potential up-to-date information. You will find many helpful tools for social recruitment there as well.

When this book makes your career a success story, let me know about it at **josef@peopleasmerchandise.com**. I can publish your own story in the extended edition of this book.

Disclaimer

The material in this book is for informational purposes only. The author and publisher expressly disclaim responsibility for any adverse effects that may result from the use or application of the information contained in this book.

Happy headhunting,

JOSEF KADLEC

Livigno Ski Resort, Italian Alps
January 9 2013

01

Introduction: It's Personal, Not Just a Business

Introduction:
It's Personal, Not Just a Business

People as merchandise, how can this not be personal? In the recruitment business you have to get results as an individual. Usually, you are not part of a bigger system where you can hide your incompetence.

Without immediate results you are out of business and this affects your life in some way. Regardless if you are a freelance recruiter, internal or agency recruiter or the owner of a company, you are forced to create instant impact.

When I was younger, I remember a recruiter crying and begging me to attend job interviews so that they could get a highly needed commission. That is not a position you want to be in. It is do or die. So when some of your competitors steal your commission, it is damn personal. You'd better be smarter than they are.

On the other side, as a recruiter you can influence other people's lives as well. In a positive way in most cases, I hope. Changing a job is not an iota. It can influence a prospect's career, family life and, not least, their happiness. So play this game right and, preferably, in the interests of your candidates. **Take care of your candidates and commissions will come automatically.**

Personnel Agencies Annihilation

The current world trend is obvious. Companies looking for new talent are cutting costs on everything, the staffing costs included. On the other hand, personnel agencies have to deal with a lack of efficiency where job advertisements are concerned.

Of course the tension is different between industries, but in general, if you are hiring experienced specialists, you would more likely face this problem. So both companies and recruitment agencies are facing the same problem. How to deal with the situation of plunging influence? The answer is **direct social search** in all its forms – executive searches, headhunting, whatever you want to call it.

Unless your company has a brand like Google, Zappos or Red Hat, which belong to the 'best employers' according to the official awards and employees in their industries, you are literally forced to use direct searches to create your candidates pipeline.

But don't worry, most of the best employers receiving thousands of resumes per day must use direct search as well. Usually for highly skilled specialists with some niche expertise and the right company culture fit or employees for not so saturated locations.

This also shows how human resource departments have to work more and more closely with marketing and sometimes sales departments as well. This is a reason why recruitment agencies have to transform to survive and recruiters should become the world's best marketers and brand ambassadors. Hiring people is not as simple as it was.

Social Recruitment = LinkedIn®

LinkedIn® (abbreviated as LI) is one of a kind. Its direct competitors Viadeo and XING have about 45 million users together. Facebook, Google Plus and Twitter are irrelevant. Monster's BeKnown is trying to penetrate the professional social networking market but it is still rather at the beginning, and the question is: 'Are these organizations capable of becoming a serious threat to LinkedIn®?'

Let's look at the facts:

- LinkedIn has over 175 million members (Jan 2013) and growing
- Two new members every second
- Impact across 200 countries
- The 13th most visited website on the Internet.

In addition, the structure of LinkedIn members is as follows:

- Average income of LinkedIn users is more than $80,000
- 69% of them earn $60,000 or more per year

- 74% of them have a college degree

- 2 million are C-level executives.

This is why LinkedIn® is our main reservoir of potential experienced candidates, and fresh university graduates who will most likely be experienced in the future.

> **NOTE**
>
> You can check how the number of LinkedIn users has been increasing since 2003 at WaybackMachine (www.archive.org). For instance, at *figure 1.1* you can see how LinkedIn looked in August 2004 when it had "only" 3.8 million users.

Find People
Clients, partners, sales leads and experts

Find Jobs
Top jobs and the most reputable candidates

Find Services
Recommended services and new customers

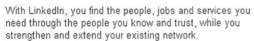

And find them through the people you know and trust

With LinkedIn, you find the people, jobs and services you need through the people you know and trust, while you strengthen and extend your existing network.

➡ **Take our tour**

LinkedIn is free   **Join Today**
Join over 3.8 million other professionals now

Figure 1.1: LinkedIn in 2004 with only 3.8 million users

I Already Use LinkedIn®, So What Do You Want to Teach Me?

Doubters, attention! You probably already use LinkedIn in some way, but the question is, can you utilize LinkedIn for recruitment with maximum effectiveness? Remember that it does not matter if you have 1,000 or 10,000 direct LinkedIn contacts and maintain a group of 10,000 or 100,000 members, as many other LinkedIn books are suggesting you do. **If it was a simple matter of the amount of contacts you had, all LinkedIn recruiters would be equally successful.**

Quantifiers like, for example, the number of LinkedIn contacts are relative to the market you are influencing. A recruiter actively working across the USA will ultimately have significantly more direct contacts than another recruiter working in significantly smaller Spain. But it says nothing about their effectiveness. The Spanish recruiter can easily be more successful in terms of hired candidates than the US one. The completely same analogy works for each recruitment industry – whether you are a recruiter in finance, IT, utilities or maybe you just seek IT specialists for the SAP platform.

The vast majority of books about LinkedIn® I have seen and read are focused on how to increase sales over LinkedIn. These books provide general best practices for making sales via LinkedIn but the problem is that as a recruiter, you have completely different requirements. Some of the so-called best practices are going against your interests as a headhunter – e.g. accepting all invitations you receive. It's rather vague advice. Additionally, you will find no real recruitment methods and strategies in such books at all; just general advice and vague descriptions of basic features, which are good only for newcomers to LinkedIn®.

I am going to show you nothing more than thorough, hands-on procedures which utilize LinkedIn for the recruitment business. Remember, **I do not work for LinkedIn so you can be sure I will not be pushing any LinkedIn paid services.** My approach is completely the opposite and independent.

There is no need to spend a dime. I tested the premium membership and other paid services for you, so I can tell you what they are worth. I will also publish some of the **"blackhat" recruitment methods** which other books do not mention, even if they are aware of them. Stay tuned.

Direct Search is Pretty Nasty

Readers of this book might or might not be familiar with LinkedIn. But I assume that they are intelligent and PC-literate, so I will not be describing general knowledge everybody knows, but I will get straight to the core of LinkedIn recruitment.

As a former software engineer and mathematician I appreciate an analytical approach, which really gave me the competitive advantage in this field; based on this, I became a successful recruiter. My background provided me with the needed 'out-of-the-box' view of the recruitment problem. As I see it from the current perspective, my recruitment approach was pretty hardcore day in, day out. It was a race. I did so many tests and experiments. Most of them failed, but if they worked, they worked big time.

Now I am at a stage in my life that I would like to share this knowledge with you. There is no way I would have done this a few years ago. Why? I was a player trying to reach the highest score amongst the other players in recruitment. More than money, the number of hired employees and commissions for them were only points for me.

This score represented successes for me. I did not want to reveal my secret key to success. I had great discipline for everyday work, not going on vacation for five years, for example, because it could ultimately influence my 'score' which was proportional to the time spent on recruitment.

It led to great results – I became the top recruiter for one IT corporation in terms of the number of placements. That was a great achievement on its own, but I ran a one-man-show against other local and international personnel agencies which have people power and all the other advantages to be successful. As you can imagine, they wanted to get rid of me.

I was a headhunter, a headHUNTER in a crowd of other hunters trying to catch a fish in the same pond. That is what we are, hunters. There is no avoiding this fact. Sometimes it is not pleasant because we must hunt to survive. On one side, we serve a company with a candidate, on the other, we hurt another company by taking their employee. It is how it is. It is impossible to do good for everybody every time. You have to choose who to support and decline the rest. I am declining offers for recruitment cooperation every month.

Frankly, I have never had friends amongst recruiters. Firstly, I came from a different business sector and secondly, I did not want to be influenced by the conventional methods of the vast majority of them. I had my own methods and procedures and now I believe it was the only way to succeed. **Going with the mainstream cannot bring anything new to the table.** So stepping out of the crowd requires thinking out-of-the-box.

For instance, immediately, at the very beginning of my

recruitment career I began with a policy of not hiding the name of the targeted company to potential candidates. My logic was that if the only tool you have to persuade a candidate to use your service is a hidden company name, you offer a lousy service. I was looking at the problem from the candidate's perspective because I had been a candidate looking for a job; this was the first dumb thing I noticed. There were more things I didn't like, but I started my recruitment business without hiding company names and... it paid off!

Of course it is not as simple as it looks, but it shows how I looked at the problems in the recruitment industry. I wanted to **change the recruitment sector in favor of candidates**. I think I achieved that, at least partially. A few years later, other recruitment agencies were implementing the same approach I started. They were naturally forced to.

Recruitment 5.0

A new direction for the recruitment business was already defined which should completely change in the near future. Some companies are already trying to implement some of the aspects of recruitment 5.0. It is not only about building and driving value.

The defining features of Recruitment 5.0:

▪ Mobile recruiting finally takes off and becomes the dominant channel

▪ Recruiting gets back to basics and focuses on building relationships. Included in this is a focus on personalization driving communications

▪ Footprints in the cloud. Companies obsessively get to know their customers/consumers, and recruiters do the same with their "corporate" talent pools

▪ Data DNA: Companies draw data to profile candidates based on online habits and trends

▪ Technological developments bring an end to the traditional ATS/CRM (Applicant Tracking System/Customer Relationship Management)

▪ Emerging markets emerge and dominate

- Augmented reality and disruptive marketing dominate recruitment marketing

- As companies seek to attract the best talent in a candidate-weak market, they set up their own courses, universities/academies, and "clone" future employees

- As talent becomes more scarce, talent becomes more contract based by nature and more flexible

- It is the end of recruiters as we know it ... maybe even the death of the recruiting profession?

Focus on Your Candidates

There is nothing better than when a candidate you placed into a company tells you that it is the biggest step forward in their life or that he/she has never met such an extraordinary recruitment service like yours. The main concern of the recruiter should be the candidate's interests; everything else should be second to that.

This is why I moved from the everyday recruitment race to the next stage of my life and started a training business, while continuing with recruiting. It wasn´t too demanding. I found ways to delegate and work in a team but the procedures did not change.

I realized that the so called recruitment score is not everything and I felt that it was time to change my life avenue again, which is the reason why I established a LinkedIn recruitment academy called LINREA.com.

I started as a technical candidate hired by an external recruiter, moved on to being an IT recruiter hiring technical candidates and finally became a recruitment trainer helping recruiters to follow the current trends in headhunting. An almost idealistic evolution, isn't it?

Similarly to recruitment, it's a great feeling when you are told that your training is the best training a trainee ever attended. These are the things that push me forward, providing top-notch and valuable services, because mediocrity is damn boring.

As I said earlier in this chapter, I had great discipline for everyday work. It was hard work to get where I am but it was worth it in the end, especially when I found myself on a great vacation on the French Riviera.

02

Modern Headhunter: Up-to-Date Recruitment with LinkedIn®

Modern Headhunter: Up-to-Date Recruitment with LinkedIn®

What you will learn in this chapter

- How to use social recruitment to hire talent

- How LinkedIn® changed the world of recruitment

- What is the principal LinkedIn® recruitment strategy

Contest: LinkedIn vs. Old-Fashion Recruitment

Recruitment is expected to increase worldwide, but budgets are not keeping pace. That is the reason companies need to find other ways of hiring people than just using personnel agencies. Personnel agencies are pushed to decrease their commissions and companies are using their own internal recruiters more and more, who are substituting external recruiters and recruitment agencies.

As an example, the company Adobe Systems, employing 10,000 people, was using external personnel agencies for their recruitment. Before the existence of LinkedIn® there was basically no other way to find suitable candidates because company job advertisements were ineffective. They simply did not work, especially for experienced candidates like IT professionals.

After a period of LinkedIn activity on the market, Jeff Vijungco, who was in charge of talent acquisition at Adobe Systems, arranged a contest between two teams. The instructions were: Find 50 suitable technical candidates for our company. One team was using advertisements and external agencies and the second was using LinkedIn®. The LinkedIn team found 50 candidates after only a few hours! The second team said that they were almost done after a few weeks of work.

That is how Adobe Systems is saving millions of dollars on recruitment costs. External recruiters must be satisfied with only 2% of recruitment volume. The list of such companies could go on and on. For instance, only every 70th candidate is hired by an external recruitment agency at the company Red Hat.

Social Recruitment as a New Trend

As you can see, you cannot ignore LinkedIn if you take the recruitment business seriously. Do not expect that LinkedIn is just a short-term thing. The LinkedIn Corporation had a very successful IPO, the value of their shares soared 64% just in the year 2012, and their revenue estimate was 895 million dollars. Their profits for 2012 were estimated at 70 million dollars which was approximately a 71 to 100% increase compared to 2011.

As an overview of the industry, the largest companies providing candidates with the 'old fashioned' methods are facing a drop in their share prices. For example, Monster Worldwide lost about 81% and Heidrick&Struggles lost 67%, which demonstrates where the market focus is.

The aforementioned data was obtained as a result of estimates from CNN, CBS, etc., which showed that only 20% of jobs are filled by people responding to job ads. This means that the other **80% of jobs are filled informally by social recruitment**, internal recommendations, etc. In alignment with these statistics, we must take into account that only 20% of all possible openings globally are advertised through mainstream advertisement channels.

Somebody recruiting electricians, welders or bus drivers can disagree with this trend by claiming that an advertisement and an old fashion interview work as well as they always have. And I agree. For those kinds of vacancies you should stick with the old methods. If you are hiring specialists and experienced candidates, switching from the old methods to LinkedIn is better suited for you, regardless of whether you are looking for candidates in pharmaceuticals, IT and finance, or if you are looking for managers and executives.

In terms of business continuity, I would trust LinkedIn more than, for example, Facebook which has about five times more users (about 900 million), but is struggling to make money. Facebook has a different philosophy which makes it an undesirable tool for recruitment. This is not just my opinion; the facts can be found in the LinkedIn® Global Recruiting Trends Survey 2011. We have to take into account that this survey was issued by the LinkedIn Corporation itself. However, there is no doubt that it is in alignment with the trend of recent years. In the survey, over 4,300 respondents were consulted with the positions of HR generalists, internal recruiters and recruiters from external recruitment agencies (*see figure 2.1*).

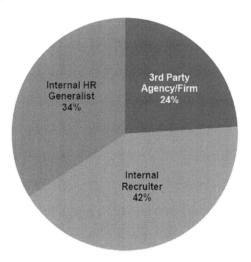

Figure 2.1: LinkedIn Global Recruiting Trends Survey 2011: Respondents Composition

These respondents were most likely to recommend LinkedIn as the major tool for social recruiting (*see figure 2.2*). This is why you should utilize LinkedIn the most.

There were some concerns about the localization of LinkedIn to languages other than English and that localization might compromise the level of network professionalism. It might have encouraged non-professionals to sign up who were not fully aware of the purpose of LinkedIn. Therefore, LinkedIn users were forced to use only English which guaranteed, to some extent, global continuity. However, these concerns were false so we do not have to expect that LinkedIn® will transform into a Facebook-like environment.

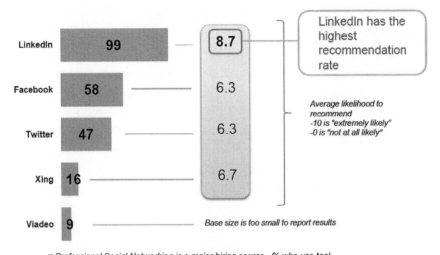

Figure 2.2: LinkedIn Global Recruiting Trends Survey 2011: Social Recruiting Tools Recommendation

Respondents to the survey also uncovered their main pressures, which correspond with my own research (*see figure 2.3*).

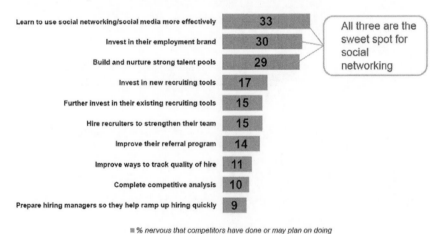

Figure 2.3: LinkedIn Global Recruiting Trends Survey 2011: Top Competitive Pressures

Gaining an advantage by mastering social recruitment, via LinkedIn® especially, is the only way to succeed in this brutally competitive industry. This trend is valid globally, not only in the USA. It does not matter if you are a recruiter in the Netherlands, UK, Canada or

Australia; you have to face the following trends:

- Utilizing social and professional networks

- Finding better ways to source passive candidates

- Upgrading employment branding

- Training recruiters and hiring managers on "How to Hire A-level Talent".

The current LinkedIn corporate strategy is to focus right on the recruitment business and completely take it over. You can see this because LinkedIn is launching a lot of new features directly targeted at recruiters and hiring companies, including all the premium or paid accounts for recruiters, such as Talent Finder, LinkedIn Recruiter, etc. Also, there are smaller features like the *Apply with LinkedIn* button which you can place on your company website and receive professional profiles directly from LinkedIn®. We will come back to these features in later chapters.

LinkedIn® Database is Better Than Any Internal Database

Now that we know that social recruitment is an inevitable trend and that LinkedIn is the major player in this sector, we can take things a step further to the core of the LinkedIn tool; and not only the tool, but the whole methodology. To see the bigger picture we will go beyond LinkedIn.

Apart from social recruitment itself we will also touch on things like:

- Online marketing

- Recruitment psychology

- Business writing

- And also a little bit of digital security.

Without crossing the borders of LinkedIn as a tool or website, you will not be as successful. You also need to be flexible. I will describe special legal hacks such as how, for instance, to override the maximal amount of invitations by using more browsers or how to uncover hidden user profiles with Google. These are the details which make a very good headhunter a great one. **These small details can mean the difference between success and failure.**

Do not flow with the mainstream.

LinkedIn provides us with hundreds of millions of potential candidates. Your internal database can only dream of being so vast. But the main advantage of the LinkedIn database is that it updates automatically. Once you buy some 3rd party database, it is already obsolete, as is the one you are maintaining internally. LinkedIn is providing you with up-to-date information, if it is the candidate's will, and you are automatically notified of any changes.

LinkedIn should become the 'diary' for the 21st century. The thing without any recruiter, headhunter or hiring company cannot image functioning. If you think about how LinkedIn changed the world of recruitment till this time, you can easily believe this.

The merit of such a database or diary is that it is not just a list of independent items. You can see the relationships between the items (i.e. users). This is crucial to recruitment nowadays, because you can easily ask for recommendations for your candidates, even before you contact him or her. Referrals are the most highly rated source for a candidate's quality. Regardless of whether your candidate is an active or passive job seeker, you can simply ask some of his previous bosses or coworkers, discretely of course.

Maybe you are wondering: 'Do I really have hundreds of millions of potential candidates at my disposal?'

Yes and no. It is not that straightforward.

The tricky part is that you are not allowed to reach all of them easily. The LinkedIn Corporation has to earn money, so they are putting obstacles in your way which can be removed by paying some sort of fee; or they can be overridden with some tricks, as we will find out later. The other reason of course is the quality of the network and security. It would not be reasonable to be able to just download all LinkedIn® users and spam them as you please.

The amount of potential users you are able to screen is dependent on the following:

- Number of your direct connections (your 1st degree connections)

- Number of your 1st degree connections' direct connections (your 2nd degree connections)

- Number of your 2nd degree connections' direct connections (your 3rd degree connections).

If you already have a LinkedIn® account, you can figure out the number of your 1st, 2nd and 3rd degree connections on your LinkedIn profile homepage in the section *YOUR LINKEDIN NETWORK* (*see figure 2.4*).

YOUR LINKEDIN NETWORK

615 Connections link you to
        3,966,823+ professionals

5,859 New people in your Network
         since January 6

Figure 2.4: Your LinkedIn Network

The first large font number is the number of 1st degree connections, the second large font number is the number of 2nd degree connections and the small font number, usually shown in millions, is the number of 3rd degree connections.

Why are they important to us? Each degree is connected with some level of restriction we as headhunters must deal with.

1st degree connections can be contacted via the *Send a message* function without any restrictions (*see figure 2.5*). You can also see a potential candidate's full profile.

2nd degree connections can be contacted only by using the *Connect* function, which itself hides some further pitfalls (which I will explain further in the text), or you can use the *Get introduced* function which is not very effective as it is dependent on other people who are not usually interested in an introduction. And finally, the *Send InMail* premium function can be used (*see figure 2.6*), although this feature is paid.

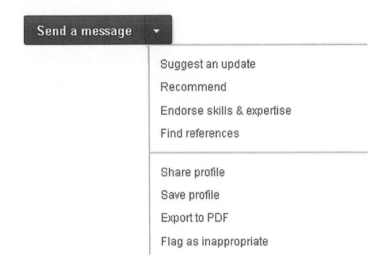

Figure 2.5: Contact options for 1ˢᵗ degree connections

Figure 2.6: Contact options for 2ⁿᵈ degree connections

Even if you pay for this premium feature it does not substitute the main networking stream for recruiters because it is very limited in terms of volume. Such a connection's profile is fully visible – only it excludes their contact information fields. If there is an e-mail address anywhere else in the profile, it is fully visible.

3ʳᵈ degree connections can officially be connected only by the *Get introduced* and *Send InMail* functions (*see figure 2.7*). Also, you cannot see the user's surname (just the first letter of it). This restriction was not there at the beginning, so you can see that LinkedIn® is adjusting their settings and literally making their restrictions stricter. Also, the 3rd degree profiles, except for a brief beginning, are not visible. But do not worry. I found an elegant trick to deal with this in the majority of cases. I will present this to you in further chapters.

Figure 2.7: Contact options for 3rd degree connections

I will show you ways to repress these restrictions so that you do not have to care about them at all. I told you, we are hunters and it is a dirty job from time to time which must be done.

> **NOTE**
>
> LinkedIn is currently on the brink, in early 2013, of implementing significant changes affecting the design of LinkedIn profiles and potentionally more. For example, there will be a completely new system of LinkedIn applications. At the time of writing this book, your profile has probably been transferred to the new type. Due to this, LinkedIn users are currently facing quite a lot of glitches which will be fixed soon, hopefully.

Six Degrees of Separation

In 2011, the Earth's population reached seven billion inhabitants, and it is still growing by about 80 million people per year. All the people are structured like a chain where each acquaintance is one degree of separation. This theory says that a random two people worldwide are connected by over five people on average. Those five people equal to six degrees of separation (*see figure 2.8*).

This means that if you are person A, and you know person B, where person B knows person C, you, as person A, are connected with person C by 2 degrees of separation.

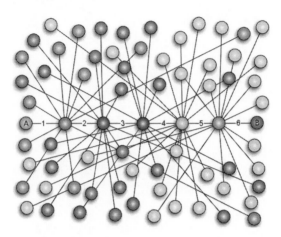

Figure 2.8: Six degrees of separation theory

This theory was demonstrated by different scientists and companies throughout history e.g. on the basis of sent letters, e-mails, instant messages or connections on social websites such as Facebook and LinkedIn. All these tests and analyses showed that the theory works pretty well. Microsoft gauged the level of separation at 6.6 degrees, Facebook at 5.73 degrees, Twitter at 4.67 and scientists agreed that the number is somewhere between 5-7 degrees. A mathematical model was created, e.g. by Duncan. J. Watts and Steven Strogatz (*http:// en.wikipedia.org/wiki/Watts_and_Strogatz_model*).

Why is this important for LinkedIn recruitment?

As I already said, there are almost 200 million LinkedIn users but you are not able to reach all of them via your account. LinkedIn limits each user to three degrees of separation (*see figure 2.9*). Due to this fact you are able to cover only a fraction of all LinkedIn® users.

Figure 2.9: LinkedIn relationship path to 2nd degree connection with new design

NOTE
If your profile has not been converted to the new one yet, your profile probably still looks like the old design (*see figure 2.10*).

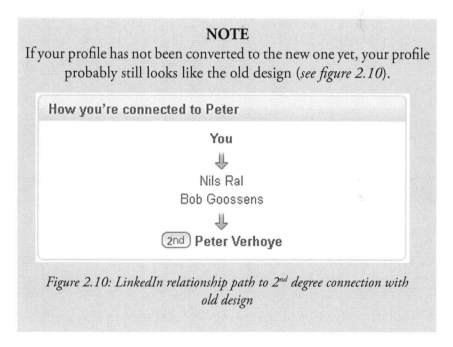

Figure 2.10: LinkedIn relationship path to 2nd degree connection with old design

It depends who you are connected to in terms of the number of their connections; whether you are connected to regular users with about one to two hundred 1st degree connections, or if you are connected to lots of power-users with thousands or tens of thousands of 1st degree connections.

Regardless of whom you are connected to with thousands of direct contacts, you will reach maximally about 20 million LinkedIn® users which is about 9% of all LinkedIn users.

The number of 3rd degree connections is not growing proportionally to your 1st degree connections.

Approx. number of 1st degree connections	Your whole LinkedIn network [in millions of users]	1st degree vs. 3rd degree connections ratio
100-200	1-2	10000
600	3-4	5833
4 000	15	3750
15 000	20	1333
43 000	27	628

For instance, having one to two hundred 1st degree connections will connect you with about 1 to 2 million users. The ratio between 1st degree and 3rd degree connections is 10,000.

And having about 43,000 1st degree connections (which the user with probably the most 1st degree connections, Ron Bates, has) will connect you with about 27 million users. The ratio between 1st degree and 3rd degree connections is 628.

As you can see, the ratio comparing the increase of 1st to 3rd degree connections is plunging alongside 1st degree connections growth. This means that when you have thousands of 1st degree connections, it is very tough for you to increase the number of 3rd degree connections (or whole network to be precise – i.e. 1st + 2nd + 3rd degree connections). On the other hand, when you have hundreds of 1st degree connections, it is pretty easy to double the 3rd degree connections by connecting with only hundreds of people.

This is caused due to the fact that when you have thousands of direct connections, your network is so large that there is a very high probability of shared connections – i.e. the acquaintances of your new connections are already in your network, or the majority of them. So the overall number of 3rd degree connections will increase just a little bit.

But do not worry; covering all LinkedIn® members is not your goal. **The recruiter's goal is to cover all or the vast majority of users in their recruitment niche and geographical location.** But that is even more complicated. Read on.

You can visualize your own LinkedIn network with InMaps (*see figure 2.11*) which is one of the LinkedIn experimental applications.

Try it using the following link: *http://inmaps.linkedinlabs.com*

> **NOTE**
>
> Due to changes on LinkedIn, the official LinkedIn applications has been turned off or converted to the new media format. InMaps is an example of an experimental application created by employees of the LinkedIn Corporation. This group of applications has not been affected by the changes so they are still working.

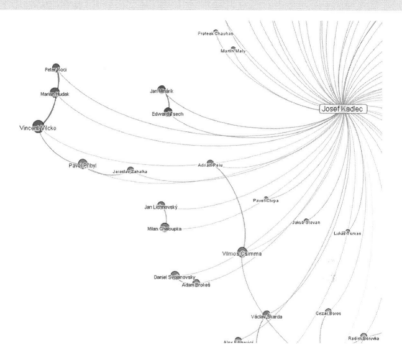

Figure 2.11: LinkedIn InMaps visualization of user network

> **NOTE**
>
> The example is just an example account with only 63 connections. If you have an extra large network, you might find a problem displaying the map. LinkedIn is working on increasing the limit, so stay tuned.

Social Direct Search is Not Stationary, It Is a Process

Being on LinkedIn as a recruiter means evolution. You should be growing on an everyday basis. Your LinkedIn® connections should be increasing. You should be choosing your connections strategically, expanding your groups, and fine tuning your profile.

You will have a different impact and influence as a recruiter with tens of connections than a recruiter with hundreds, most likely thousands of 1st degree connections. Your success at hiring people will also be different based on the structure of your connections. Do your connections include mostly your potential candidates, irrelevant people or your competitors?

This process requires quite a regular, daily routine. It is simply not possible to build a high quality LinkedIn® account over night. It takes some time. Of course there are some shortcuts which might help us to speed up the process and I will describe them further in this book. Anyway, get used to doing regular tasks.

Quantity Matters but Quality More

There are two main goals which a headhunter wants to aim for in terms of LinkedIn networking:

- To reach all potential candidates within their niche and location

- To avoid other recruiters parasitizing on your network.

By 'reaching', I mean to have them as 3rd, 2nd or at best, 1st degree connections. Members other than your potential candidates and other recruiters are sort of irrelevant to you, but you will take advantage of some of them on your way to your desired position on LinkedIn.

As an example, you might need to boost your LinkedIn network in a new location, let's say Russia. The majority of your current connections are from a different area so you are not able to effectively search the new location. The solution is to find the power-users in Russia and connect with them. The power-users are usually so called *LinkedIn Open Networkers* (known under the abbreviation LION). They are easy to find and they will most probably accept your invitation even if it can take more time as these people are receiving a huge amount of invitations every day.

The same procedure can be used when you are new on LinkedIn® and you have only very few candidates.

Very active recruiters and headhunters are often power-users within their niche and location. I am, for instance, a power-user in the Czech

Republic, Central Europe. This means that connecting with me will provide you with an entrance to this market – the Czech Republic, especially the IT sector.

The problem with recruiters is that they will not accept your invitation if they are smart. They will not let you pick cherries from their garden.

I will get back to that in detail in the chapter *05, Cultivate Your Hunting Ground: LinkedIn® Networking Strategy for Recruiters.*

A Candidate's Success Story

This is a true story demonstrating not only recent trends in recruitment but mainly the great power of LinkedIn. It's about my friend Radim Boruvka, one of my former colleagues at a company called Acision, where we worked as software engineers. He was not actively looking for a new job at all. On the other hand, he was not closed to offers. He was a typical so called *passive candidate* (see next section for an explanation). But there was basically no channel for him to potentially receive such offers because he had not set up a LinkedIn profile. It was 2008 and not all IT professionals had a LinkedIn profile even if the percentage was significantly higher than in other industries, such as finance, automotive and so.

Now, penetration of LinkedIn® amongst IT professionals is converging on 100% I would say. This is because nobody can afford to miss some of the great offers which can come through LinkedIn. By 2008, I myself knew almost all of my potential candidates within my recruitment niche by name in Central Europe. OK, not literally, but you get my point. Potential candidate saturation was way lower than it is now. Of course, the number of recruiting competitors was also significantly lower. Now you can expect that 8% (source: Adler Group survey) of all LinkedIn users are recruiters in all their forms.

Anyway, back to my story. Radim created a LinkedIn profile, connected with me as a power networker which quickly connected him with the LinkedIn world. It took three days, just three short days and Radim received a kick-ass job offer proposing three times the ordinary salary for the job he was doing. A very lucrative engagement! He passed all the interviews and got the job. His new life avenue began.

Active vs. Passive Candidates

Radim was a typical so called *passive candidate*. Such a person is currently employed, usually at least one year and is not actively seeking a new job. At that moment LinkedIn® for him is just a tool for networking and watching the career changes of his colleagues. On the other hand, such a person is not closed to new job opportunities. He is open to discuss them.

The second group of candidates is *active candidates* who are actively looking for a job. They are sending their CVs everywhere so that personnel agencies and hiring companies have them in their ATS (Applicant Tracking System).

But why focus on passive candidates when the active ones are replying to our ads on their own?

Again, it is just math because about **80% of the work force is passive candidates.**

The second critical reason is that with these candidates you have a better chance against the competition to place them because you can be the first to persuade the candidate to go with a job opportunity.

On the other hand, when you are contacted by an active candidate, it is very probable that they already sent his CV to other recruitment agencies and targeted companies as well. Imagine that one candidate sends their CV to three personnel agencies specialized in the IT sector – one of those agencies is where you work. If all agencies have the same response reaction, it is just a matter of coincidence that you will be the first person to get their CV. Of course, brand power and the size of budget spent for job ads has some influence and can change the odds in your favor, but at what cost?

It works in a similar way for hiring companies as well. Being dependent just on active candidates is not feasible any more, especially in very demanding sectors like IT which suffers from a lack of experienced IT specialists globally. These people are usually active candidates just at the very beginning of their career. Then they become passive candidates till the end of their productive lives.

The advantage of hiring companies is that, more than personnel agencies; they have better options to promote a very strong brand which makes their company attractive for potential employees. The pipeline of active candidates is significant, sometimes huge in terms of volume. But as we already know, quality over quantity, these companies have to focus on passive candidates as well. And do not think that between these companies belong only global players like Google, Microsoft or Apple. Each location and each country has some attractive companies, sometimes being awarded 'Employer of the Year' or sometimes just small but quickly growing startups.

For example, the San Francisco area is known as a Mecca for tech companies and start-ups. The current 10 most attractive startups for IT specialists are as follows:

1. Arista	6. Pinterest
2. Nicira	7. Violin
3. Box	8. Palantir
4. Cloudera	9. Hortonworks
5. Square	10. Splunk

How many of these companies do you know?

If you are an IT recruiter from the Bay area, you should probably know all of them. The bottom line is that you should be aware of such companies within your recruitment niche and location because:

1) It is difficult to take people from these companies in general. These people are more loyal to their current employer than others. However, it is not impossible to attract some people, especially those who are with a company for more than three years. Even if they have a strong relation to the brand and company culture, they might like to have some change in their life. These employees are super passive.

2) These companies will not be your ideal clients for recruitment because they have a strong pipeline of active candidates (e.g. Google receive over 10,000 job applications a day) they are not dependent on external recruitment agencies. This means that unless you focus on very specific skills in combination with region, your income from these companies will be an iota. They have the leverage to push your commission down.

It is a very valuable experience to be an internal recruiter or HR employee in these kinds of companies. You will not be working just in the HR department but you will experience the great synergy between

HR and marketing which is an inevitable trend in modern recruitment.

We are already aware of super passive candidates, so we know that not all so called passive candidates are easily approachable.

So let's look at the full structure of all candidates:

- 20% **Active** - actively looking for a new job (almost non-approachable)

- 15% **Tiptoer** - thinking about changing job (easily approachable)

- 45% **Explorer** - not looking for a new job but open to discussion (easily approachable)

- 20% **Super Passive** – satisfied at their current position and not willing to discuss new opportunities (almost non-approachable).

As you can see, we have a nice 60% of approachable candidates from the groups of all potential candidates including the active ones.

With a passive candidate you can create a competitive advantage among other recruiters by improving your LinkedIn® skills including search, candidate processing, and of course your ability to persuade the desired candidate to change their job and possibly change it via you. It does not mean that you have to convince them at the moment and, if they are not interested, discard them. Today's recruitment requires a more long-term strategy. You must become a sort of 'advisor' for your potential candidates so that they will get back to you in the future.

As we already know, professional social networking is a major hiring source. About 86% percent of recruiters are already using it at least to some extent (*see figure 2.12*). The question is, how are they successful in terms of their efficiency in hiring passive candidates.

In summary, the point is that there is space to establish a lasting competitive advantage by improving your LinkedIn abilities, including searching in alignment with the knowledge of the labor market and your persuasion. For example, if you are able to discover candidates who your competitors are not, you are gaining a competitive advantage. You can do this by improving your LinkedIn skills. Otherwise, there is no advantage over the competition as we all have access to LinkedIn, so improved LinkedIn skills make the difference. It is like with cars – use it like you stole it.

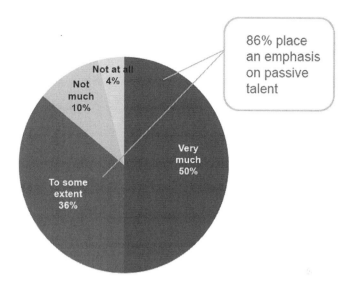

Figure 2.12: LinkedIn Global Recruiting Trends Survey 2011: Passive Talent

Social Recruitment Strategy

Before we truly start with LinkedIn® social recruitment, there are a few prerequisites. Some of you are internal recruiters at hiring companies, some of you are working for personnel agencies and some of you are maybe on your own; so each of you has a different recruitment strategy.

Internal Recruiter

Your strategy is simple. You promote the company which you are working at only. The best scenario is to work in cooperation with your marketing department. All other companies with potential relevant candidates are your targets.

Employee Recruiter at Personnel Agency

Your strategy is basically set up by your employer. Often, the problem is that if the personnel agency is economically stronger, they have contracts with a lot of companies. Their strategy works on the basis "more is better". That of course works for gathering active candidates, but pure headhunters at such companies can have a disadvantage because they are allowed to contact potential candidates at companies which are not current (sometimes also past) clients of the personnel agency. The recruitment contracts usually have a fine for actively contacting an employee of your current client; therefore you might be very limited in direct searching.

Owner of a Recruitment Agency or Headhunter Freelancer

You have the chance to set your strategy up on your own. That is also my case as the owner of a personnel agency and previously as a recruitment freelancer. If your main strategy is to focus on passive talents, which is the only way in some very competitive industries such as IT, you should create a shortlist of companies you would like to contact for recruitment, and the rest of the companies utilize as a candidate reservoir. I know it sounds cruel, but that is the reality. The shortlist does not need to be huge. If we consider large corporations, they are hiring and firing a large amount of people so the employee fluctuation is significant. With them you can establish a sufficient volume of vacancies.

If you are a freelance recruiter, it is sometimes better to have a smaller number of contracted companies, because in terms of the *contacted vs. hired employees ratio* it can lead to better results. For one person it is more difficult to properly know more than ten companies and follow them on a daily basis. On the other hand, there is a risk if one such company is firing or not hiring currently, you face significant outage in your revenues. Therefore, consider your clients carefully.

General Rules When Hiring Passive Talents

Mark Zuckerberg has established Facebook based on the idea that it does not matter WHAT is in a message but WHO the message is from. In your case you have to focus more on what is in the message because the world of recruiters might be pretty homogenous from this point of view. What I'm saying is that it is difficult to become famous or known as a recruiter even only within your industry.

It does not matter if you work for a small or a large and well known recruitment agency or if you are a senior HR person. It has little impact on a candidate's decisions. Candidates give a hack more or less. You can only try to differentiate at least a bit. For example, instead of saying *I am a Recruitment Consultant* I started to call myself a *Career Advocate*. Or depending on the industry and niche you recruit in you can adjust it even more specifically to get closer to the candidate – e.g. *Unix Career Advocate* or *Finance Career Advocate*.

You will become more memorable and interesting for candidates. So step out of the unanimity of never-ending recruiters and consultants if your situation allows it.

This might be different from country to country, culture to culture, but I can honestly say that when I was working as a software engineer, I was contacted by loads of recruiters and I do not remember a single one! They're all the same.

The exception is when a candidate is contacted by e.g. a department manager or director or a regular employee from the same field of expertise of the hiring company (i.e. not a personnel agency). It gives a completely different credibility to the message and you can expect that such a candidate will consider the opportunity more seriously.

To support the credibility of the sender you can:

1) Write the message on behalf of a credible person. Do not take it personally, but we as recruiters are nobody to our candidates. The exception might be some headhunters focusing on top level management where the situation is at least equal. C-level managers have to actively co-operate with executive search consultants to get the desired job.

For example, if you are contacting a software engineer, you can send the message on behalf of the company's R&D director or chief software architect, if you have approval to do so, of course. Trust me that words of flattery will sound more honest from a person with the same expertise than from an anonymous recruiter who's only interested in their commission.

2) Try to utilize your background as much as you can. If you became a recruiter from a different job, your background is probably in some expertise such as pharmaceutical, finance, accounting, IT, architecture, etc. Try to communicate with the candidate as if he/she was your colleague, not from the position of a recruiter forcing the job on the candidate. Use jargon he/she understands and let them know that you understand their role. For example, mention some actual news from the industry he/she is working in.

3) Hire people from the position of the targeted company. Targeted company hiring of employees will always have better credibility than recruitment agencies. If you are an internal recruiter, you have no dilemma. If you are an external recruiter, you can try to be considered as connected with the targeted company. You can adjust the website of your agency in favor of this regardless of how many company clients you have. Usually, a company is more important than another from the perspective of the number of open vacancies. You can pick just the most important one(s).

Spend more time and effort publishing targeted company references and successes, company culture and why this company is beneficial for potential new employees. A company promotional video and, my specialty, which is a reference from a real employee, are useful tools. You can ask a regular employee from the hiring company a few questions about working for the company, for example:

a) What are the main advantages of the company? Why would you recommend it?

b) What could they do better?

c) Share with us the company atmosphere.

I pushed this strategy for some of my company clients so far, that my recruitment agency webpage was ranked better than the original webpage of the targeted company, and was taking first place in Google searches.

Even if you apply some of these strategies which support your credit as the sender, your main focus, which can influence a candidate's decisions, will be the content of the message you are trying to put across.

What are the key elements driving career change for passive talents?

1) They want to make an impact. This does not mean that they need recognition for their contributions. It means that they want to be useful with meaningful results. Being an insignificant part of a product which nobody knows and maybe will not be even released, is not that case. So highlight impact over a skill-focused job description.

2) They want a culture that fits their personality. Times when just a salary matters are over. Company culture matters more than at anytime in history and more and more companies are seriously improving this aspect. They have to. And sometimes in cooperation with external company culture experts. Emphasize culture and how your candidate can fit into it.

3) More likely to want challenging work. Competition is part of human nature. A sufficing job place is not attractive for passive talents. Therefore, emphasize the challenging aspects of the job offer.

Communication with passive candidates should be like a long conversation. You should not only be a recruiter, but mainly an advisor. The majority of contacted potential candidates will decline your offer, but they can accept any other time, so you should take care of them too. Timing is crucial, you must make timing work for you. This means that you must develop a system.

Regardless of which ATS you use, you should develop a system where you have e.g. four basic groups:

1. Candidates who did not reply to your message yet
2. Candidates who are in touch with you
3. Candidates in the application process
4. Candidates who were successfully hired.

Each candidate is only in one of these groups. Each group of candidates will require different care. Your goal is to try to get all of the candidates from the first group to the last one. It is never going to happen, but this approach will help you to maximize your results.

A common mistake of the majority of recruiters is that once they recruit a candidate, they don't keep in touch with him/her anymore. They are missing out greatly! Usually, such candidates are not usable for 1-2 years, but after that, they are possibly looking for a new challenge again and you should be there to assist. Do not forget, that because you helped them once, it is much easier for you to then persuade them again. You have a comparative advantage over your competition.

This is why you should devise an aftercare program and ideally assist such candidates till the end of their productive life. With this approach you can also better scale the workload among your employees or coworkers, for example:

- One person or team is trying to pipeline new candidates to the system .

- Another person or team is communicating with candidates and solving specific opportunities until they are hired

- And the last one, organizing aftercare for hired candidates and once they are prepared for another challenge, forwarding them to team number two.

Based on these points, what follows are a few more suggestions you should take into account:

Never cry for commission, it will never cry for you. Push a candidate only when it makes sense. I already mentioned this story, but I remember a situation from my time in information security and forensics when a female recruiter was crying on the phone trying to persuade me to at least go to an interview and try it. It wasn't going to happen because I was already almost hired somewhere else. Never cry for money, it will never cry for you.

Force a candidate only upon individual consideration and with your head up. Be friendly, casual and personal, but not sleazy and get under the candidate's skin. If a candidate is not interested in changing their current job at the moment, suggest a term of a few months ahead when you will contact the candidate again.

The AAA rule – Advisor, Ambassador, Advocate. Become an advisor to your candidates accompanying them through their career path. Become a brand ambassador for your company clients and be prepared to support their brand. The same works for internal recruiters because human resources and marketing have to work hand in hand. And because you represent both sides: company clients and candidates as well, be prepared to become an advocate who will need to e.g. negotiate salaries and to try to close deals. So basically be advisor to your candidates, ambassador to your company clients and an advocate for both.

Process all candidates without exceptions. I hate the statement of many recruitment agencies *"If we do not contact you in two weeks, we are not interested."* What the heck!? That is really appealing to candidates, right? Do not be short-sighted. If your recruitment duty is not a one-time temporary job, you need to think a few steps ahead to be successful.

The worldwide trend is to be prompt. Not only when speaking about recruitment but about any customer care or support. And I can tell you, your candidates will appreciate it and it will increase your efficiency. The slogan of my recruitment agency is *"We provide all job candidates with prompt feedback EVERY TIME!"*

A junior candidate or fresh graduate will become, in a few short years, a regular and later a senior candidate. Build the trust at the beginning, funnel them into your process and you have a great chance to make a profit from them in the future.

Customize communication with all candidates. It depends on how many candidates we are seeking and what time and man capacity we have, but you should individualize your communication as much as you can. Even bulk e-mails can be individualized to some extent. I believe this is one of the main strategies, increasing the effectiveness of your proposals.

Measure your recruitment activities. Take your recruitment activities as processes and improve them on-the-go. Once you compose an opening proposal offering specific opportunities to candidates and you are not satisfied with the number of replies, adjust it and evaluate the results again after the next run. You cannot manage what you do not measure. Be patient when waiting for replies, but if you do not get a reply to your first message, do a second shot with a modified proposal. I will describe powerful ways of gauging your efficiency later in this book.

Consider relevant candidates effectively. When I said to reply to all candidates who contact you it does not mean to be extreme and contact everybody with justification just in case. These candidates include employees who have been working for a new employer only for a few months or offering a regular full-time job to a contractor. These candidates usually have two or more current employers in their LinkedIn profile. And of course, don't offer non-relevant jobs in terms of desired expertise. Also, do not discard candidates with poorly written LinkedIn profiles.

Do not overwhelm candidates with a plethora of information. Less is more sometimes. Do not overwhelm candidates with tens of job proposals from several companies. It is better to choose one company and a whole proposal structure in this regard. In any case, you cannot easily promote more than one company in one e-mail; that would be too much information. Also, do not simply copy and paste original full proposals. Highlight just the bottom line and provide the candidate with a link to the full proposal on **your website** (meaning the website of your agency or company website).

How exactly you should structure your messages to candidates and how to analyze each part, including communication channels you can use is described in more detail in the chapter *07, Shoot to Kill: How to Reach Candidates with LinkedIn® Every Time.*

Requirements for Successful Social Headhunting

For proper usage of LinkedIn® and maximizing the success ratio, I recommend the following:

1) Description of the vacancy available via a weblink reference. The best place is your website as you can support the description with other lures to persuade your potential candidates.

2) Do not hide the name of the targeted company. I started with this strategy first here in Central Europe while everybody was telling me that it is nonsense and that candidates would bypass me. But they did not. I was offering added value in providing them with comprehensive information about the company itself and about the interview, so I was considered a specialist by the targeted company. So it is a no-brainer for candidates to bypass me because they gain nothing by such behavior.

3) Have a hiring company description available on your website as well. Nowadays candidates, especially those who are really experienced, are interested in their employer. Not only in the specific job role. Therefore, offer company success stories, references, a company presentation video (most corporations have one) and offer information about the company from the perspective of the employee. Show off, show off and show off.

Mention all facts which might be attractive for potential employees, such as:

i. Approximate salary package (salary range if possible) plus any other income from the employer such as on-call wages, performance bonuses, etc.

ii. All benefits including technical courses and certification possibilities or flexible working hours.

iii. Describe the workplace (attach photos if possible) and company culture – maybe they use an unconventional open space, their premises are at a nice location, they do not require a dress-code or they allow you to have your own Linux on workstations.

iv. Mention the technology which is normally unavailable for normal people. Maybe the targeted company uses the latest hardware technology which the potential candidate would be in touch with as an engineer.

v. Sometimes there are things which one candidate considers attractive and others not. For instance, the possibility of going on business trips. Mention those as well.

Be thorough otherwise it will sound like some PR information which is not our aim. It must look as if you really know the company from an insider's point of view and that you are giving them something more than can be gathered from a company flyer. To gather such information, it is best to be in touch with some of the employees – meaning not only HR employees; and of course, to visit the place in person and start a discussion.

4) Offer some bonus which does not have only informational value. For example, each successful candidate can receive a Kindle with e-books for a discounted price or an Apple iPod. It needn't be pricey. The goal is to show that you share your success and care about your candidates. They will get this bonus after their trial period which is usually also your warranty period within the recruitment contract. By offering such a bonus it will be easier to get a reference including the candidate's photo.

Figure 2.13: Jobs Consulting candidates get Amazon Kindle e-books and this geeky mug

5) Mention reasons why the candidate should choose your recruitment agency. The bottom line can be that you provide detailed information about the targeted companies, including salary.

Next you will provide the candidate with detailed information about the first round interview. You should also mention that you have skilled recruiters who know the industry (meaning the industry of the opening – finance, automotive, IT, etc.) very well if you feel confident about this.

Furthermore, mention that you negotiate and reply promptly every time. Even if you do not place the candidate at the moment, this is a feature which candidates appreciate very much because there is nothing worse than contacting a personnel agency or a recruiter and them not getting back to you… or getting back after a long time.

Mention that you communicate and do the first consultation by telephone and e-mail. This is valid, specifically for industries like IT where the preliminary personal interview is waste of time. I started with this procedure as one of the first in Central Europe and the competition just did not keep up. When an agency invited a candidate to a preliminary interview, I had already sent the candidate to the hiring company!

And lastly, mention the loyalty bonus I talked about in point 4 of course.

6) On your website it's also a good idea to mention references to your other candidates. The references have to be genuine, so a full name and photo would be advantageous. I also recommend publishing one larger reference in the form of a short interview with an employee of a hiring company. You have the chance to emphasize the pros of the company and it will support the rest of the hiring company description. It can include just three questions e.g.: What are the main advantages of working for the company? Why would you recommend it to other potential employees? Could you share with us information about the company's culture?

> **NOTE**
>
> To save time, if you ask a candidate for a reference, prepare one for them in advance according to your needs and mention that any changes are welcomed from their side. In 99% of cases they will just accept the reference and it is done.

7) You can also offer a mediation of the non-formal meeting with some employee of the targeted companies to the potential candidate. If you are hiring for a corporation there is a big chance that the potential candidate knows someone from the hiring company. This is not always the case or the person they know is not from the same department or team. However, this can be a powerful weapon if you have such an employee at your disposal.

Chapter Summary

- LinkedIn® is more effective than traditional advertisement-based recruitment

- LinkedIn® is the leading medium in the field of social recruitment

- The networking goal of a headhunter is to cover most of the LinkedIn® users from his/her industry and geographical location

- Social direct search has to be understood as a process and improved on-the-fly

- The vast majority of potential candidates are so called passive talents

----

03

Skills Check-up: An Assessment of Your LinkedIn® and Recruitment Preparedness

Skills Check-up: An Assessment of Your LinkedIn® and Recruitment Preparedness

---

What you will learn in this chapter

- How well you are prepared to start with LinkedIn® recruitment

- What your knowledge is of LinkedIn® for recruitment

- You will be provided with suggestions based on your individual results

---

This chapter contains an evaluation form consisting of fifteen questions to help you estimate how well you are prepared for social recruitment with LinkedIn®. It will test your current LinkedIn® profile, networking development and necessary recruitment knowledge, as well. Based on this assessment you will be put into one of three groups where each group represents a different level of LinkedIn recruitment experience.

Take into account that such automatic assessment is not able to cover all aspects of your LinkedIn profile and knowledge, and is a bit sensitive to the specific region and niche you recruit in. Therefore, look at your results from a distance and do not take them as dogma.

NOTE
This assessment can also be done online on
www.PeopleAsMerchandise.com

Answer the following questions and find out where you stand. The duration of the assessment is approximately fifteen minutes including checking the results.

> **NOTE**
>
> If you are a complete LinkedIn novice and you do not have a LinkedIn account yet or you have just created one, you have zero points and going through the evaluation questions does not make sense for you.

Assessment question		Points
LinkedIn Profile		
1.	**Is your profile strength at _All-Star_ level** (or 100% _profile completeness_ if you still have an older profile)? (yes = 1, no = 0)	
2.	**Do you have at least ten recommendations?** (yes = 1, plus 1 additional point for each next 5 recommendations up to 3 additional points as maximum, no = 0). E.g. if you have 23 recommendations, you write down 1 + 2 = 3 points.	
3.	**Do you use at least one rich media (e.g. video, presentation, audio, portfolio) on your LinkedIn® profile?** (yes = 1, no = 0).	
4.	**Do you have at least 10 skills and expertise set up?** (yes = 1, no = 0).	
LinkedIn Networking		
5.	**Do you have at least 500 1st degree connections?** (yes = 1, plus 1 additional point for each next 1,000 1st degree connections up to 3 additional points as maximum, no = 0 points). For example, if you have 3,743 1st degree connections, you fill-in 1 + 3 = 4 points.	

Assessment question		Points
6.	**Do you have at least 13,000,000 3rd degree connections?** (yes = 1, plus 1 additional point for each next 1,000,000 3st degree connections, no = 0 points). For example, if you have 16,543,502 3st degree connections, you fill-in 1 + 3 = 4 points. This number can be found when you click *Home* in the main menu and see the section *Your LinkedIn Network*.	
7.	**Do you receive at least one invitation a day (i.e. approximately seven a week)?** (yes = 1, no = 0).	
8.	**Do you have at least 700 invitations left to send?** (yes = 1, no = 0). If you have your last 1,000 invitations or less, you are notified anytime you want to send an invitation. Otherwise, you still have more than 1,000 invitations.	
9.	**Have you joined at least 30 groups?** (yes = 1, plus additional 1 point if you have joined 50 groups, no = 0).	
10.	**Do you own or manage at least one group with a minimum of 1000 members?** (yes = 1, plus 1 additional point up to three as a maximum for each next group, no = 0).	
LinkedIn Recruitment		
11.	**Do you use Boolean operators (at least two of them - AND, OR, NOT, quotes, parenthesis) in LinkedIn Advanced People Search?** (yes = 2, no = 0).	

Assessment question		Points
12.	Do you know how to display the full LinkedIn profile view of a 3rd degree, or out of network, connection without upgrading to a premium account? (yes = 2, no = 0).	
13.	Do you have at least one LinkedIn Saved Search Alert set up? (yes = 2, no = 0).	
14.	Do you know how to locate LinkedIn® users using Google or any other search engine, i.e. a so called X-ray search? (yes = 2, no = 0).	
15.	Do you have at least one extra LinkedIn profile to be used as a honey pot for monitoring the activity of your competitors? (yes = 2, no = 0).	
Total Score		

Results

If you scored more than 30 points, you are easily part of the group of well rounded LinkedIn recruiters. Although, as this assessment form covers only basic aspects, there is always something to improve. So keep going to advance your LinkedIn profile and social recruitment capabilities.

If you scored 15 to 29, that's not too bad, you are probably on the right road to the highest social recruitment league, but there is still a lot to improve. Keep going and gather the necessary knowledge you need to become a world class LinkedIn® recruiter.

If you scored less than 14, then the good news is you have lots of potential to improve. The bad news is that you are missing out. You have to take action now. Establishing your profile for proper social development cannot be done overnight so do not waste more time and start right away.

04

Prepare Your Arsenal: How to Fine-Tune Your LinkedIn® Profile for Recruitment

Prepare Your Arsenal: How to Fine-Tune Your LinkedIn® Profile for Recruitment

---

What you will learn in this chapter

- What are the most important LinkedIn® profile sections for recruitment

- How to promote your profile strength to 'All-Star'

- LinkedIn® symbols and their meanings

LinkedIn® is currently in the process, for 2012 to 2013, of making significant changes influencing not only the design of all LinkedIn® profiles, but also some functionality. If you used applications such as *Amazon Reading List* or have a video on your profile, they are probably not available at the moment and were disabled or transformed to work with the new LinkedIn media system. This will cause different behavior of these parts; for example, video does not start playing automatically when somebody opens your profile.

The process of transformation of LinkedIn profiles from the old look to the new one takes a while. So at the time of writing this book, there are LinkedIn users with the old version of the profile and the new one as well.

If you have the new one, which you probably have at the time of reading of this book, you can check by seeing if you have a *profile strength* indicator (new) instead of a percentage *profile completeness* indicator (old) on your LinkedIn profile.

The partial aspects of your LinkedIn profile might vary according to the phase in which you stand at the moment. If you decide to become a LinkedIn OpenNetworker (so called LION) temporarily to penetrate the market and strengthen your contact base, or if you are a settled recruiter with a strong contact base of potential candidates, your headline or any other field with your name will be different. All the networking strategies will be explained thoroughly in the next chapter 05, *Cultivate Your Hunting Ground: LinkedIn® Networking Strategy for Recruiters.*

Bear in mind that as there are resume writers and resume writing services, the LinkedIn profile writers showed up. Their primary focus is to help job seekers with LinkedIn profiles to maximize their chances that they will be contacted by recruiters or at least well presented in front of potential employers.

Their intentions might be quite different from those of recruiters. So as a recruiter forget about such services and do what it takes. You have to understand all aspects and the psychology of your profile to be a solid LinkedIn recruiter. Otherwise, it is like being a cook who does not know how to chop meat and vegetables properly.

NOTE

I need to add, please do not copy all the aspects of my personal profile (*http://www.linkedin.com/in/josefkadlec*) precisely. I am still doing some research and testing so I am changing things all the time and these things might not correspond with the best practices all recruiters should keep to. On top of this, I am not only a recruiter but also a training services provider so I am going after other goals rather than just seeking candidates. These things influence the look of my LinkedIn® profile somewhat.

All-Star Profile Strength A.K.A. 100% Profile Completeness

Other sources state that having your profile 100% complete (the LinkedIn terminology) is the most crucial aspect of your success on LinkedIn. This may not necessarily be the case for recruiters. Having your profile 100% complete will guarantee that your LinkedIn profile will be about 40% more likely to be found. However, being found is not the primary goal of headhunters because usually they will be the ones who look for people in the vast majority of cases.

> **NOTE**
> With the transformation to the new LinkedIn website design, the Profile Completeness indicator changed to Profile Strength, which does not show percentages anymore. However, it is analogical.

Nevertheless, there is no reason not to fulfill all criteria. Maybe it has an impact on other LinkedIn functions? Nobody knows exactly what is behind the LinkedIn algorithm. Overall, the 100% complete profiles (i.e. All-Star rank in terms of the new LinkedIn profiles) are preferred so it is worth doing.

On top of that, for those of you who have just created a LinkedIn® profile, it is an easy step-by-step guide about how to create the content of your profile. So, regardless if you have just created your LinkedIn profile or you are an experienced LinkedIn user, your primary goal is to have your profile 100% complete. This is indicated by the progress bar in your profile (you must be logged-in) with the old profile style (*see figure 4.1*):

Figure 4.1: The progress bar of profile completeness for old LinkedIn profiles

…or by the new diagram with the All-Star degree for new profiles (*see figure 4.2*).

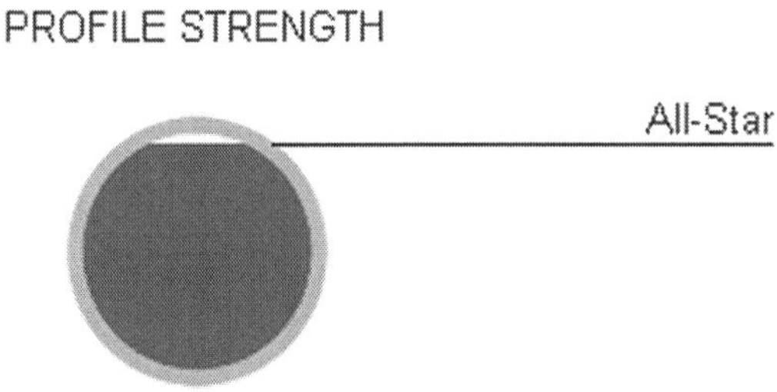

PROFILE STRENGTH

All-Star

Figure 4.2: The indicator of profile strength for new LinkedIn profiles

How do you reach this status?

To have your completeness progress bar at 100% or to be ranked as an 'All-Star', you must have filled the following profile fields:

- Photo
- Summary
- Skills and Expertise
- Education
- Three recent positions
- Three recommendations.

When you are new on LinkedIn® or you do not care about your profile, you start with the rank of Beginner (*see figure 4.3*).

PROFILE STRENGTH

Beginner

Figure 4.3: Profile strength - Beginner

As you build up your profile you move up to the rank of Intermediate (*see figure 4.4*). PROFILE STRENGTH

Intermediate

Figure 4.4: Profile strength - Intermediate

…and then to the rank of Expert (*see figure 4.5*).

And finally, up to the highest rank, All-Star (*see figure 4.6*).

PROFILE STRENGTH

Figure 4.5: Profile strength - Expert

PROFILE STRENGTH

Figure 4.6: Profile strength – All-Star

Beware! LinkedIn might change criteria for these ranks after some time even if your profile is boosted to maximum at the moment. One year ago, I noticed that my profile was 90% complete from the previous 100%. I had to confirm two of my current posts to get back to 100%.

Just filling in the required fields to achieve the highest rank does not guarantee success. You also need the right profile content. A few words filled in the required fields may count toward a computer's view of 'completeness', but it won't be effective if your profile still contains the minimum information. Therefore, let's move on to profile 'compactness'.

Profile Compactness

In my opinion, the most crucial aspect of the correct LinkedIn® profile is its compactness. A compact profile looks solid and trustworthy. But what is a compact profile? A compact profile contains only that much information which is necessary. Having an incomplete profile or having a profile with too much information are excesses which are not beneficial.

Let's go through each field in detail.

Photo

Having a picture uploaded is an absolute must. Firstly, the uploaded picture is a part of your All-Star profile strength. This makes your profile more reachable because it will be seven times more likely to come up in searches and you will also have more click throughs to your profile. Secondly and mainly, you will be more reliable to your potential candidates.

I did a quick search and it is amazing how many recruiters still have profiles without a picture!

Your photo is about expression, so it should look professional and create positive feelings for your audience. In searches your photo avatar is pretty small, so if you want to be recognizable make sure your head and face is covering the vast majority of the photo space. Of course, that is if you decide to have a headshot.

Full body pictures are pretty useless to be honest because nobody will recognize you properly. Also, do not use your ID photos as these photos have some strict limitations. For example, you are not allowed to smile so that they often look awkward and stifled. Photos with a low resolution e.g. made by a web camera, do not look good either. So find something suitable.

General things you should avoid when choosing photos:

- Group photos

- A photo of your baby

- A photo of you with your pet

- A photo of your logo or product

- A photo with bad resolution or composition

- An obsolete photo

- A wedding photo

- A too serious face photo

- A cartoon photo.

NOTE

Some of the following photos were originally colored and others were black & white, which is not recognizable in the book properly. Take into account that black and white composition does not flatter everybody. I am one of these people for instance.

Do not forget that photos are about feelings. No matter what is in the photo, it is right if you provoke positive feelings to your audience. So try to look naturally relaxed and happy (*see figure 4.7*)

Figure 4.7: Good examples of LinkedIn profile pictures

Next, look at the bad examples which have really poor composition, colors, resolution or they are not appropriate in terms of background, occasion or clothing (*see figure 4.8*).

Figure 4.8: Bad examples of LinkedIn profile pictures

In the last category I will show you a few controversial photos which cannot be said to be good or bad (*see figure 4.9*). They are simply different and it depends what your intentions are when using such pictures.

Figure 4.9: Controversial examples of LinkedIn profile pictures

The first picture is a picture of mine which I used on my LinkedIn® profile for some time. If you are confident using a 'controversial' or unusual photo it could work in your favor by quickly initiating some non-formal communication.

Name

This is pretty simple. Just use your real name or an alias if you are recognizable under that one. Anyway, fields *First Name* and *Last Name* can be used for additional information also. For example, LinkedIn OpenNetworkers mark their profile with the [LION] abbreviation to be easily recognizable. This abbreviation is usually put after the last name (*see figure 4.10*).

 Josef Kadlec [LION] 1st

I'm providing Unix/Linux developers, testers and support engineers with new great opportunities.

Czech Republic · Information Technology and Services

500+ connections

Current: Linux Career Advocate at ... more
Past: Platform Integration at LogicaCMG /... more
Groups: Adobe Flex Developers · Volvo Owners
▶ **19** shared connections · Similar

Figure 4.10: The [LION] abbreviation after the last name

But the *First Name* form field can be also used for any kind of marking (*see figure 4.11*).

Josef (LION) Kadlec (1st)
I'm providing Unix/Linux developers, testers and support
engineers with new great opportunities.
Czech Republic · Information Technology and Services
500+ connections

Current: Linux Career Advocate at ... more
Past: Platform Integration at LogicaCMG /... more
Groups: Adobe Flex Developers · Volvo Owners
▸ 19 shared connections · Similar

Figure 4.11: The (LION) abbreviation after the first name

The use of ASCII and Unicode symbols is also allowed with your
name. However, you can step out of the crowd easily and be considered
as unreliable if you use them too much, so don't overuse these symbols
(*see figure 4.12 and figure 4.13*).

★ Josef Kadlec ★ (1st)
I'm providing Unix/Linux developers, testers and support
engineers with new great opportunities.
Czech Republic · Information Technology and Services
500+ connections

Current: Linux Career Advocate at ... more
Past: Platform Integration at LogicaCMG /... more
Groups: Adobe Flex Developers · Volvo Owners
▸ 19 shared connections · Similar

Figure 4.12: Using ASCII codes can provide solid differentiation

Josef Kadlec ✓ (1st)
I'm providing Unix/Linux developers, testers and support
engineers with new great opportunities.
Czech Republic · Information Technology and Services
500+ connections

Current: Linux Career Advocate at ... more
Past: Platform Integration at LogicaCMG /... more
Groups: Adobe Flex Developers · Volvo Owners
▸ 19 shared connections · Similar

*Figure 4.13: Using ASCII codes can also provide a more sophisticated and
decent look*

> **NOTE**
> You can copy and paste these special ASCII symbols from LINREA.com, a LinkedIn recruitment academy website.

Use only the basic versions of the symbols to avoid errors when displaying them. If you see the symbols correctly on your PC, it does not necessarily mean that everybody else can see them in the same way. So rather check it on other computers as well. You do not want your presence on LinkedIn with incorrectly displayed symbols (*see figure 4.14*).

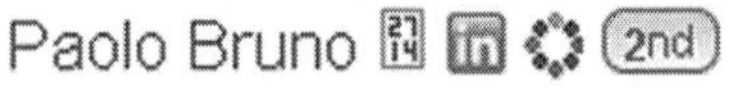

Paolo Bruno 🗓 🔳 ✲ (2nd)

Figure 4.14: ASCII code is not displayed properly

Incorrect display of symbols usually means that the browser does not support the encoding and must be set up individually.

There is also an option to use only the capital letter of your last name (*see figure 4.15*) under the condition you do not use a public profile (read further to discover exactly what a LinkedIn® public profile is).

Oscar B.

Figure 4.15: Anonymous name with only last name capital letter

However, this is not an interesting option for us as recruiters. The LinkedIn Corporation does regular automatic searches where they scan to check if users use their real names. Therefore, if you have something unusual in the form fields supposed to be used for your first name and last name, you can be notified by e-mail (*see figure 4.16*).

More aspects of the LinkedIn User Agreement are analyzed in the *Breaking LinkedIn® User Agreement or Not?* section.

Headline

This field is important right after your name because it is the first thing any visitor to your profile sees. In addition, the headline is not just a part of your full-view profile it is also viewable in search results and in the search prompter (*see figure 4.17*).

LinkedIn Notification

Dear LinkedIn Member,

LinkedIn periodically reviews accounts on the site, and we have found that the first and/or last name on your account is not in compliance with our User Agreement. All LinkedIn accounts must be listed under your real first and last name.

We ask that you do one of the following to correct this issue:

- Update the first and last name fields on your account
- Transfer your group to another account and Close the invalid account after group is transferred
- Close your account

If you're looking to promote your business with LinkedIn, we recommend that you Create a Company Page instead.

IMPORTANT: If no changes are made to your account before it is reviewed again, your account and group(s) will be subject to restrictions or termination.

Thanks in advance for your cooperation.

Sincerely,

LinkedIn Trust & Safety Team

Figure 4.16: E-mail warning about non-standard usage of LinkedIn names

Your headline creates an immediate impression and any potential candidate should be aware of your expertise from the headline alone. Take into account that there are a plenty of recruiters and headhunters on LinkedIn, so labeling your name with a headline such as *"HR Professional"*, *"Senior Recruiter"* or *"Consultant at XYZ Company"* is not differentiating you at all; especially when you are not working for a company which is recognized as an authority in a specific industry.

You have one hundred and twenty characters, so you should make the most of them. If you take your time creating a high quality headline, your visitors will notice it. This is valid for any other part of your LinkedIn profile.

Examples of quality headlines for recruiters are:

I'm providing Unix/Linux developers, testers and support engineers with new, great opportunities.

Recruiting Java/J2EE Developers in London

If you want to combine more roles and information, use a separator:

Author of the #1 LinkedIn Book | Founder of XYZ Agency | IT Career Advocate

Figure 4.17: LinkedIn search prompter

The ASCII or Unicode signs can also be used to emphasize your profile, but do not overdo it:

★ *Author of the #1 LinkedIn Book* ★ *Founder of XYZ Agency* ★ *IT Career Advocate*

If you are in a phase of being a LinkedIn® Open Networker, you should state simple facts why other open networkers should connect with you and you should also publish your e-mail address there to make the process of connecting with you as easy as possible. Such a headline could look as follows:

▶ *I will accept your invitation. 5,000+ direct contacts. example@gmail. com* ◀

Such a headline has a nice feature for open networkers. When you are updating the number of your direct contacts (5,000+ direct contacts, 5,200+ direct contacts, 5,300+ direct contacts, etc.), your current contacts are notified by LinkedIn about changes to your profile, and based on these changes, they are visiting your profile.

This means that your profile displays more in the "*People also viewed*" (the obsolete "*Viewers of this profile also viewed...*") section which results in more new users seeing your profile and sending you their invitations.

On the other hand, sometimes it might be beneficial to hide such changes to your profile. For example, you might be making some changes and fixes to your profile which you do not want to be shared with others. In this case, see the section *LinkedIn® Profile Settings* in this chapter.

Summary

This section, part of the *Background* panel, should contain an overall summary of your professional profile and expertise. As a recruiter you should publish all relevant facts which might be interesting for your potential candidates. But do not make it too long. Nobody will want to read more than one or two short paragraphs. Use bullet points and simple text formatting which is easy to read.

In the past, the summary was broken down into two sections *Professional Experience & Goals and Specialties*. The two separate sections weren't of much use so they were merged into one section called just *Summary*.

State the following facts in the *Summary*:

▪ One or two sentences about yourself
Find a few things about yourself which might be appealing to your potential candidates. If, for example, you are looking for salespeople and you are a former sales professional, mention it. If you have some awards in this field, mention those as well.

■ **The list of job positions you seek candidates for**
Show your candidates what your area of recruitment is. The easiest way is to publish a list of the types of vacancies which you usually fill. Do not mention the names of targeted companies as it is not important at this stage but mention the industry or technology. This is not a list which you would maintain every day as an actual list of your openings, just examples like so:

Software Engineer (C/C++)
Key Account Manager (oil and gas)
Project Manager (banking)

■ **Mention the geographical area of your openings**
It should be immediately clear what the geographical location of your openings is. Are you recruiting for companies in Paris or in Belgium? Mention this also.

■ **Description of your company**
Regardless if you are working for a recruitment agency or for a company which is hiring, mention a few appealing facts your candidate should feel good about. Maybe your personnel agency is working for leading companies in the industry or your clients belong to Fortune 500 companies. Maybe your company was awarded as the best employer in your country.

■ **Contact**
Provide your potential clients with your e-mail address, mobile phone number and the website where they can find an actual list of openings and further information.

Some LinkedIn users also put a special paragraph into this section called 'keywords'. Here they list keywords which are relevant to their profile. This is simply to assist with LinkedIn® search optimization. Anyway, this is not important for recruiters because candidates do not search for recruiters using LinkedIn search, or very rarely. You, as a recruiter, search for candidates, not vice versa. I would focus on what is good for your candidates instead of what is good for the LinkedIn search engine.

Some users fine-tune their profiles by mentioning keywords many times in their profiles – e.g. 100 times. This might result in them being number one when someone searches for that keyword but their LinkedIn profile is ugly and unusable.

Some examples of such SEO-friendly but very user-unfriendly profiles are:

http://www.linkedin.com/in/kennyboykin
http://www.linkedin.com/in/davidwalz
http://www.linkedin.com/in/ank1t

From my experience, this does not pay off for recruiters, so rather avoid making your profile such a mess.

The pattern for an effective *Summary* could look as follows:

✉   *firstname.surname@agency.com*   ☎   *001-650-223-1711*

As a former Linux engineer and Linux community proponent, I am representing the Linux/Unix professionals in front of the largest Linux employers in the United States such as Red Hat, Oracle, Google and HP.

Looking for a new attractive Linux-based opportunity? Feel free to contact me anytime.

Permanent job vacancies
Java/J2EE Software Engineer
Linux QA Engineer / Software Tester
C/C++ Software Engineer
Linux/Unix Support Engineer / Administrator
and others.

More at www.agency.com

Enjoy a new experience with a job change!

Feel free to contact me anytime at firstname.surname@agency.com, 001-650-223-1711.

Experience

Publish up to five of your employers or job roles. Again, think which of them might be interesting for your potential candidates. Frankly, your potential candidates will be glad when they see that you were not a recruiter your whole life. If you were in sales and you are recruiting a sales force at the moment, definitely mention it.

The description for each item within the *Experience* section should be brief with bullet points. Mention what a particular company was about, your tasks and some references. Show off a little bit.

Education, Publications, Languages and Certifications

These fields are not so important but fill them in to make your profile look compact. Some of your potential candidates could have e.g. studied at the same university as you, so you can increase the chances that they will reply to your invitation. All of this data might be used as a less significant discussion opener which will bring you closer to your prospective candidates.

Recommendations

To support your credibility in front of your potential candidates you should have a number of recommendations, but do not overstate them. More does not necessarily mean better. The optimal number of recommendations is about fifteen. You should definitely not exceed twenty recommendations. The reason is simple, clear arrangement. If you have more than twenty recommendations your LinkedIn profile will simply be too long when somebody expands it and they have a hard time going through it. This is a little bit volatile based on the overall textual length of recommendations even though LinkedIn® has improved how recommendations are displayed. Recommendations are not displayed fully expanded by default any more.

Next, try to have at least one recommendation for all of your job roles published on your LinkedIn profile. This can support your complete career history. And, if you worked outside the recruitment industry, you can boost your credibility by being recommended by people from the specific industry you were part of.

But how do you get such recommendations?

LinkedIn offers you the option *Ask for recommendations* where you can ask your connections to endorse you. "But who the hell has time to do that?" I hear you say. The best way is to prepare a shortlist of users who you think might endorse you. For you as a recruiter, there are your peers, representatives of your clients and, mainly, your successfully hired candidates. Such candidates usually have no problem accepting your recommendation requests.

On top of this, if you give your successful candidates a gift e.g. as a kind of 'loyalty bonus', you can expect a 100% success rate.

The crucial part of such requests is to prepare the text of recommendations in advance. People have no time to write them themselves, so providing them with an option just to say "I agree" or "I disagree" is the best way to succeed.

Let's say you are asking your successfully hired candidate for a recommendation, such an inquiry might look as follows:

Dear Oliver,

I hope you enjoy working for company XYZ.

I would like to kindly ask you if you could endorse me on LinkedIn. I am aware of the fact that time is money, so I prepared such a recommendation for you:

"Finding a good continuation of your management career is not a single-shot action, especially when both you and the hiring companies have very high expectations. Josef's dedicated work and close cooperation gave me a significant advantage on the job market. Additionally, his motivation and ambition boosted my confidence and helped me to achieve the best from the available job opportunities."

Would you agree with such a recommendation?

If yes, please paste it as a LinkedIn recommendation to my latest job role. Any modifications are welcomed.

Thank you.

Best regards, Josef

I guarantee you that nobody will decline such a request. The same procedure can be used to get testimonials on your website (*see figure 4.18*) where you publish your vacancies. In this case, you should also ask for a picture and state the candidate's full name, the name of the job role and year of the recommendation.

I do not publish the name of the company where the candidate works because stating their name with a picture is enough to prove that such a testimonial is not a fake. To save the time of the person you are asking for a recommendation, you can also say that you will use the picture from his/her LinkedIn® profile, so it is not necessary for them to send it separately.

A real example of such a website testimonial would look as follows:

"I would like to thank these people for finding me a great job. It was also a great opportunity to meet with highly skilled professionals who are able to initiate my further career growth."
Kostyantyn Fomin, Sustaining Engineer, 2009

Figure 4.18: Website testimonial promoting your recruitment services

Do not bother with the wording of testimonials that much. I usually highlight something specific for the particular candidate in terms of how I, as a recruiter, helped them. Plus, add some more boasts. The truth is that nobody will be reading recommendations that carefully. It's a fact!

If you want to artificially increase the number of LinkedIn® recommendations, you can find people on the Internet who do that for you for a small fee. However, always take into account that a recommendation from a non-relevant LinkedIn user must make sense to you. If not, such a recommendation can usually be easily recognized as a fake. Such a service can be found on *www.fiverr.com*, for example.

If you want to get customizable and industry relevant recommendations, check out my special offer:

SPECIAL DEAL

I will swap an Amazon review of this book for a LinkedIn recommendation of your profile. It is simple. If you like this book, write a book review on Amazon and I will write you a LinkedIn recommendation from my *main* LinkedIn profile. Send me an e-mail to *josef@linrea.com* stating SPECIAL DEAL in subject.

Skills & Expertise

This section is not so important for you as a recruiter aiming to find potential candidates. However, it might be useful for your company clients. The *Skills & Expertise* section went through a large overhaul in 2012. Basically, you can create a list of the expertise you are focused on. As a recruiter it will probably be some of the following:

Recruitment	Job Search
Headhunters	Jobs Search Strategies
IT Recruitment	Executive Search
Technology Recruitment	Career Development
Talent Acquisition	Staffing Services
Strategic Hiring	Human Resources

Also, other users can endorse you for each of these skills and expertise separately (*see figure 4.19*). Let's say thirty people endorsed you as a specialist for IT Recruitment. You are ultimately gaining credit in this field.

On the *LinkedIn Skills & Expertise (More -> Skills & Expertise)* page you are able to check who has credit in particular expertise and also how many users sign up to such expertise.

This will not be that effective for recruiting itself, but it might bring you some new contacts or strengthen your current ones.

Contact Information

This part is a formality which needs to be properly filled-in.

Website – Publish the website of your recruitment agency or company, but do not do it using the *Company Website* option but as *Other:* (*see figure 4.20*).

In this way, the link to your website will show the text *JobsConsulting.org* and not *Company Website* which is not appealing, especially when you have more than one company website.

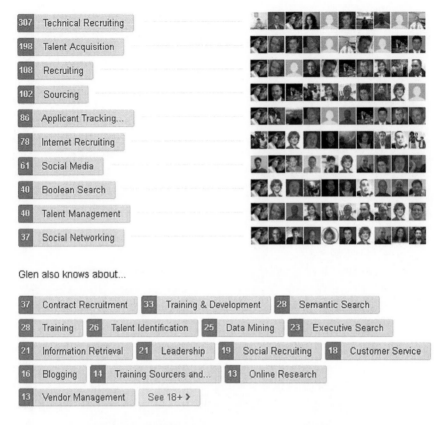

Figure 4.19: Skills & Expertise on your LinkedIn profile

Figure 4.20: How to set your websites up

Twitter – If you recruit in a country where Twitter is a popular medium, you should take this into account and use it to spread the word. By linking to Twitter with LinkedIn®, you can post a copy of LinkedIn updates (short messages you can write on LinkedIn) to one or more Twitter accounts. If you are not interested in sending a copy of such updates to Facebook or other social media channels, it is a great solution which saves you some time and effort. LinkedIn updates can be used for publishing new vacancies and news from your recruitment area.

Email, IM, Phone, Address - Simply fill-in the contact information based on your preferences. Some recruiters prefer only the e-mail channel and use phones only for candidates who are in the process of application. This simply saves time which you might spend on the phone with candidates in the preliminary phase – i.e. before they are even interested in a particular job.

Your Public Profile URL

Firstly, it is important to say that you should have your profile public. What does this mean? A public profile can also be seen by people who are not on LinkedIn (or, to be precise, not signed up to LinkedIn). Therefore, if somebody types your name into Google, your LinkedIn® public profile will be included in the search results. On the other hand, users with a private profile cannot be found via search engines. Our desire as recruiters is to be found, so set your profile as 'public'.

Each LinkedIn public profile has its own URL (Uniform Resource Locator). The problem is that, by default, it is a lengthy mixture of letters and numbers like the following:

www.linkedin.com/pub/zuzana-matousova/9/112/93b

Edit your *Your public profile URL* in such a way that it is short so that you can use it e.g. as part of your e-mail signature. The best scenario is to use your first name followed by your surname:

www.linkedin.com/in/josefkadlec

If this version is already used for your name, find another short version – use only the capital letter of your first name or use only your last name, etc.

If your profile URL starts with *ca.linkedin.com, uk.linkedin.com,* etc. just rewrite it to www.linkedin.com to make it more general and overall nicer.

You can also use *Profile Badges* for linking to your LinkedIn profile from an e-mail signature, website or anywhere else.

Other Parts of Your LinkedIn® Profile

You have a chance to fill other profile parts in as well, but they are not so important for the recruitment community. These parts include:

- Education
- Languages
- Certifications
- Organizations
- Additional info – Interests, Personal details, Advice for contacting you
- Projects
- Honors & Awards
- Test Scores
- Courses
- Patents
- Volunteering & Causes.

It really depends if you have something meaningful to highlight. Otherwise, filling in just anything can make your profile unnecessarily complicated.

Groups and Following

The *Groups section* of your LinkedIn® profile is a list of groups you are a member or the owner of. The *Following* section is where a list of companies and news you are following is published. More about LinkedIn Groups and Companies is explained in the chapter *08, Plunder at Your Own Will: Utilizing Groups and Companies for Recruitment.*

LinkedIn® Applications are History

LinkedIn Applications are being replaced with a new feature that lets you add media links to images, presentations, videos, and documents. So do not try to install any LinkedIn applications because you will just get the message:

You have reached the limit of applications on your homepage and your profile. Please remove an application from both pages before adding another application.

This new feature is only available if you have the new LinkedIn profile type. If you previously had LinkedIn® applications installed on your old LinkedIn profile, for example, *Amazon Reading List,* they will not be available on your new profile.

The LinkedIn Corporation completely migrated old LinkedIn applications to the new rich media system which is going to support different 3rd party applications that were unavailable until now.

NOTE

If you have the *Slideshare Presentations* or *Portfolio Display* applications on your current profile, that content will be migrated to the *Summary* section of your profile once you have the new profile design. However, video using the Slideshare application will not start playing automatically as it did previously.

How does it work at the moment?

The sections *Summary, Education* and *Experience* and their items include the icon in the edit mode (*see figure 4.21*).

⊡ Add your videos, images, documents...

Figure 4.21: New rich media add interface

This is the new and only interface which can be used for adding content you used to add with LinkedIn applications including: presentations (*SlideShare, Google Docs*), the list of books you are currently reading (*Amazon Reading List*), export of your blog (*Wordpress, Blog Link*), other files for download (*Box.net Files*), etc.

Everything is available by pasting links (*see figure 4.22*), so you do not need to install applications anymore.

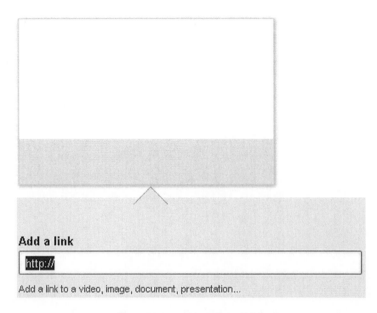

4.22: New rich media add link

Unfortunately, not all of the former applications are supported anymore. So, for instance, if you had a video over on the SlideShare application which was automatically started when somebody viewed your profile, such a video does not work anymore. It has been moved to the *Summary* section and migrated to the new media system, which avoids automatic starting of such videos. If anybody wants to start such a video, they have to click on it and it starts in an external frame. I would say that for a user viewing a profile, it is a bit less user-friendly.

The list of supported media formats is pretty long and, based on the LinkedIn Corporation's modifications, the list is being expanded.

How to Add a Video to Your Profile

As you can see from the video provider's list further in this section, there are lots of video providers. Probably the easiest way to publish your own video is to put it on YouTube (*www.youtube.com*) and then use the icon *Add your videos, images, documents...* to add a video to your profile.

Once you add the link of the video to the *Add a link* field, it switches automatically to provide you with *Title* and *Description* fields for your video (*see figure 4.23*). These fields can be edited according to your requirements.

Once you have entered a *Title* and *Description*, hit *Save* and you are done.

In the very same way you can use other video providers including:

- ABC News
- AllThingsD
- Animoto
- Atom
- bambuser
- big think
- blip
- Boston
- Bravo
- brightcove
- CBS News
- Clikthrough
- Clipfish
- ClipShack
- Clip Syndicate
- CNBC
- CNN
- CNN Edition
- CNN Money
- Colbert Nation
- CollegeHumor
- Comedy Central
- Confreaks

- Crackle
- Dailymotion
- Dipdive
- distrify
- dotsub
- Fora.tv
- Forbes
- funny or die
- GameTrailers
- GodTube
- Hulu
- Jardenberg
- justin.tv
- Khan Academy
- KoldCast TV
- LiveLeak
- Logo FierceTV
- Panorama
- Washington Post
- Zero Inch
- TED
- Telly
- The Daily Show

- mobypicture
- New York Magazine
- NZ On Screen
- Overstream
- PBS Video
- Revision3
- SchoolTube
- ScienceStage
- ShowMe
- snotr
- Socialcam
- Spreecast
- VEVO
- Viddler
- viewrz
- Vimeo
- Washington Post
- XTRANORMAL
- Youku
- YouTube
- Zapiks
- Coub
- The Escapist

How to Add a Presentation to Your Profile

Presentations can be added in the same way as videos, it just depends which presentation provider you are used to using.

There are four of them at the moment:

- Google Docs
- Prezi
- Scribd
- SlideShare

Of course you can also add a video to your presentation and publish such a presentation on your LinkedIn profile.

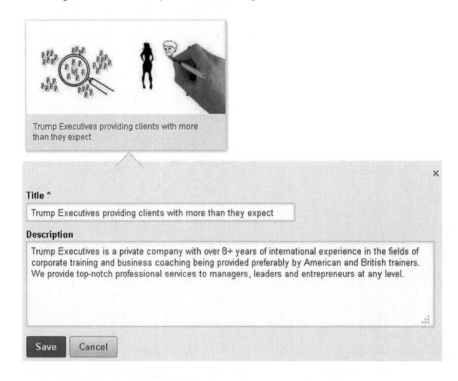

Figure 4.23: Add a video to your LinkedIn profile Figure

How to Add Audio and an Image to Your Profile

If you want to put audio or an image to your profile, use the following audio and image providers.

Audio Providers:

- AudioBoo
- Band Camp
- Free Music Archive
- gogoyoko
- Grooveshark

- Hark
- Huffduffer
- Mixcloud
- RadioReddit
- Rdio

- SoundCloud
- Spotify
- Zero

Image Providers:

- 23hq

- pikchur

- twitpic

- meadd
- mlkshk
- mobypicture
- ow.ly

- Pinterest
- Questionable Content
- somecards
- twitgoo

- TwitrPix
- Twitter

How to Add Other Media Formats to Your Profile

There are a few other media providers which can be used to add media content to your LinkedIn® profile, including:

- Behance – portfolio publisher

- Issuu – any document presented in the form of a magazine

- Kickstarter – the funding platform

- Quantcast – enables you to buy and sell targeted audiences in real time.

How to Add a Blog to Your Profile

At the moment it is not possible to add a blog output as we were able to with the old LinkedIn profiles. If you self-host a *WordPress* site, you can enable auto posting to LinkedIn through the *Jetpack* plugin from *Automatic*. If your site is on *WordPress.com*, simply enable the *Publicize* setting for LinkedIn from your *WordPress.com* dashboard. This will simply share the link to your blog posts in the LinkedIn activity section. It is not analogical to what we were used to before, when we could create a stable blog section in our LinkedIn® profile containing about five of the latest blog posts.

How to Add Your Business Trips to Your Profile

You will be able to continue to post *TripIt* updates to your LinkedIn network and profile by linking your *TripIt* and LinkedIn accounts. So if you want to share your business trips with your LinkedIn audience, set up a link to LinkedIn from your account on *TripIt* (*www.tripit.com*).

If I were writing this book a few months earlier, I would also recommend the *Events* application which was helping with event arrangement. However, this feature has been removed by the LinkedIn Corporation.

LinkedIn® Profile Settings

The *Settings* section hides some quite interesting and useful options which you are probably not aware of, even if you are an experienced user. See the subsection *Profile -> Privacy Controls items*. I will mention just the relevant items for recruiters:

Turn on/off your activity broadcasts – If you want to hide the fact that you are making changes to your profile, just turn off your activity broadcast. As a recruiter, you will not use it that often. However, there might be times when you want to hide that you are connecting with somebody or making changes to your profile which you do not want your connections to know about. If you want to stay under the radar, just turn this option off.

This option is especially useful for your potential candidates, when they want to hide that they are connecting with certain recruiters, following companies, gaining recommendations and improving their profiles which might indicate a willingness to change their current job. And, ultimately, cause problems for them with their current employer.

Select who can see your activity feed – Activities you are executing on LinkedIn are also stored in a tab called *Josef's Activity* (i.e. using your own name e.g. *John's Activity* or *Jane's Activity etc.*) and are displayed underneath the top section of your LinkedIn® profile. It is the same story as the previous point, if you need to stay under the radar and don't want to show what activities you are doing, choose the option where only you can see your activity feed. You can set it back whenever you need.

Select what others see when you've viewed their profile – In general users can normally see who is visiting their profiles. Using your own profile, just go to the *Who's Viewed Your Profile?* tab and click on the relevant link. In the same way you are visible at profiles you have visited. If you want to stay under the radar when browsing employees of a particular company, change this setting to *You will be totally anonymous*. Once you are done, you can change the setting back as it is beneficial for networking to be visible. Plus, if you want to see who is visiting your profile, you need to be visible - i.e. *Your name and headline (Recommended)* option.

Select who can see your connections – 1st degree connections are normally allowed to see the list of your connections. This option allows you to hide your connections from them, meaning that no one can see your connections. But don't get confused. **Those connections still appear in the search results of your connections.** That is why this is NOT that powerful a weapon against your competitors. It is more complicated than that. I will come back to this later.

You can keep the rest of the settings as default. Changing them makes no major difference and they are mostly of a cosmetic nature.

Move the Position of LinkedIn® Profile Sections

You can select the position of your profile sections such as *Skills & Expertise* or *Publications* across your LinkedIn profile according to your needs. You can also move the items within each section. This means that you can sort your work engagements at will.

There is no best practice rule to say where a particular section should be placed. If you think that your *Publications* section is bringing added value, move it to the beginning of your profile. If you think that the listing of your job experience is making a difference, move the *Experience* section to the top.

Try to embody the potential candidates who see your LinkedIn profile and find out what is the best placement of sections for you. Clear, well arranged and compact profiles win. So do not overcomplicate your profile by adding lots of sections.

LinkedIn® Marking

When browsing LinkedIn profiles you may notice different signs and badges next to user's names (*see figure 4.24*).

Tom Dupuis 🔲 ⚙ (2nd)

Alexis Ndekwe 💼 ⚙ (2nd)

Shachar B. (GROUP)

Josef Kadlec [LION] (YOU)

Figure 4.24: LinkedIn marking next to users' names

It is probably obvious what each sign means, but some of them are critical for recruiters to realize what they mean exactly.

1st 2nd 3rd	These signs mark your relation to the particular LinkedIn user.
GROUP	This sign marks a LinkedIn® user who is out of your network (i.e. they are not a 1st, 2nd and 3rd degree connection) but he/she is in the same group as you. This is important because such a user can be easily contacted by a message even if he/she is out of your network. This becomes one of the most powerful aspects of your recruitment process.
❖	This badge indicates that a user is a member of the so-called OpenLink network, meaning that anybody can send him/her an InMail® message (a type of paid LinkedIn message) for free. You have to purchase a premium LinkedIn account to be able to be part of the OpenLink network.
in	This badge indicates that you purchased one of the LinkedIn premium accounts. It can be turned on and off.
💼	This badge indicates that the member is looking for a job. It is available only for premium accounts, so you cannot benefit from it significantly.
YOU	This icon just highlights your profile in your searches. Simple.

NOTE

Get your LinkedIn profile reviewed by a professional. If you want your LinkedIn profile checked by an independent, 3rd party professional from the recruitment field, visit LINREA.com. For a couple of dollars you can get a review of your LinkedIn profile with suggestions for improvement. Avoid paying big money to LinkedIn consultants who do not have any experience with recruitment.

Chapter Summary

- Your LinkedIn® profile should be upgraded to All-Star rank

- Avoid an incomplete LinkedIn® profile or a profile with too much information

- Pay attention to all important profile sections including *Recommendations, Name, Photo, Summary,* and *Experience*

- Keep your LinkedIn® profile public and set up your public profile URL

- Adjust your profile due to the recent LinkedIn® profiles update

05

Cultivate Your Hunting Ground: LinkedIn® Networking Strategy for Recruiters

Cultivate Your Hunting Ground: LinkedIn® Networking Strategy for Recruiters

---

What you will learn in this chapter

- What are the recruiter's main networking goals

- How to effectively increase the number of connections without being banned

- How you should act based on your actual individual LinkedIn® network development

---

Networking strategy is one of the main parts of LinkedIn® recruitment and it is directly connected together with other pieces of the recruitment puzzle. The whole **LinkedIn recruitment method has to be taken as a process** which is not static. Not only because it is an ongoing, never-ending process, but also because it really depends where you stand at the beginning of the process. A LinkedIn® user with just a few 1st line contacts lacking market penetration should stick to a different behavior than a user with thousands of connections from his/her recruitment niche. In the same way, users somewhere in the middle should follow different rules.

You can read from other sources basically just one simple rule and that is: connect with anybody, send your invitations in different directions and gain volume.

Wrong!

This might work for people from sales in some way but not for recruiters. If everybody behaves like that, which is not rocket science because everybody can do it, where is the differentiation separating superstars and losers?

You have to step out of the crowd to be successful. In such a competitive industry, which recruitment definitely is, it does not mean just working hard but also working smart.

What We Want to Achieve in Recruitment

Firstly, it is important to realize and analyze what each individual recruiter or team of recruiters is limited to, what is their 'playground' regardless of LinkedIn.

Each recruiter has some **recruitment niche** such as finance, retail, IT, automotive, etc. Or he/she can, for example, act across industries while seeking managers, HR managers, accountants or just be a general recruiter for various types of job openings. Also, IT professionals do not work only for pure information technology companies but can also work at automotive, logistics, and finance industry companies like banks etc. So things might be a little bit confusing. Therefore, you should become crystal clear about your target group and, if it is possible to determine also, which companies are the primary source of such people within your location.

Next, you are limited to a location, which can be a continent (Europe, Northern America, Asia, etc.), a country (United Kingdom, Germany, Japan, etc.) or just a city or area (New York City area, Paris, Prague). It can also be a combination of e.g. two cities or two countries. This basically reflects the company location of your clients.

This can be further divided into two groups where the first one includes primary locations where there are no distance and commuting barriers for new employees (usually the same city where the employer is located or sometimes a state or a country) and the second one, which is extended and belongs to a location not so close to the employer premises but in which people still might be interested in relocating to.

Usually the reason for commuting or relocation can be going from a small city to a larger one which can mean better prospects in terms of future career. On the other hand a candidate might move from a larger city to a smaller one to fill a very specific role, i.e. it might be a higher quality opportunity.

Once you are clear about these facts, you can set up shop. **You're optimal networking goal as a LinkedIn recruiter is to have your target group within your location reachable via LinkedIn but isolated from your competition.** You do not want others to parasite on your hard developed network.

Maybe you are wondering what I mean by 'reachable'. Of course, the most ideal status is to have your complete target group as 1st degree contacts. Unfortunately, this is hardly possible. The realistic scenario is that you have the majority of your potential candidates as 1st and 2nd degree contacts and the rest as 3rd degree contacts. Some of you may have obstacles such as not seeing even a surname for 3rd degree contacts. This is on purpose and LinkedIn made this happen a few years ago. But still, there are ways to uncover the full name of 3rd line contacts and I will show you how to do this in the chapter *07, Shoot to Kill: How to Reach Candidates with LinkedIn® Every Time.*

So imagine a network where you can reach any of your potential candidates, this network is growing automatically as new people are joining LinkedIn itself or just entering the industry and target group you are focused on; and, there are no other recruiters directly (i.e. meaning 1st degree connections) connected to you, which is changing the odds in your favor.

Automatic growth occurs naturally because it is highly probable that someone is entering your target group (e.g. someone became a software engineer which is your target group) and is a 1st degree connection with some of your 1st or 2nd degree connections, which makes him/her your 2nd or 3rd degree connection.

Of course, your never-ending goal is to convert your connections to 1st degree connections and ultimately increase the number not only of your 1st, but also 2nd degree connections.

But how do you get to this desirable state? Especially when you have zero, tens or a few hundred connections, which means that you are not penetrating the market significantly. Or maybe you have thousands of connections, but lack targeted ones.

Take a look at your LinkedIn® connections and analyze them from this perspective. How do you stand? If you search for potential candidates on LinkedIn, are you getting a lot of people with 3rd degree connections (those without their surname) or worse, people marked as out of your network? How many 1st degree connections do you *really have*? Tens, hundreds or thousands?

The number of 1st degree connections is not a 100% determinative parameter dividing better users from worse ones. In reference to the previous information, you can have a better quality network with fewer 1st degree connections and paradoxically also a higher impact in terms of the number of your 2nd and 3rd degree connections. The key factor is how many 1st degree connections your 1st degree connections have. It is just pure math.

Image this example to simplify the problem. User A has two 1st degree connections. User B has three 1st degree connections. It can seem like user B has a bigger market impact in comparison to user A. But user A has a better quality network where each of his/her connections (1st and 2nd degree ones) have three 1st degree connections. User B has a lower quality network where each of their 1st and 2nd degree connections has just two 1st degree connections. The math says that the overall impact of user A is 26 users, while user B has only 21 users in his network (*see figure 5.1*).

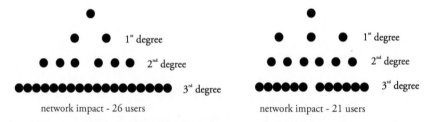

network impact - 26 users   network impact - 21 users

Figure 5.1: LinkedIn network impact simulation

And I am not counting things like groups, which are other powerful tools for recruiters. I will explain how to benefit from groups in the chapter *08, Plunder at Your Own Will: Utilizing Groups and Companies for Recruitment.*

The number of overall 1st degree connections can determine, to some extent, who is a complete beginner not using LinkedIn® much (zero to a few 1st degree connections), a user using LinkedIn on an average basis (tens to a few hundred 1st degree connections) and a user actively using LinkedIn (five hundred or more 1st degree connections).

Increase LinkedIn® Connections without Being Banned

There are several more or less natural ways to establish and develop your LinkedIn network.

1) Connect with Your Acquaintances, Colleagues and Former Colleagues

Probably the very first step leading to an increase in your LinkedIn connections is your friends and colleagues. You should be sure that these people are going to accept your LinkedIn invitation without any problems. Search for them and connect with them in the standard way.

If you use *Gmail, Yahoo Mail* or any other mainstream webmail service, you can easily browse your e-mail connections by adding your e-mail to your LinkedIn profile (*Contacts -> Add Connection*). You can also import contacts from *MS Outlook, Apple Mail* or contacts stored in a file (*Contacts -> Add Connection -> Upload Contacts File*). Or you can invite anyone else simply by adding his/her e-mail (*Contacts -> Add Connection -> Invite by individual e-mail*) or by sending bulk e-mails.

Choose your connections wisely from the beginning. As you have only a limited number of invitations, it does not pay to connect with friends who have approximately ten 1st degree connections.

Anyway, if you are a recruiter, your colleagues are probably also recruiters. Do not forget that **you do not want to let other competitive recruiters take advantage of your network.** On the other hand, when your network is weak or average, let's say up to five hundred 1st degree connections, it is beneficial for you to connect with other recruiters having five hundred plus 1st degree connections.

For instance, I have over three hundred pending invitations from recruiters of varying LinkedIn network quality who want to connect with me. At the moment, when my LinkedIn® network is providing me with 100% market coverage in my recruitment niche and location, they simply cannot bring any added value. Be aware that if you accept such invitations, you are offering your network at their disposal which might be expressed by lost opportunity costs. In such a case, just leave the incoming invitations as pending (*see figure 5.2*).

Of course, a really unfriendly recruiter could hit *Report Spam* which should complicate the sender's life a little bit as he/she can be suspended from sending more invitations. But I prefer a way that does not let us parasite on ourselves, but also does not harm others. The latter I prefer only in a boxing ring but that's another story.

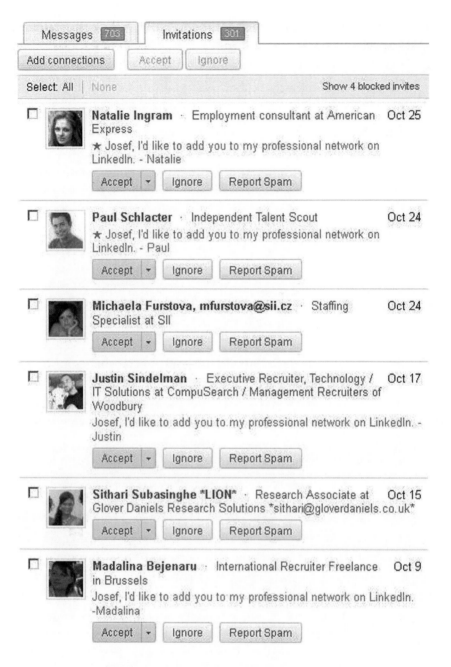

Figure 5.2: LinkedIn pending invitations from recruiters all over the world

Now, you needn't be afraid of sending me your invitations because I am in a different situation at the moment. My personal career changed from a full-time headhunter to the owner of a recruitment and training agency, and also the trainer for a LinkedIn recruitment academy, LINREA.com. So feel free to send me your invitations if you wish. But think carefully before accepting invitations from other recruiters, especially those with weak connections. Guard your territory.

How to Track the Real Number of Connections for Users Labeled with 500+

The fact is you are not able to track the number of connections of other users when they reach five hundred 1st degree connections so easily. They are just marked with a *500+* label so you do not know if such a user has six hundred or six thousand 1st degree connections at first sight.

New LinkedIn profile

However, if you really need to know the number there is a way to find out. Unfortunately, with the new LinkedIn® profiles it is more demanding than with the old ones. Open the LinkedIn profile of the user being reviewed and scroll to the *Connections* part (*see figure 5.3*).

Then click the *NEXT* button and count the number of clicks till the end of the list. If someone has e.g. 10,000 connections, you need to click 1,000 times which is pretty awkward. But the method works.

Old LinkedIn profile

If the user you want to check still has an old profile, you need *See all Connections »* (in the right-hand table) and you can see a full list of the user's 1st degree connections, including all the shared ones. If there is no such option, it means that the user disabled other users from browsing his/her connections (see the section *LinkedIn Profile Settings* in the chapter *04, Prepare Your Arsenal: How to Fine-Tune LinkedIn® Profile for Recruitment*). You can see the tab with all the user's connections and the tab with the shared user's connections.

Simply by counting all user connections you will get the real number of a user's 1st degree connections. Just multiply the number of pages by twenty five which gives you the lump sum of all connections (to be precise you should take into account that the very first and very last page does not probably have twenty five connections, but less). So when somebody claims that they has ten thousand 1st degree connections, you can easily verify this.

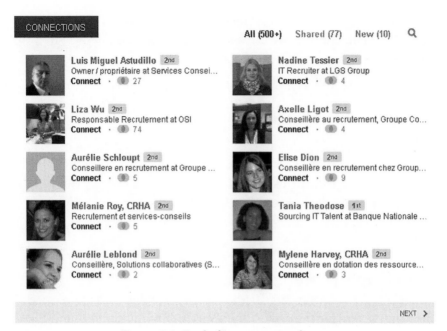

Figure 5.3: LinkedIn connections listing

When you develop a solid network you are confident with and these connections are of no value to you, you can erase such temporary connections to avoid them using your network. I know it is dirty but don't forget that the number of connections is not the only aspect which separates a successful recruiter from a less successful one, but it is also the skill of utilizing connections effectively.

How to Remove Connections

It sounds like a simple operation, but sometimes it is difficult to find this function on LinkedIn. Click *Contacts* on the main menu, wait till your address book is loaded and then hit *Remove Connections*. Select connections you want to erase and hit the *Remove Connections* button (*see figure 5.4*).

Always take into account that you have only a limited amount of invitations you can send. So choose wisely who you send invitations to. **The maximum number of invitations is three thousand.** When you exceed two thousand sent invitations, you will be notified by a countdown for the last one thousand invitations.

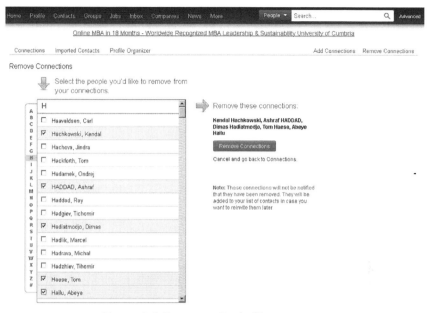

Figure 5.4: Removing LinkedIn connections

How to deal with this?

There are ways which I will show you at the end of this chapter.

2) Recruitment Network Building

Enlargement of your LinkedIn® network is directly connected with LinkedIn recruitment itself. One of the main ways to approach your potential candidates is to send them a LinkedIn invitation. With this approach, your 1st degree connections naturally grow.

However, as always, it is not that black and white. First you need to maximize the number of accepted invitations (option *Accept*) – this means trying to avoid the person keeping your invitation as pending. He/she could just reply to you with a message (option *Reply*) or, at worst, hit the *Report spam* or *Ignore* buttons.

Recruitment methods will be thoroughly explained in the chapter *07, Shoot to Kill: How to Reach Candidates with LinkedIn® Every Time*.

3) Connect with People from Your Recruitment Niche

The best way to approach a community which is your target group is to be one of them. My former background is in IT, as a software engineer, so it was pretty easy to connect with my peers. However, receiving invitations from recruiters is sometimes like receiving invitations from a stranger.

On top of this, they usually do not have a good reputation. That is why you need to provide added value for your potential candidates to discreetly force them to accept your invitation or to appear as one of them.

If you worked in the same field where you are executing recruitment, take advantage of that big time. Try to connect with as many professionals as possible from such a target group without offering them any job. Just as if a banker is connecting with a banker or an IT professional with an IT professional.

One ethically questionable method for pure recruiters who did not work in the industry they are recruiting for is to temporarily create a profile which does not look like that of a recruiter but e.g. a finance professional; or at least to create a former background from the industry which gives them higher credit as a recruiter in a specific industry.

4) Connecting with the Regional Top Open Networkers

One way to penetrate a specific market with potential candidates is to connect with the regional top open networkers with significant numbers of 1st degree connections. These are users who have a lot of 1st degree connections, especially from a specific region – e.g. North America, Central Europe, greater New York City area, etc.

If your market penetration is not sufficient, it means you have up to about five hundred 1st degree connections (it might vary based on the size of the specific region); you might take advantage of strong open-networkers, but how to find them?

These users are open networkers so they accept invitations from anybody. It is often not immediate though, sometimes such users can receive lots of invitations every day. Open networkers mark themselves with the term *LION* which is usually a part of their surname.

To find open networkers in a specific region and sort them by their number of connections, just use the following search. Open *Advanced People Search* and fill-in the following fields (*see figure 5.5*):

Last Name
LION

Location
Located in or near

Country
Select country (for example, Brazil)

Postal code
If you want to specify e.g. a city, use a postal code. Bear in mind that not everyone fills this field in their profile so that such people will not be included in the search results.

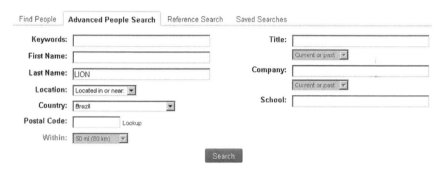

Figure 5.5: Searching for LinkedIn open networkers

When the results show up, sort them by connections - option *Sort by: Connections* (*see figure 5.6*).

To display more open networkers, you can search with *LION* filled in the field *Keywords*. However, this might also display users who are not open networkers because it takes only the presence of the term *LION* on such a profile. So, for example, when there is a recommendation from a user *John Mattison [LION]* on a profile, the owner of this profile will be included in the search results even if he is not an open networker.

You will also get results when you put *LION* into the form field *First Name* or *Title*. You can also use other keywords in the field *Keywords* to display such users. These keywords include words like 'open networker', 'networker', 'toplinked', etc.

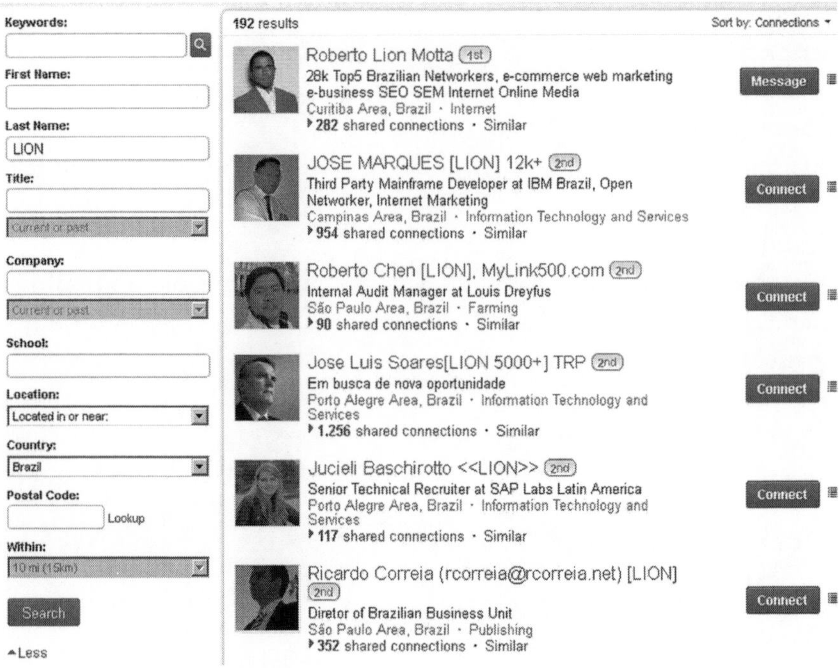

Figure 5.6: Sorting LinkedIn People Search results

Even if you have zero 1st degree connections, you are able to do this. The only difference from the screenshot will be that all of your connections will be marked as *out of your network*. Anyway, it is not an obstacle to connect with them.

Some of those open networkers might also be recruiters. In reference to behavior towards other recruiters, I would connect with such recruiters only temporarily or completely avoid them if you can substitute them with non-recruiting open networkers.

To find recruiters in a specific region and sort them by their number of connections, just use the following search. Open *Advanced People Search* and fill-in the following fields:

Title
(Recruiter OR recruiting OR recruitment OR sourcer OR sourcing OR talent OR career OR headhunter)

Location
Located in or near

Country

Select country (for example, Spain)

Postal code

If you want to specify e.g. a city, use the postal code. Bear in mind that not everyone fills this field in their profile, so such people will not be included in the search results.

When the results show up, sort them by connections - option *Sort by: Connections* (*see figure 5.7*).

The title might vary according to the local language in the country you focus on. If you want to display recruiters from e.g. Spain, you should include other terms in the Boolean search (in *Title*) like 'reclutador', 'reclutamiento' and other local expressions.

Figure 5.7: Seeking recruiters and sorting results by connections

If you have a brand new LinkedIn® account or your LinkedIn 1st degree connections are close to zero, you will have problems connecting with the vast majority of these people as you cannot see their names and profiles and you are not able to send them an invitation (*see figure 5.8*).

131

As you can see, you can still send invitations to people who are part of the OpenLink Network, which is a function available to LinkedIn® premium users. So you can connect with top recruiters in terms of the amount of connections from your region and potentially also from your recruitment niche.

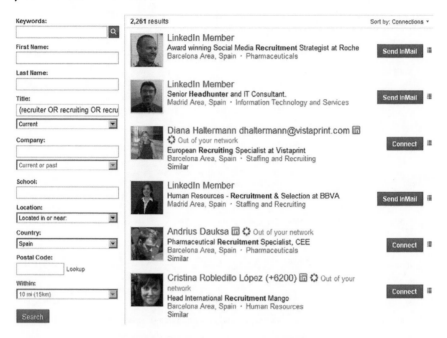

Figure 5.8: Search results with a weak LinkedIn account

5) Become a Recruiters-Free Open Networker

Maybe you wonder how it is possible that someone has five thousand, ten thousand or thirty thousand 1st degree connections when it is possible to send just three thousand invitations? You basically have to persuade others to send invitations to you.

Another approach to expand your network is to become an open networker or an open networker not accepting recruiters. This is beneficial primarily for recruiters with a global scope of work who want to gain maximum impact globally.

In the chapter *04, Prepare Your Arsenal: How to Fine-Tune LinkedIn® Profile for Recruitment,* I showed how to mark yourself as a LinkedIn Open Networker. Having LION next to your name is not the only thing you should do as an open networker.

Furthermore, open networkers group themselves in LinkedIn groups.

Here is a list of the most significant ones:

- **TopLinked.com (Open Networkers)** 134,100+ members

- **OpenNetworker.com** 66,400+ members

- **LION500.com (Open Networkers)** 60,000+ members

- **Leading International Open Networkers (LION)** 23,330+ members

- **LIONTM Worn with Pride! [Choose wisely ...] < BEWARE** 21,770+ members

- **InvitesWelcome.com (Open Networking)** 20,740+ members

You may also find the local open networking groups valid for particular countries and cities. If you join these groups and you are marked as a LinkedIn open networker, you might expect that invitations will start to come.

There is one limit which the majority of you needn't bother with and it is the maximal number of 1st degree connections you can have. That **limitation is thirty thousand connections.** When you reach this number you would only be able to replace the old connections with new ones. This limit was not there when LinkedIn began, so you might find some people having more than thirty thousand and also forty thousand 1st degree connections, such as Ron Bates with forty three thousand 1st degree connections.

Here you can see an interview with him:
http://j.mp/CNN_Interview

Anyway, this is not possible anymore. But not to worry, this limitation is an enemy of recruiters but it is unlikely to ever affect you. In 99% of cases, you will not need to worry about this limitation.

There are services for open networkers (they are not created or maintained by the LinkedIn® Corporation) whose purpose is to provide an easy way for open networkers to connect between themselves.

One of the most significant of these services is *TopLinked.com* (reachable also via their sister site *OpenNetworker.com*). As a non-paid member you are able to download a list of open-networkers which you can easily import into your LinkedIn account. It will send an invitation to all the users from a shortlist which the users should accept. As they are marked as open networkers and they pay to be on the list, there is almost a 100% guarantee that they will do so. If you want to be on the list as well, you need to pay $9.95 for one month or $49.95 for one year.

You might find similar services with lower significance. But as I said, it pays off only for recruiters with a global impact. Of course, if you enjoy being an open networker, you can use these services. But take into account two limitations – your maximal number of sent invitations is three thousand, so do not waste them on worthless or less important contacts. And your maximal number of 1st degree connections is thirty thousand, which is, of course, a limit you will not reach in a few days. The bottom line is to focus on your recruitment goals and modify your approach to those.

Dealing with a Limited Amount of Invitations

If you are an active recruiter, running out of LinkedIn® invitations is inevitable. But it does not mean you are done. Firstly, sending invitations is not the only way to contact your potential candidates. It is one of the major ones, though. I will describe all potential ways in the next chapter *07, Shoot to Kill: How to Reach Candidates with LinkedIn® Every Time.* And secondly, we can deal with the lack of invitations on our own.

How do you find out how many invitations you already depleted?

Just check your *Inbox -> Invitations -> Sent invitations.* At the bottom you can see the overall number of sent invitations – e.g. 1 - 15 of 2,395 which means you sent 2,395. I'm assuming you do not erase any invitations from this folder.

NOTE

When you have your last one thousand invitations, you will be notified about your remaining invitations after sending any single invitation.

When you run out of invitations, you can ask LinkedIn for a few more. However, this will not cover your recruitment needs at all.

So, how to deal with this? You need to simply create another duplicate LinkedIn account. But don´t worry, you needn't do this to boost your network from the beginning to have good market coverage and be able to search people effectively. You will use your main well established account to make the searches, but the invitations themselves will be sent over to the new account. This is how you can do it. The very first rule is **not to completely deplete your invitations on your original account!** If you know that you are down to your last five to eight hundred invitations, stop using them for actual recruitment and save them for other networking purposes like connecting with top open networkers which might bring added value to your searches in a particular area.

You should aim to have one LinkedIn account maximized for search purposes in your recruitment area – i.e. you have all of your potential candidates maximally as 2nd degree connections. Just a minority of them should be 3rd degree connections, and none of them should be out of your network. Your other LinkedIn® accounts should be utilized for a new set of three thousand invitations.

Try to have some logic in your duplicate accounts. For example, if your original account is covering mainly the finance sector in the USA and you want to penetrate the Canadian region also, simply allocate the second LinkedIn account for the Canadian region.

As it is not possible to strictly cover only the USA, you will use your original account to find first Canadian connections for the second duplicate account and as your network base of the second account is growing, you will slowly reach a deeper market penetration in Canada than with your original account. It means that when you need to find some potential candidates or specific people in Canada, you will use your second LinkedIn account for that.

It works anywhere else in the same way. For instance, I covered the IT sector in the Czech Republic with my main account. And the IT sector in Romania and Bulgaria with my two 'side' LinkedIn accounts. Of course, it is not necessary to scale it like that. If you are lacking invitations on your main account, you will use other LinkedIn accounts just for the new set of invitations and you will stay in the same region and recruitment niche.

So it is time to create your new LinkedIn® account. It can look basically the same as your original account, but I recommend using another picture, title and also use different symbols with your name. This will help you to recognize which LinkedIn account you are logged into at the moment (*see figure 5.9*).

Figure 5.9: LinkedIn duplicate account differentiation

And your additional LinkedIn accounts will not seem so suspicious and confusing when they appear in search results (*see figure 5.10*).

Figure 5.10: LinkedIn duplicate account appearance in search results

Once you have two LinkedIn accounts, sign into the original one, open Advanced People Search and make your search. I will explain how to proceed with effective searches in the next chapter *06, Chase Down Your Targets: How to Target Candidates with LinkedIn*® so I will not be explaining this in detail at the moment.

No matter which internet browser you are using (I recommend *Mozilla Firefox* but *Google Chrome* or *MS Explorer* do the job just as well), open each of the potential candidates you want to contact by invitation in a separate tab (right click on the candidate's name and click *Open Link in New Tab* or you can use the middle button of your mouse to do the same thing). Just make sure you are still logged in with your original LinkedIn account.

Let's say, for example, we are seeking a general manager in Brazil (*see figure 5.11*).

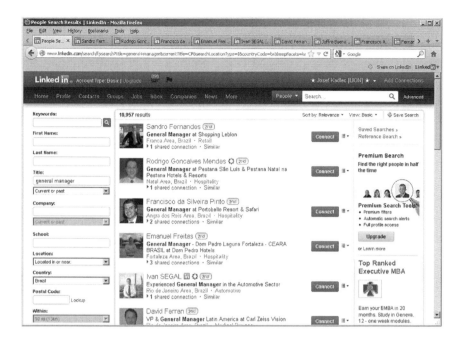

Figure 5.11: Search results including Brazil general managers

Now use the very first tab of your browser and sign out from your original account (*see figure 5.12*).

Then hit sign in and login with your duplicate LinkedIn® account. If you use a different picture and e.g. symbols before and after your name, you should see that you are logged with your new account.

Now you are logged in with your new account (*see figure 5. 13*). You want to use this account for sending the invitation because you are running out of invitations on your original one. Now just simply skip to the tab with the first profile and hit the *Connect* (earlier called *Send Invitation*) button (*see figure 5.14*).

It is important that you do not refresh the site. If you refresh the browser tab with the opened profile, it will be loaded with your duplicate profile which means you cannot see the *Connect* button as this user is not a 2nd degree connection, but a 3rd degree connection or even out of your network, toward your duplicate account most probably (*see figure 5.15*).

Figure 5.12: Sign out off your main LinkedIn account

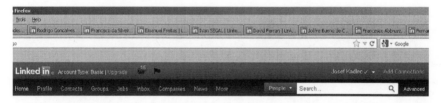

Figure 5.13: Log in with your duplicate LinkedIn account

So, just skip to that tab and hit the *Connect* button. You will get to the details of the invitation where you can choose the reference which the invitation will be sent to the potential candidate in. You can reference that you are a friend of the potential candidate, former colleague or schoolmate or you've done business with them (*see figure 5.16*).

Also paste a personal note, which is very important to maximize the response rate. I will describe the most effective strategies for sending invitations in the next chapter, *07, Shoot to Kill: How to Reach Candidates with LinkedIn® Every Time.*

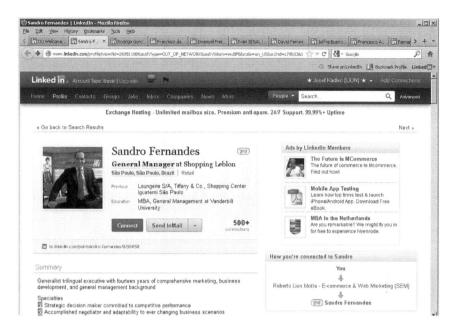

Figure 5.14: Open the first tab and hit the Connect button

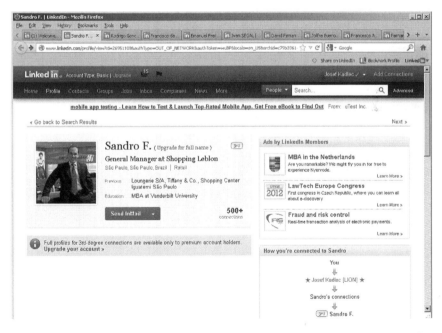

Figure 5.15: Refreshed site using your duplicate account avoiding you using the Connect button

In the same way, you will proceed with the other tabs. As you can see, you are utilizing the strong penetration of your original account, but using invitations of the new account. With this procedure you will never run out of invitations. Of course, you need to do the prior development of your original account to gain the maximal network penetration and see the vast majority of your potential candidates maximally as 2nd degree connections.

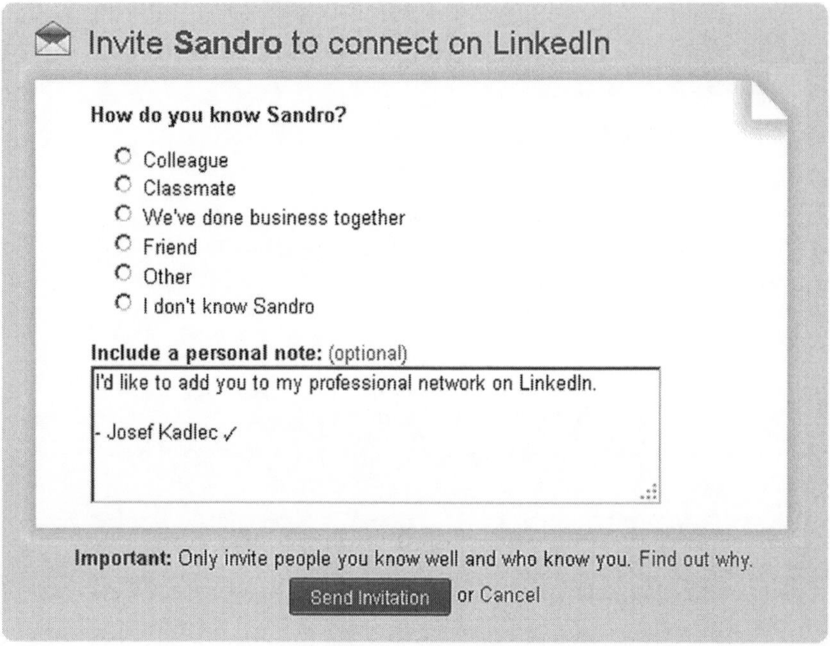

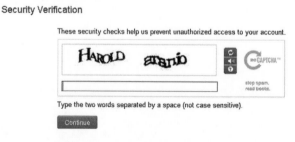

Figure 5.16: Invitation options

When sending many invitations from one account, you can be asked to verify that you are not a robot. You need to simply fill-in a so called CAPTCHA (*see figure 5.17*).

Figure 5.17: LinkedIn CAPTCHA when sending too many invitations

I found out that it is sufficient to type the second word only to get through the security verification. This might speed up your activity a little bit.

> **NOTE**
>
> Creating duplicate LinkedIn accounts is probably not directly against the LinkedIn User Agreement, but the user agreement could be modified at some point. You would need to analyze it to find out. To be 100% safe, I recommend you use a different IP address and password for each duplicate account.

The best way to use more internet identities (i.e. more IP addresses) is to use the application TOR Browser (*https://www.torproject.org/projects/torbrowser.html.en*). This application looks like an internet browser which uses a different IP address to your regular internet browser. So you can easily separate and operate with more LinkedIn accounts without the possibility of being tracked and someone discovering that there is one person behind both accounts. When using TOR Browser for LinkedIn, you might be requested to verify your e-mail address once more.

Should I connect both of my LinkedIn® accounts together?

Maybe you are asking if it is beneficial to send and accept invitations between your original account and the duplicate one, or any other account you have. For the described method it is not necessary. The only benefit is when you want to start using the new account more independently, i.e. making searches with this account that you can provide your established network through the original account. It will help you to boost the growth of your network in the new account.

On the other hand, there are some risks when doing this. I will explain in the section *Breaking the LinkedIn® User Agreement or Not?* So I would avoid doing it if it is not necessary. If you are using the new account just because you are lacking invitations, it is just a new source of free invitations for you. If you are using the new account to penetrate new geographical regions or recruitment areas, you will slowly establish much better penetration focusing on that region with your new account than with the original one. So basically, there is no merit in connecting your LinkedIn accounts together.

What if I Get Banned for Sending Too Many Invitations?

When sending loads of invitations, you will face restrictions from LinkedIn®. There are two ways that you can be banned. When too many users (in fact, five users) flag your invitation as spam (*Report Spam button*) or hit the button *I Don't Know [user's name]* - currently placed when you hit the *Ignore* button (*see figure 5.18*).

Figure 5.18: Actions you can do with incoming invitations

NOTE

In terms of LinkedIn jargon you can sometimes see the term 'no IDK', usually in the title of open networkers. This abbreviation means 'No, I don't know' which verifies that the user will not flag you with 'I don't know' or spam if you send him/her an invitation.

A restriction means that you are not able to send other invitations without specifying the e-mail of the user you are sending the invitation to. Instead of getting the aforementioned invitation form, you will get a slightly different form (*see figure 5.19*).

You can meet the same behavior when you've already sent an invitation to a user. You are not allowed to send another one without filling in the user's e-mail address.

This is also one of the ways you can find out that your account has been restricted. When this happens and you think that it might be because your account has been restricted, you need to contact LinkedIn customer support and ask them to unrestrict your account.

You can do this using their form at:

http://www.linkedin.com/unrestrict?display

Basically, nothing needs to be specified so it is pretty straightforward and fast.

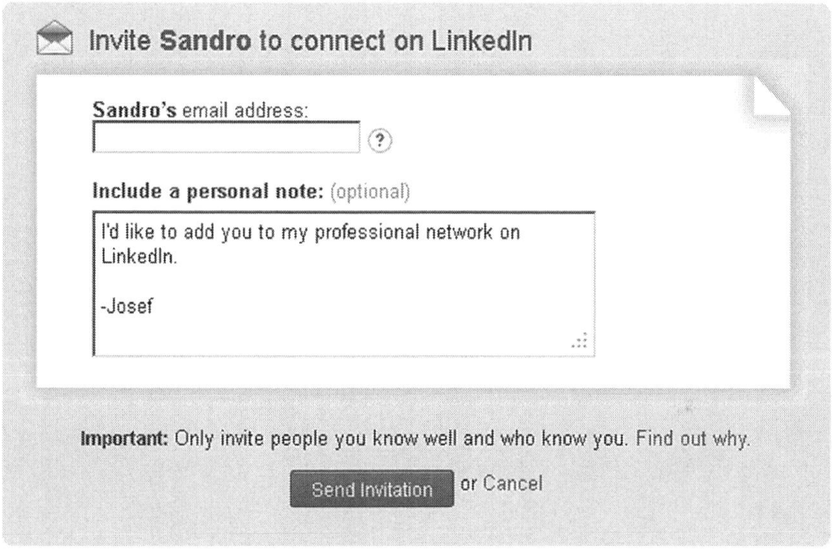

Figure 5.19: Restricted possibility to sending invitations

Or you can use the following e-mail addresses. In any case I would recommend supporting the previous method by sending an e-mail to one of the following:

cs@linkedin.com
customer_service@linkedin.com

The content of the e-mail should look similar as follows:

Subject: Unblocking of my LinkedIn invitation functionality

Dear Sir/Madam,

I would like to request you to unblock my LinkedIn functionality "Invitation". I sent a bunch of invitations to my company colleagues and probably some of them hit the button that they don't know me.

I agree with your T&C.

Thank you.

Best regards,
Josef Kadlec

Stating that you agree with LinkedIn® T&C (Terms and Conditions) is very important. Otherwise, you will be questioned about it in their next reply which prolongs the actual unblocking process. However, you need to take into account that it takes them about a week to unblock it.

From my experience you can repeat this procedure as many times as you want. In the chapter *07, Shoot to Kill: How to Reach Candidates with LinkedIn® Every Time* I will explain how to compose targeted and effective invitations so you will need to solve this just exceptionally.

Sending Out Requests to be Invited

There is also an option to send other users a message with a request to send you an invitation. You will get such requests usually from people who share some LinkedIn group with you. The reason is simple. These people are allowed to send you messages. They usually claim that they are already out of invitations and they are kindly asking you for an invitation.

I do not think that it is an effective strategy for gathering a significant amount of new connections. You have to contact group members one by one. Anyway, if you have time or capacity to do this, you can try to strengthen your connection base using this method.

Breaking the LinkedIn® User Agreement or Not?

As we delve deeper into LinkedIn problems for recruiters, it is probably time to mention some aspects of LinkedIn terms and conditions.

You probably already noticed that we already touched on the *LinkedIn® User Agreement* when we described how to unblock a restricted LinkedIn account. If you need to do this, it means that you did something against the LinkedIn User Agreement; LinkedIn noticed it and restricted your account accordingly.

I am aware that this seems like a little bit of a grey area.

But is it really?

So why do we do such things? We are a moral society. We do not violate rules on purpose and we do not want to on principal. But it can be said that many LinkedIn users and all or the vast majority of recruiters break LinkedIn T&C on some level.

Breaking these rules means just e.g. writing your e-mail address in another form field than it should be in or sending invitations to people you do not know. Oh yeah, recruiters do this big time. Or do you think that they gathered ten thousand, twenty thousand or thirty thousand 1st degree connections naturally?

It is the point of their job. The bottom line of headhunters is to connect with strangers. And these strangers see it as normal and accept it. In general, they are glad that they are connected with and offered job opportunities.

And not only recruiters are in this group. Open networkers break the rules heavily as well, and are not ashamed of it, nor criticized. Nobody has a problem with that.

So what is the problem?

We have to understand the existence of LinkedIn T&C from the LinkedIn Corporation perspective. Firstly, there must be some rules set to avoid lawsuits which can come from running such a social network site – e.g. privacy issues. Secondly, LinkedIn® Corporation exists to make money, so they try and force you to use their paid options to contact people.

The problem is that, from my experience, these paid methods (e.g. sending InMails) are significantly less effective than non-paid ways (e.g. sending invitations).

Plus, I am not counting the fact that you have a very limited number of InMails you can send and this facility does not fulfill your general requirements as a recruiter.

I am not suggesting anybody break LinkedIn Terms & Conditions, not at all! But I want you to be aware that your behavior might be against official LinkedIn rules. If you do break the rules in some way, most probably, nobody will care about it. However, LinkedIn has the right to sanction you if they wish.

In my personal opinion, the written rules are one thing and the moral aspect is the second and more important one. LinkedIn® is constituted by us, LinkedIn users. If we accept our behavior as alright and nobody complains, LinkedIn will have no problems either, especially when it is in alignment with their business growth.

There are other things which can be taken as an affront to the LinkedIn User Agreement. Some of them might be a little surprising for you. Throughout this whole book I will inform you which actions might be against the LinkedIn User Agreement prior to mentioning them.

What can be considered as 'against' the LinkedIn user agreement:

- Sending invitations to people you do not know

- Sending unwelcomed communications to other LinkedIn users

- Providing inaccurate and dated information in your profile

- Not protecting your sensitive personal information such as your e-mail address, telephone, street address or other information that is confidential in nature

- Uploading a profile image that is not your likeness or a head-shot photo

- Creating a false identity on LinkedIn

- Initiating any content that falsely states, impersonates or otherwise misrepresents your identity

- Adding to a content field content that is not intended for such a field (e.g. submitting a telephone number in the *Headline* or any other field)

- Deep-linking to the Site for any purpose, (i.e. including a link to a LinkedIn web page other than LinkedIn's home page) unless expressly authorized in writing by LinkedIn or for the purpose of promoting your profile or a Group on LinkedIn as set forth in the Brand Guidelines

- Using manual or automated software, devices, scripts robots, other means or processes to access, 'scrape', 'crawl' or 'spider' any web pages or other services contained in the site.

What a list! And this is just my shortlist of rules which you as a recruiter should be familiar with. Abusing any of these rules might cause some sort of penalty from LinkedIn. Anyway, many of them are just a formality – e.g. you cannot expect any restrictions for publishing your e-mail in a different form field than it is supposed to be in or publishing a deep-link (e.g. a link to your account) anywhere on the web.

So, How Should I Behave According to My Current LinkedIn® Situation?

As we already know, the overall number of your connections itself is not your primary goal. But it will help me to simplify different scenarios and how to behave in each of them.

0 to 49 Direct Connections

Your recruitment power is very weak and it is quite hard to proceed with powerful LinkedIn® recruitment. Especially when you are not connected to high quality users with plenty of connections from your recruitment niche and location, too many potential candidates are not properly visible to you – their profile is not visible including their name (*see figure 5.20*).

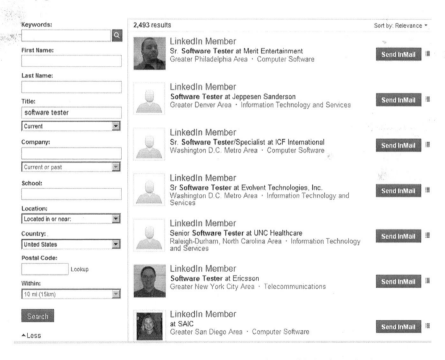

Figure 5.20: People search results using a weakly established LinkedIn account

Even if I show you how to uncover these profiles in the chapter *07, Shoot to Kill: How to Reach Candidates with LinkedIn® Every Time*, for everyday recruitment you need to make market penetration so deep that you are able to see the vast majority of users as 1st, 2nd or 3rd degree connections in your searches.

As you are lacking market penetration, you need to focus on gathering high quality contacts so that you can start with actual recruitment which will lead to the natural growth of your network base.

Therefore, focus on gaining high quality contacts from:

- Acquaintances, colleagues and former colleagues
- Open-networkers from your region
- Top recruiters from your recruitment industry and region.

50 to 499 Direct Connections

Your market penetration is sufficient to start proper LinkedIn recruitment. Your overall network should already cover several million LinkedIn users.

The start of recruitment itself will result in ongoing connections growth by highly targeted users. This should be your major source of new connections.

500 to 3 000 Direct Connections

Bear in mind that this is not a race about who will have the most 1st degree connections. Network size is important, but at some point when you have more than five hundred 1st degree connections, the differences are minor. For instance, the difference between a user with four thousand and five thousand 1st degree connections (lets assume that both have average quality contacts) is just several hundred thousand maximally in the overall number of connections (i.e. 1st, 2nd and 3rd connections in summary).

When you have just hundreds of connections, you are able to take such big steps by connecting with only tens of connections. With a larger network you are facing more and more shared connections (i.e. mutual connections) with users you are going to connect with. That is why the network size grows slower with the growing number of your 1st degree connections.

You can support your network growth by becoming a recruiters-free open-networker. Of course you continue to enlarge your network by proceeding with recruitment and converting your connections from 3rd to 2nd degree and 2nd to 1st degree connections.

You should also set a weekly regime to accept incoming invitations. It is not efficient to accept every single invitation once the notification comes to your mailbox.

3 001+ Direct Connections

Having more than three thousand connections means that you are not only sending invitations but also receiving them; this is because you can send only three thousand invitations (not calculating that LinkedIn can provide you with extras when you run out).

With such a number of connections you are an appealing subject to the top open networkers and also appearing in search results more often. Because of this you can expect more incoming invitations from various users.

At this moment you should fine tune your brand as a top recruiter in your industry and focus on other LinkedIn® options such as groups.

With this network base it is beneficial to export your contacts for further usage, such as for bulk emails.

How to Export LinkedIn® Connections

People think that you can export your whole network, this is incorrect. You can export only 1st degree connections. Nevertheless, having thousands of 1st degree connections is a solid base for a quality database which can be used off LinkedIn® for various purposes. At this moment you will appreciate the purity of your connections.

If you are a technical recruiter from the USA and over 90% of your 1st degree connections are technical professionals, you can say that you have a highly targeted network which can be nicely used outside of LinkedIn. The other 10% can include open-networkers and other top networkers. In the best scenario, it does not contain any recruiters. That would be silly to let other recruiters take advantage of such a well developed network.

Exporting can be done simply by hitting the button *Export connections* which can be found at *Contacts* available from the main menu. You can choose from several .CVS and .VCF formats (*see figure 5.21*).

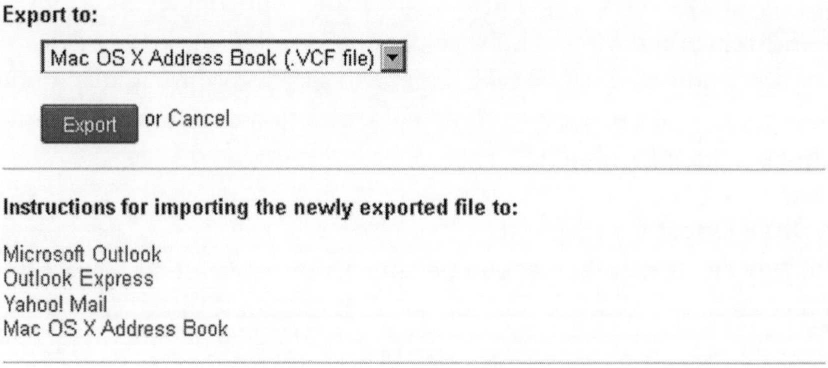

Export to:

Mac OS X Address Book (.VCF file) ▾

Export   or Cancel

Instructions for importing the newly exported file to:

Microsoft Outlook
Outlook Express
Yahoo! Mail
Mac OS X Address Book

Figure 5.21: Export connections

Chapter Summary

▪ Optimal networking goals of each recruiter are to have their target group reachable and, meanwhile, isolated from their competition

▪ Becoming an open networker is a way to rapidly increase the your number of connections

▪ If you run out of invitations, establish another LinkedIn® account to continue networking

▪ Some actions recruiters take on LinkedIn® might be against the LinkedIn® User Agreement

▪ Customize your networking procedure based on your actual LinkedIn® situation

06

Chase Down Your Targets: How to Target Candidates with LinkedIn®

Chase Down Your Targets: How to Target Candidates with LinkedIn®

What you will learn in this chapter

- How to use LinkedIn® Basic and Advanced People Search to target potential candidates

- What is a Boolean search and X-Ray search and how to benefit from them

- What is user diversity and what challenges does it bring

Once we have our LinkedIn® account fully prepared and also established from the perspective of LinkedIn networking, we can take the step of searching for potential candidates.

Take into account that LinkedIn itself or a premium LinkedIn account is not the competitive advantage you have (at least not among other LinkedIn recruiters because we all have access to that). We all can purchase a premium LinkedIn account if we want to. What makes **the difference is HOW you use LinkedIn** and how you use LinkedIn search. So the difference is you and your skills.

Everybody can find candidates. Everybody is able to put something into the search form and get results. So finding potential candidates is not a problem, obviously. But beware that there are other recruiters getting the same results and contacting the same people.

When I started with LinkedIn® recruitment, there were no other recruiters around in my region, Central Europe, so I was satisfied with all the results I got. You bet I harvested as much as I could.

But the situation now is a little bit different. The saturation of LinkedIn recruiters is significant. The Human Resources industry accounts for 3% of all LinkedIn users. Even if each recruiter has his/her own recruitment niche and is recruiting for different companies, the situation where a candidate is contacted several times with the very some job opportunity is more and more common.

A nice analogy is to compare LinkedIn® to an apple tree. The first apples to be picked are from the bottom where everybody can access them. But for the apples which are at the top of the tree you need a ladder. So if you use just a basic search with basic keywords, you will get to the same people as the majority of your competitors. These are the easily accessible apples.

This is about 20-30% of all potential candidates. But if you make more of an effort and structure more advanced searches, you step out of the crowd of your competitors and reach candidates who are more difficult to find. These people are the apples from the top of the tree.

The solution is to uncover candidates who are not so easily visible with basic searches; and also your **reaction time** which is related to search automation which I will explain further in this chapter.

Once a job opportunity is open, you have to act immediately and in large volume – i.e. contact as many candidates as possible, but only the relevant ones for sure. You must be effective to be successful; work smarter, not harder.

Sometimes it is also beneficial to gather candidates prior to publishing a job opening. If you have long-term clients, you can predict which professionals will be needed. This is also related to search automation which is the point of the section *Candidates Search Automation*.

You must realize that **you are seeking neither the most accessible candidates nor those who have their LinkedIn profiles best completed.** You are seeking people who are suitable for the specific opening or sometimes you are looking for the best talent in general. Such candidates can have an expertly filled, accessible LinkedIn profile, but can also have a fragmented one with minimum information and on top of that, information which you would not expect. For instance, a Java software engineer can have his/her profile completely without mentioning the word Java.

So our first task is to get results which we can use for further processing – i.e. contacting them, which is the goal of the next chapter.

Firstly, choose a job opening you need to fill. Think of who are the potential candidates for the specific role from the perspective of expertise and also from the perspective of previous professional experience. Each job opening might require a different type of search; usually it is useful to combine more of them.

Each job post you are going to fill has some key requirements from potential candidates which are mandatory. They might be from the family of hard skills which are the primary ones you are going for and are easy to search – e.g. the knowledge of some operating system such as GNU/Linux or experience with finance accounting procedures. I would add to this section also e.g. master's degrees from universities.

There are also soft skills which are difficult to use as a search filter, unfortunately. If you are looking for someone with good communication and leadership skills, you have to go after people with managerial posts. This is possible to realize with LinkedIn.

Usually the most difficult searches are based on **candidate diversity**. This includes e.g. gender diversity (i.e. filtering men and women), religious diversity, etc. LinkedIn® usually does not provide you with options to filter upon these criteria. You have to help yourself on your own and with your own imagination.

Once you know what you are looking for, you can move to the search itself. There are basically three types of searches:

- **Basic Search**

- **Advanced People Search**

- **X-Ray Search.**

Basic and Advanced LinkedIn® People Search

A Basic Search is simply the field you can see in the upper right corner of your LinkedIn profile (*see figure 6.1*). You will normally not use this search for detailed candidate searches. However, if you start to use advanced LinkedIn operators which I will explain further in this section, you will be using this field on a regular basis.

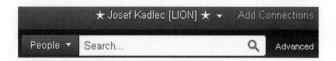

Figure 6.1: Basic People Search

Nevertheless, as a recruiter, the Advanced People Search will be your main interface. You can access this search via the *Advanced* link next to the basic search input field.

Seeking Professionals by Job Title

This is one of the basic searches where you seek candidates by a job title.

All fields are not case sensitive in terms of keywords so it does not matter if you insert *"Software Engineer"*, *"software engineer"* or *"Software engineer"*.

Using quotation marks ensures you that you will get results with the exact term. Typing *"software tester"* (*see figure 6.2*) in the *Title* field finds users who labeled their job post as *Software Tester* or *Senior Software Tester*, but will exclude candidates who work as *Tester – Mobile Software*.

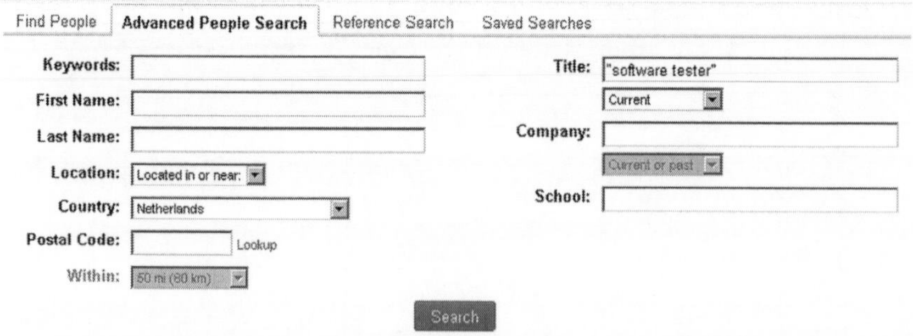

Figure 6.2: Advanced People Search – using quotation marks in Title

Sometimes it might be beneficial to type the keywords without quotes to get better results (*see figure 6.3*).

Not using quotation marks (i.e. *software engineer*) will include in searches users whose title or titles contain the words software and tester; for example, a user with a title *Software Quality Tester* or mentioned *Tester – Mobile Software*.

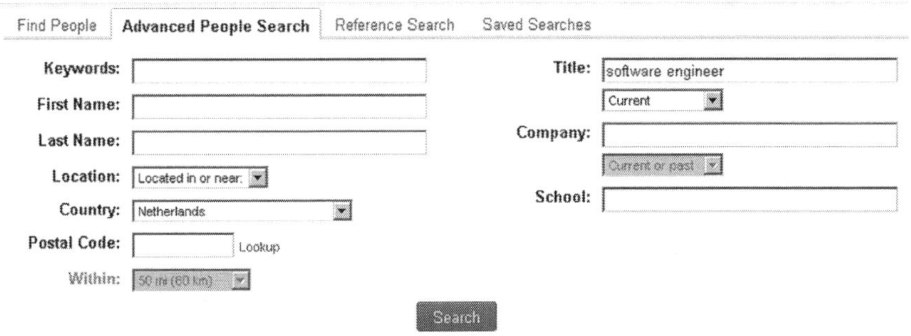

Figure 6.3: Advanced People Search – not using quotation marks in Title

One user can have more current job titles in LinkedIn and this searches through all of them. So in our case, our results will include people who also work e.g. as *People Manager* and besides that, as *Software Contractor.* Both job posts include one of our stated keywords.

The same logic is valid when you search not only through current job titles, but also through past ones (*see figure 6.4*).

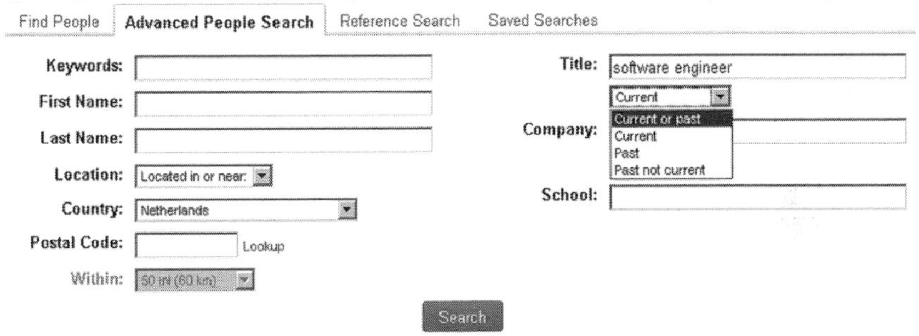

Figure 6.4: Advanced People Search – include current or past job titles

Such searches include all LinkedIn® users whose current or past job titles all together contain the words *software* and *engineer*.

However, using just the option *Current* will be more common for you because the option *Current or past* will produce more non-relevant results.

Not using quotation marks will most probably include also irrelevant results but you will also uncover relevant potential candidates who are not included in the search with quotation marks. **This is the difference which can make you successful because the majority of recruiters just try the simple search and do not bother with its modifications.**

NOTE

Maybe you are wondering if you could specify just a country without any keyword and display a complete list of LinkedIn users from a specific country. That could be a very nice list for any recruitment purposes. This is not possible with embedded LinkedIn searches. You have to type a keyword to get relevant results. Otherwise, results will contain just a fraction of LinkedIn users from the country, completely excluding people outside your network.

Take into account that **with a non-premium account you can see only one hundred LinkedIn users in the search results**. To be more precise, you can see the first one hundred LinkedIn users within your search results.

Each of you will have a different set of one hundred users for the very same search due to relevance sorting based on each individual LinkedIn® network. So with a non-premium account, the first hundred result slots are your playground and are based on your search skills and to what potential candidates you can get there. You have to be able to change the search parameters in a way that you can utilize these one hundred slots to uncover thousands of candidates with similar professional profiles.

With a premium account you can upgrade this number up to a thousand. In my opinion, this is one of the best features next to extended saved searches you can get from the premium LinkedIn account to increase the user-friendliness of LinkedIn recruitment. BUT we are able to override both of these premium functions so it is not necessary to upgrade to premium at all. The pros and cons of LinkedIn premium accounts will be explained in the chapter *10, Arsenal Upgrade: Pros and Cons of LinkedIn® Paid Services*.

In any case, you can be sure that in terms of potential candidates, **you get the very same results with the basic as with the premium account**. So you do not need to pay for different/better results but for the number of visible users, search filters, etc.

One of the ways to get around this limitation is called *X-Ray Search*. This search uses regular search engines such as Google to locate LinkedIn candidates. I will get back to this powerful technique in the *X-Ray Search* section. It also depends which specific professionals you are seeking in your area. If you are getting too many results (over a hundred) and you do not have a premium account, you need to modify the search to cover individual smaller volumes which will lead to a more significant volume of candidates. The number of results is shown when you proceed with a search at the top (*see figure 6.5*).

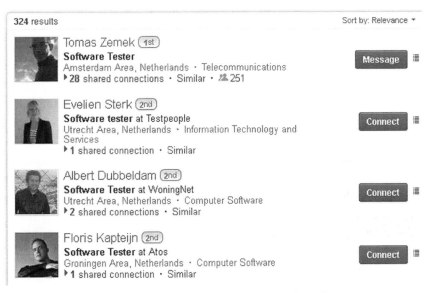

Figure 6.5: Search results – number of results

NOTE
You can also support a search by gathering more contacts manually using the *People also viewed* section (former *Viewers of this profile also viewed...*) in user profiles. You can find there users who have similar professional profiles to the current profile including this section. Often they are current and former colleagues and peers. This is called a non-linear search.

Modifying a search means changing any field of the search which changes the results while you are still getting to the relevant results; for instance, if you change the *Title* field from *Current* to *Past not current*. Of course you can expect that not all results will be relevant because a user's current job role might be on a different level – e.g. senior one, promoted to a managerial post and so he/she might not be interested in the offered opening.

The overall strategy is to make the most generic search for the specific opening as a first step and then make more specific searches which are subsets of the generic one. This means that firstly you seek just the current title from one country. Then you can narrow it down by inserting a specific keyword. Then you can specify a particular company and choose *Current or past*, *Current*, *Past* and *Past not current* for this field.

Then you should eliminate unwanted users such as senior professionals if you are looking for a junior one. Or you might want to eliminate directors, contractors, sales staff or also recruiters from your search.

To display more potential candidates you can also switch the sorting of the results. Because you can see only a limited number of LinkedIn® users, let's say a hundred for the basic non-premium account, by changing sorting, you can see, to some extent, a different hundred users.

The default sorting is by relevance. Every time you do a search, you will have results sorted in the following order:

- 1st degree connections

- 2nd degree connections

- 3rd degree connections

- Group members

- Users based on profile completeness from the highest to lowest

- Everyone else with an *All-Star* profile strength (former 100% complete profile)

- Everyone else with low profile completeness.

All-Star profiles always rank above incomplete profiles connected via the same degree.

> **NOTE**
> Group members are LinkedIn users who joined the same groups as you. Take into account that some of the 1st and 2nd degree connections might be group members as well. Being a 1st or 2nd degree connection has a higher priority so you can see the batch GROUP only for 3rd degree connections and users out of the network in the results.

You can change the relevance in the advanced people search form (*see figure 6.6*)…

Figure 6.6: Changing relevance of search results prior to search

…or you can change sorting when the results are displayed (*see figure 6.7*).

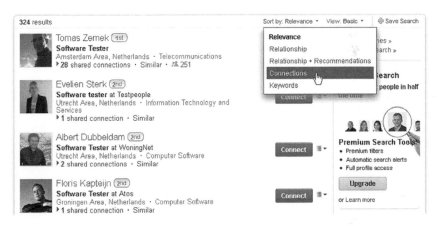

Figure 6.7: Changing the relevance of search results after a search

Search Filters

As you might notice, there are also filters under the Advanced People Search (pre-search phase). Filters are also on the left side of the search results (post-search phase).

As you can see, most of the filters are available only for premium members. But do not worry, you are not missing out. Most of the filters are not beneficial. For instance, the *Industries* filter is an example of a problematic option. Imagine that you are a software engineer for mobile applications working in a bank. Which industry are you working in: Banking, Information Technology and Services or Telecommunications?

As you can see, it is very confusing and in the same way it is confusing for LinkedIn® users. A similar case is the *Seniority Level* filter.

The only beneficial filters in the pre-search phase are *Groups,* which I will describe in the chapter *08, Plunder* at *Your Own Will: Utilizing Groups and Companies for Recruitment* and the *Relationship* filter which can be used to break down the results so they can fit into the hundred user results limitation.

This means that firstly, you filter just 1st degree connections, then 2nd degree connections, then Group Members and lastly 3rd degree connections with everyone else. With this one-by-one procedure, you can display more profiles of potential candidates than displaying all LinkedIn members all together.

There are also post-search filters at your disposal (*see figure 6.8*).

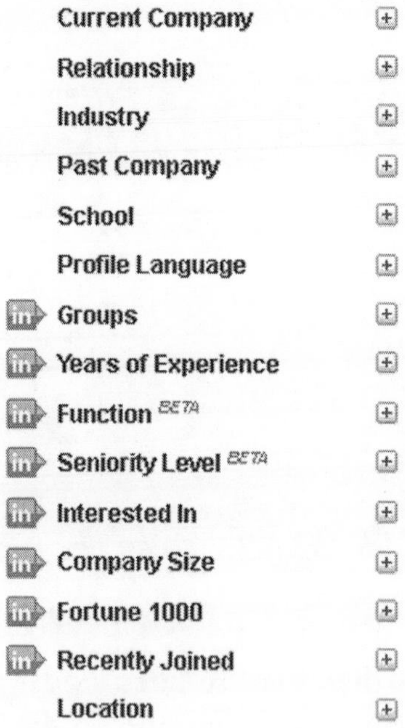

Current Company	+
Relationship	+
Industry	+
Past Company	+
School	+
Profile Language	+
Groups	+
Years of Experience	+
Function *BETA*	+
Seniority Level *BETA*	+
Interested In	+
Company Size	+
Fortune 1000	+
Recently Joined	+
Location	+

Figure 6.8: Advanced People Search post-search filters

As you can see, you can use all pre-search filters in the post-search phase as well. There are also additional filters such as *Current Company*, *Past Company, Location*, etc. The mentioned filters are very useful and I will describe their usage later in this chapter.

You have to take into account that the same job role might be titled differently at another company. For instance, a *Software Tester* might be called elsewhere a *Verification Engineer, Quality Assurance Engineer, QA Engineer, SW Tester*, etc. You need to use them all to get the best results.

In a similar way, this is how you should proceed when searching for other openings. For instance:

- Vice President, V.P., VP, SEVP, EVP, SVP, CVP, FVP, AVP, etc.

- Software Engineer, SW Engineer, Software Developer, SW Developer, Coder, Developer, Programmer, etc.

- Technical Support, Help desk, Helpdesk, Support Engineer, Support Consultant, Operations Engineer, etc.

International corporations usually use English names for the job roles. However, if you recruit in a region where English is not the primary language, do not forget to also include position names in the local language, e.g. *Developer* can be called *Programador* in Spanish.

It is possible to merge the search into one command. You can fill-in the title with the following string to cover all mentioned job titles:

"Software Tester" OR "Verification Engineer" OR "Quality Assurance Engineer" OR "QA Engineer" OR "SW Tester"

This will include LinkedIn® users in the results whose title includes one of these exact terms. The problem is that this will enlarge the number of users in search results. On the one hand this is good because you can be sure that there are enough potential candidates on the market. On the other hand, within one search you can see a limited number of users (one hundred users for non-premium accounts and five hundred, seven hundred, a thousand for premium users based on the specific premium plan for recruiters). So you have no other choice than to break it down and also exclude unwanted profiles.

Let's say we want to exclude anyone working as managers, senior candidates and also as recruiters. In such a case, we would type the following string into the *Title* field:

"Quality Assurance Engineer" NOT manager NOT senior NOT recruiter

The same command can be converted into a more transparent one with dashes:

"Quality Assurance Engineer" -manager -senior -recruiter

To cover all potential users, your goal is to fit into this limit with every one of your searches. In practice, it usually means to break the search down into smaller searches as mentioned. Using such complex commands including the OR modifier is beneficial only in cases where you can expect a maximum of one hundred potential candidates.

I am also not counting that for a particular job role you can seek candidates not only with the same title, but also candidates working at different job posts. You can predict that they have the necessary knowledge required for the position. For instance, a tester can be potentially hired also as an IT support engineer, a software developer, etc. So this can make your pool of potential candidates even larger. Of course, you have to start with searches where you can expect the highest success ratio.

Boolean Search

We mentioned the operators OR and NOT so it is a good time to uncover what are all the operators (also called modifiers) which you have at your disposal, and how they work. It is time to get into so called Boolean searches, named after George Boole, an English mathematician.

We already know OR and NOT. There are more of them and if you want to proceed with high quality searches, you need to get to the core and use them on a regular basis.

There are five modifiers which can be used with LinkedIn®:

- quotes - " "

- parenthesis - ( )

- OR

- AND

- NOT

You can also use a dash (-) instead of NOT. You can use them in all fields for Advanced People Search. You have to **use them in upper-case.** Keywords themselves are case-insensitive but Boolean modifiers are case-sensitive.

There are no wildcards such as *, $, % to be used. If you want to use wildcards and stemming, you have to skip to X-Ray Search (see the section *X-Ray Search*).

Quotes – We already know when to use quotes; preferably when we want to search for an exact phrase. For example, you can put the following phrase into the *Title* field:

"Account Representative"

We do a search with the option *Current*. With this term you will find current *Account Representatives* but you will exclude e.g. *Account Managers* or *Sales Representatives*. On the other hand, not using quotes will have the effect of finding any profile including the words *Account* and *Representative* in the current title/titles.

Let's say we change the option from *Current* to *Current and past*. So, for example, if there is a potential candidate who worked as a *Sales Representative* and after that became an *Account Manager*, they will be included in the search results as well as anyone who is working as an *Account Business Representative*.

AND – You will use AND when you search for LinkedIn profiles including all terms connected with the AND modifier. For example:

Software AND Engineer

This is actually the completely same thing as stating:

Software Engineer

If there is no modifier between terms we assume there is AND. But let's say we are looking for someone who worked or works as a *Java Software Engineer* and a *Python Software Engineer*. Both of the following syntaxes can be used:

"Software Engineer" Java Python

"Software Engineer" AND Java AND Python

Maybe you are thinking, why not only type:

"Java Software Engineer" "Python Software Engineer"

or

"Java Software Engineer" AND "Python Software Engineer"

In comparison with the first example, these commands will exclude candidates who labeled their job titles as e.g.:

Software Engineer – Python

Java Senior Software Engineer

Senior Software Engineer – Python, Java

OR – If you need to find profiles including one or more terms you are going to use the OR modifier.

For example, you are looking for somebody who is working for Facebook or LinkedIn®. You would structure your search in the *Company* field like this:

Facebook OR LinkedIn

We said we are looking for users currently working in either of these companies, so we choose the *Current* option. You can combine it with quotes for multiple word terms, for example:

"British Petrol" OR Shell

NOT – If you want to exclude a particular term from your search, you can use NOT or a dash before the excluded term. Dash is not officially known.

It is pretty beneficial when you want to target employees of a particular company, but exclude those who worked at another specified company, e.g.:

Coca-Cola NOT *PepsiCo*

The following syntax has the same effect:

Coca-Cola -PepsiCo

Parentheses – You can combine more modifiers. Sometimes you are forced to use parentheses to structure such searches; but let's say we are looking for potential *Key Account Representatives* or *Key Account Managers*.

We can use the following syntax:

"Key Account" AND *(Representative OR Manager)*

Any multiple OR structures have to be grouped by parentheses.

Seeking Professionals by Keyword

Now that we know the theory about LinkedIn® Boolean searches, it is time to practice again.

Sometimes you need to use a keyword alone or next to a specific title to make the search as targeted as possible. Imagine the similar example from the previous section. We are seeking a *Software Tester* but with knowledge of the Unix platform. In this case you can specify the term *unix* in the *Keywords* field (*see figure 6.9*).

Another great usage of the *Keywords* field is when you seek candidates by expertise. For example, you seek a suitable candidate for a *Software Tester* opportunity with knowledge of the HP Quality Center (a special application for testing purposes used especially in corporations), you can specify it as a keyword to get the relevant results (*see figure 6.10*).

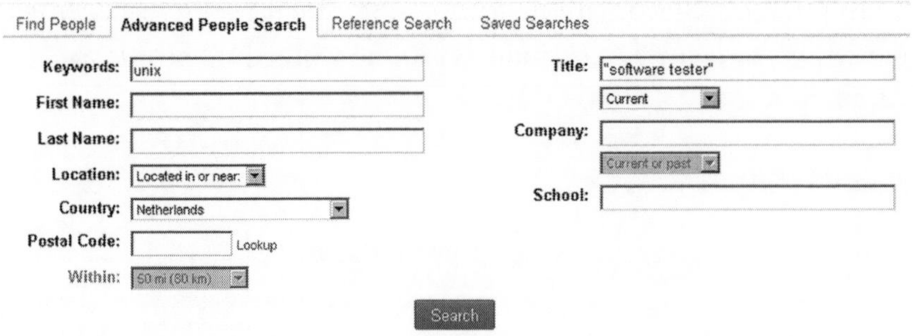

Figure 6.9: Advanced People Search – searching with keywords

Figure 6.10: Advanced People Search – searching with keywords

Or when you consider that it might be beneficial to get more generic results, you do not need to specify a *Title* in this case. Your search will include all professionals who were in touch with the 'HP Quality Center'. From this we can assume that they worked as testers, so there is no need to specify this.

Keywords can also be used in more complicated forms. Maybe you are seeking a *Software Tester* with knowledge of Unix and the HP Quality Center as well (*see figure 6.11*).

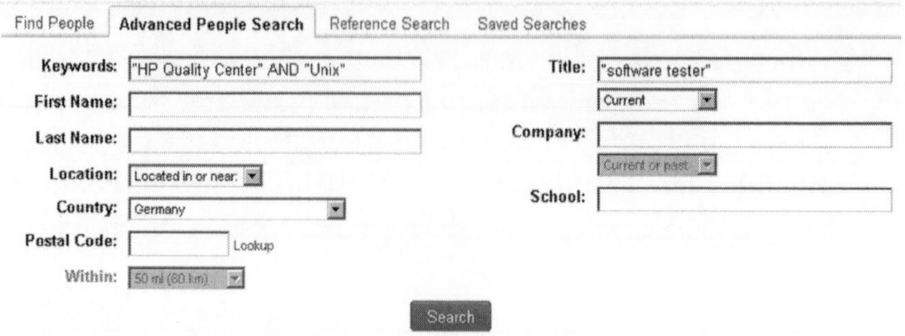

Figure 6.11: Advanced People Search – searching with keywords

Another example might represent a search for a team manager with knowledge of Android and either Unix or Linux (*see figure 6.12*).

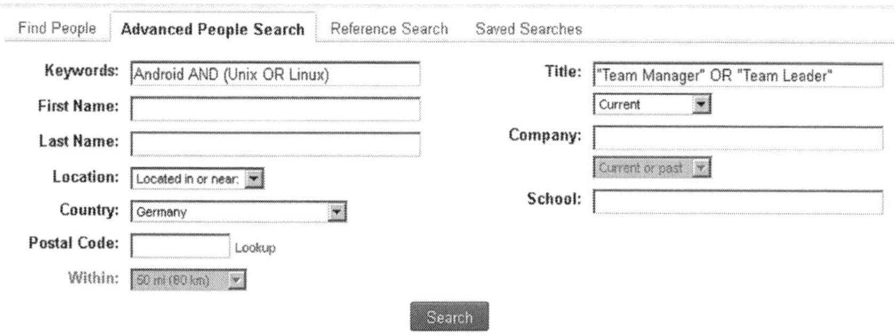

| Find People | **Advanced People Search** | Reference Search | Saved Searches |

Keywords:	Android AND (Unix OR Linux)		Title:	"Team Manager" OR "Team Leader"
First Name:				Current
Last Name:			Company:	
Location:	Located in or near:			Current or past
Country:	Germany		School:	
Postal Code:	Lookup			
Within:	50 mi (80 km)			

Search

Figure 6.12: Advanced People Search – searching with keywords

As you can see, the quotation marks can be used only for terms with more than one word. A quoted one-word term has the same meaning as a one-word term without quotation marks.

The *Keywords* field can be used as a general field which you can use to find not only expertise but also job posts and companies. The real benefit of the *Title* and *Company* fields is that you can choose between the options *Current or past, Current, Past* and *Past not current.* However, if these things aren't important, you can use just *Keywords.* Such a search is equal to cases when you use the option *Current or past.* When this option is what you need, you can try typing the following command into *Keywords*:

"HP Quality Center" AND (Microsoft OR IBM) AND ("Software Tester" OR "QA Engineer")

Using keywords makes LinkedIn® a very powerful tool for finding professionals with some very special expertise. Sometimes there are only a few such experts in a country. For such job posts, it is especially difficult to find candidates with advertisement-based recruitment.

However, you have to think from the perspective of the candidates; what and in which exact form they can mention some detail about their professional profile. One term can usually be expressed in many different ways.

If you are looking for someone with Unix knowledge, you may look for the keyword *Unix*, but someone may express this as **NIX* or just

NIX or they might mention the exact name of the operating system from the Unix family, such as *AIX* or *HP-UX*. So take this into account because the more you dive into the details, the more successful you will be because you will uncover candidates who are difficult to find and the odds will be in your favor.

Another example can be with Java developers. A lot of Java developers do not even state the term Java in their profiles because it can be expressed using many other, more precise terms:

Java Enterprise Edition, J2EE, J2SE, J2ME, JEE, Java EE, Java SE, Java ME, JEE6, Java EE 6, JDK, JRE, etc.

Or someone can just specify some Java libraries and experts know what is going on:

Spring, Hybernate, etc.

Someone working with these libraries is also most likely a Java developer. You would not believe how many of such Java developers, not mentioning the term Java in their LinkedIn profiles, are there.

Keywords is the field where you as a user of LinkedIn®, can make the difference which will boost you ahead of your competitors. Think of what your potential candidate could mention in their profile. If you are seeking a Java developer, they might not mention the word Java in their LinkedIn profile because their job post might be called e.g. *Software Engineer* and they did not provide more information about their expertise.

But maybe they acquired some Java certification which says that their expertise is most probably Java. So let's try the following keyword command:

SCJA OR SCJP OR SCJD OR SCWCD OR SCBCD OR SCDJWS OR SCMAD

The terms between the OR operators are abbreviation terms for particular Java certifications as they were called when Java was owned by Sun Microsystems. After Oracle purchased Sun Microsystems these certifications were possibly renamed. You can find the new names and upgrade your keywords command for even better search results. However, do not erase the old ones as they are still valid regardless if they are called by different names currently.

Finding Synonyms and Related Terms

Take your time to find synonyms and related words to those keywords to make your search as complex as possible. For such purposes, you can use Wikipedia (*www.wikipedia.org*). For example, when you are seeking *Ruby on Rails Developers* and you have no idea what Ruby on Rails exactly is, put it into Wikipedia and find synonyms, abbreviations, related terms and some more information about the technology.

Another way to effectively find synonyms for skills and expertise is by using the following LinkedIn site:

http://www.linkedin.com/skills

Put there the name of the skill or technology you are looking for, let's say C++, and see the related terms (*see figure 6.13*). Some of them might be used as a keyword in your search.

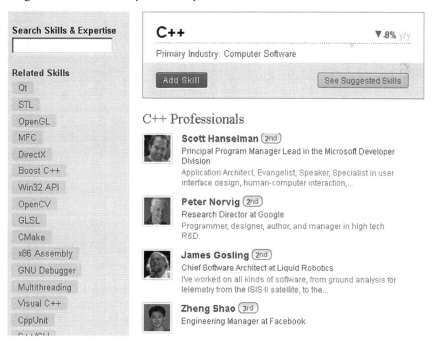

Figure 6.13: LinkedIn Search Skills & Expertise

When you want to find synonyms for job posts, you can use dictionaries such as *Thesaurus.com* or *dictionary.sensagent.com*. Simply type the name of the position, e.g. *Developer,* and see the suggested synonyms. Some of them will be relevant.

Do not forget to also use terms in the regional language; not all companies and people state their posts in English. For such purposes, you can use Google Translate (*translate.google.com*).

Finally, you might be interested in specifying companies where you want to hunt for candidates. As a recruiter you should know the companies where your potential candidates work and you should upgrade such a shortlist on a regular basis. You can use a specific Google search command to find more companies related to the specified one (*see figure 6.14*).

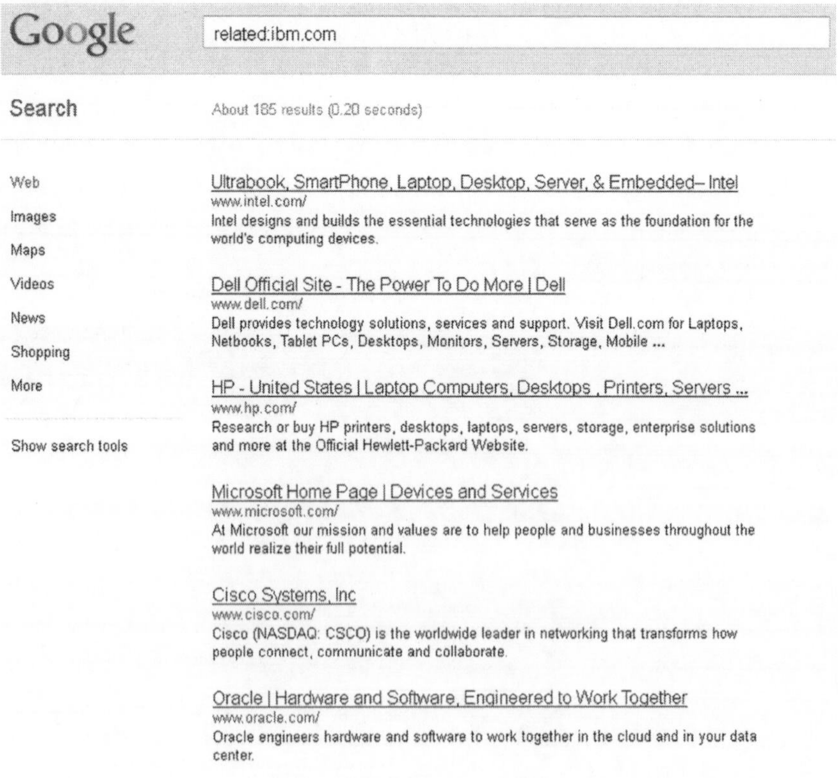

Figure 6.14: Searching relevant companies with Google

You can see that results include many potential competitors and related companies. Take into account that when looking for potential candidates, you have to focus across industries. C++ developers can be found in banks, in IT companies or in the automotive industry.

So do not be afraid to go deeper than just a job opening title. Get to the ropes of each vacancy details and try to find keywords which can be used for your search.

I mentioned candidate diversity, such as seeking only men or women. Keywords can be used to reach these types of candidates even if they are not as precise as if you were using a filter. Unfortunately, there is no filter for sex, religion, race, etc. If you want to target only women, you can utilize the fact that women's profiles will most probably contain the word *she* or *her*. So you can put the string (*she* OR *her*) into the field *Keywords* to filter only women. It is not 100% reliable, but it does the job.

> **NOTE**
> Please be aware that discrimination against people in the recruitment process by sex or religion etc. is illegal in many countries. The reason I included this topic is mainly technical. I wanted to illustrate how you should think with LinkedIn search. How not to fall into the mainstream but to always be looking for alternative ways of defining your searches.

You would proceed with other diversities in a similar manner. You have to think which terms a specific group of people has in common, and based on that, modify your search.

Seeking Professionals by Company

We already touched on filtering by companies in the previous section about keywords. Another powerful way to target your potential candidates is by over specifying companies in the form field *Company*. You should know your market, so you should know which companies in the targeted region employ professionals you are interested in.

And frankly, LinkedIn® will help you to get this knowledge. From the start of using LinkedIn as a recruitment tool, you will gather a lot of knowledge about your potential candidates. You not only get to know which companies you should be interested in, but also find out how they describe each particular job post so that you can use this in your searches.

You can also easily find out when there is some new company on the market which is hiring your targeted group of candidates. You can also study which companies professionals leave; this can mean that employees are not satisfied there. Maybe the salary level is not of sufficient; this makes them an easy target for your headhunting activities regardless whether it is a prestigious company or not. I could tell you how I literally plundered whole teams including team managers from one European IBM support center.

Take into account that you can use up to **two thousand characters in the fields _Keywords, Title, School_ and _Company_**. That is quite a lot. If you keep a shortlist of companies which employ professionals you are interested in, you can use them in the search command. You can target about a hundred companies. This is of course based on the individual length of company names but you should get to a number around one hundred.

We are using the IT area as our example, so let's stick with it. Let's say you are interested in employees only from a specific list of corporations. In this case, you would paste the following into the form field _Company_:

Microsoft OR Oracle OR "Hewlett-Packard" OR IBM Support Center OR Google OR AVG OR CA OR "CA Technologies"

And you would select the option _Current_.

Notice that I used the term _CA_ and also _CA Technologies_, which represents the same company. This is on purpose and it must be done to proceed with high quality searches. Imagine the globally known corporation PricewaterhouseCoopers. This company can be represented by many name forms such as _PwC, PricewaterhouseCoopers, Price Waterhouse Coopers, Price Waterhouse, PricewaterhouseCoopers International Limited, PwCIL and also misspelled forms such as Price Waterhouse Cooper, PricewaterhouseCooper, PricewaterhauseCooper, Price Waterhause Coopers_ and _Price Waterhause Cooper_.

Let's do some quick research on how many current or past employees of PwC use each of the names globally. We will use LinkedIn® and its basic people search (_see figure 6.15_).

Figure 6.15: Searching LinkedIn users using the keyword "PWC"

PwC – **203 674 users**
PricewaterhouseCoopers – **197 404 users**
Price Waterhouse Coopers – **27 797 users**
Price Waterhouse – **25 008 users**
PricewaterhouseCoopers International Limited - **53 users**
PwCIL – **22 users**
Price Waterhouse Cooper – **564 users**
PricewaterhouseCooper – **773 users**
PricewaterhauseCoopers – **16 users**
Price Waterhause Coopers – **4 users**
Price Waterhause Cooper – **1 user**

These numbers are relatively precise to the date I did the search. I also took into account that some of the terms might be included in others – e.g. *Price Waterhouse* is included in *Price Waterhouse Coopers* and *Price Waterhouse Cooper*. This particular item is done precisely by the search command:

"Price Waterhouse" NOT (Cooper OR Coopers)

This command ensures the terms *Price Waterhouse Cooper* and *Price Waterhouse Coopers* will be excluded.

Another point is that the searched terms might be included in a LinkedIn profile multiple times. It means one user can have both *PricewaterhouseCoopers* and *PWC* included in his/her profile on multiple job posts. In this case, such a user will appear in searches for PWC and for PricewaterhouseCoopers as well, which will distort the numbers a little bit. But it is not a major difference.

As you can see, if you use just the term *PWC* as the name of your company, you are missing out on half of all potential candidates. Similar analogies can be found for many company names on the market. You should include them all in your search.

Therefore such a search command in the field *Company* would look as follows in the case of PWC:

PWC OR PricewaterhouseCoopers OR "Price Waterhouse Coopers" OR "Price Waterhouse" OR "PricewaterhouseCoopers International Limited" OR PwCIL OR "Price Waterhouse Cooper" OR "PricewaterhouseCooper" OR "PricewaterhauseCoopers" OR "Price Waterhause Coopers" OR "Price Waterhause Cooper"

This command could be shortened by the terms which are included in one another but if you want to be sure, use the full search command.

Now, back to our search operators; imagine you are seeking a team manager and you are interested in someone who currently works at Oracle or Hewlett–Packard (*see figure 6.16*).

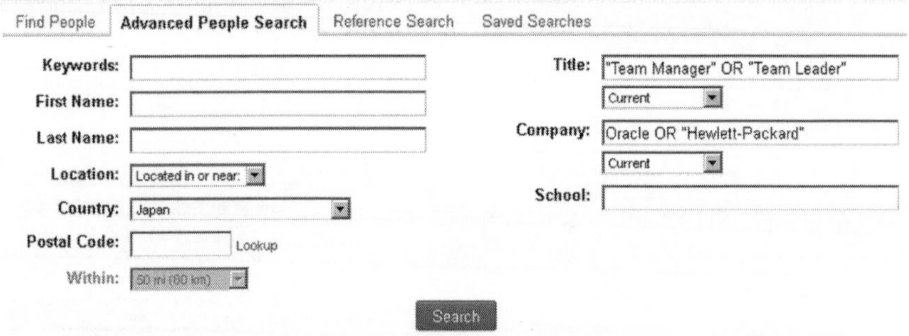

Figure 6.16: Searching candidates by Company and Title fields

This is just a simplified example to show you how operators can serve you well. But again, be aware that the company *Hewlett–Packard* is often represented not only with the term *Hewlett–Packard* but also as *HP* or the misspelled versions *Hewlet Packard, Hewlett Packard, Hewllett Packard, Hewllet Packard, Hawlett Packard* or *Hawlet Packard*.

Other mutations of companies formed into a search command might be, for example:

"JP Morgan Chase" OR "JPMorganChase" OR "JP Morgan" OR "JPMorgan" OR JPMC

"Weil Gotshal & Manges" OR "Weil" OR "WGM" OR "Weil Gotschal & Manges"

"Red Bull" OR RedBull OR "RedBul" OR "Red Bul"

Maybe you seek a potential candidate for a team manager job opening and it does not matter if such a candidate is currently working for Oracle or Hewlett–Packard or they worked at either of these in the past. In such case you would use the option *Current or past* with the field *Company* (*see figure 6.17*).

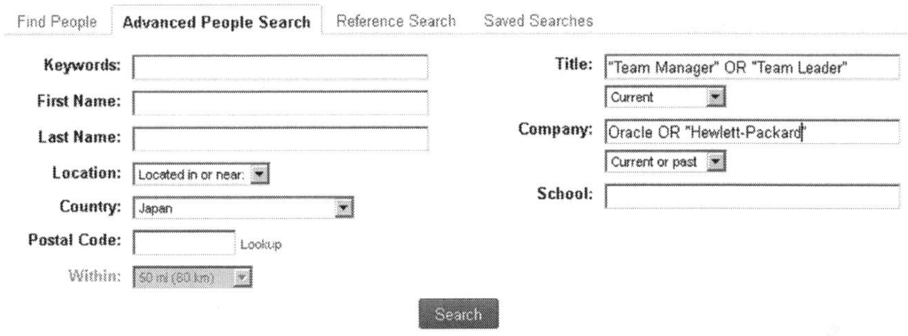

Figure 6.17: Searching candidates by Company and Title fields

There is also the possibility to use the post-search filter to separate potential candidates by a company where they work or worked. For example, I am seeking accountants in Canada. I do a search and expand the *Current Company* filter (*see figure 6.18*).

As you can see, you can include or exclude employees of different companies without knowing the company name in advance and putting them into a search form in Boolean search format. When you cannot see a company you would like to have on the list, simply add it there via the input field.

NOTE

The LinkedIn® company filter can include only users who linked their current or past company with the company's LinkedIn Company Page. This is usually done by LinkedIn requests where you confirm that you work for a specific company. However, some users do not confirm this or they use a slightly different term for the past or current company such as PWC instead of PricewaterHouse Coopers, etc. So take into account that using the LinkedIn company filter might exclude hundreds of potential candidates. The way to avoid this is to use the *Company* field in the Advanced People Search where you can fill the name of the company and its other modifications.

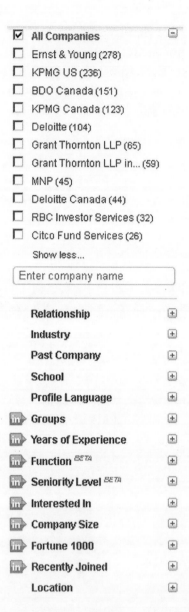

Figure 6.18: Post-search filter Current Company

This filter can also be easily used to find names of companies from a particular industry. Try to add the keyword telecom to the Basic People Search and expand the *Current Companies* filter where you should see companies from a desirable industry (*see figure 6.19*).

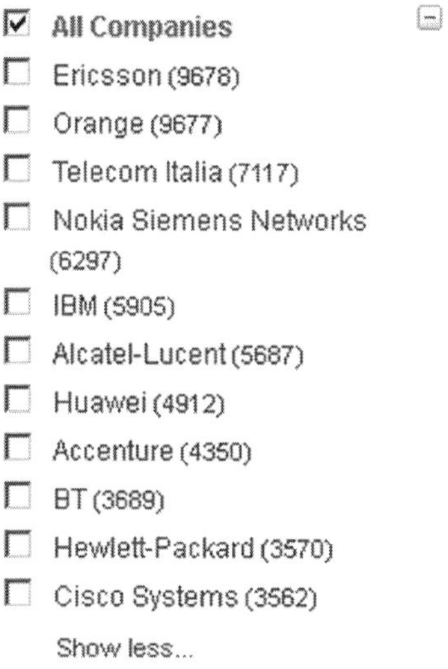

☑ **All Companies**   [-]

☐ Ericsson (9678)

☐ Orange (9677)

☐ Telecom Italia (7117)

☐ Nokia Siemens Networks (6297)

☐ IBM (5905)

☐ Alcatel-Lucent (5687)

☐ Huawei (4912)

☐ Accenture (4350)

☐ BT (3689)

☐ Hewlett-Packard (3570)

☐ Cisco Systems (3562)

Show less...

Figure 6.19: Post-search filter Current Company

Another situation is when you are seeking candidates and you want to exclude people who currently work for some companies – these companies might be your clients whom you are seeking candidates for, so it is nonsense to include them in results.

Let's say that you are seeking *Team Leaders* for Google, but IBM is also one of your clients, so you are forbidden to contact any employees from IBM and Google. Your talent pool, the place we plan to suck candidates from, is Microsoft in this example; more specifically, current employees of Microsoft. On top of that, our requirements include also knowledge of Java and the Linux platform (*see figure 6.20*).

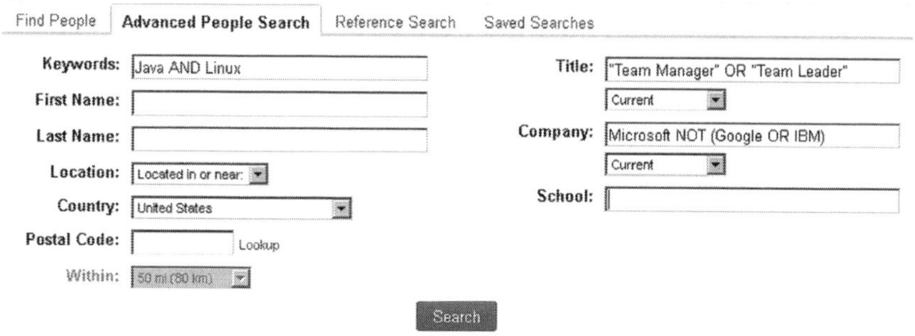

| Find People | **Advanced People Search** | Reference Search | Saved Searches |

Keywords: Java AND Linux	**Title:** "Team Manager" OR "Team Leader"
First Name:	Current ▼
Last Name:	**Company:** Microsoft NOT (Google OR IBM)
Location: Located in or near ▼	Current ▼
Country: United States ▼	**School:**
Postal Code: Lookup	
Within: 50 mi (80 km) ▼	

[Search]

Figure 6.20: Excluding keywords with the NOT operator

You can get the same results with the operator "-" (*see figure 6.21*).

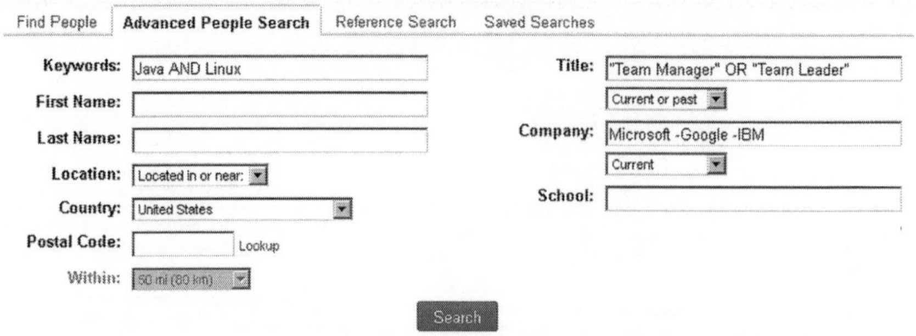

| Find People | **Advanced People Search** | Reference Search | Saved Searches |

Keywords:	Java AND Linux	**Title:**	"Team Manager" OR "Team Leader"
First Name:			Current or past
Last Name:		**Company:**	Microsoft -Google -IBM
Location:	Located in or near:		Current
Country:	United States	**School:**	
Postal Code:	Lookup		
Within:	50 mi (80 km)		

Search

Figure 6.21: Excluding keywords with a dash operator

As you can see, search operators or so called modifiers are a powerful part of LinkedIn recruitment. They will allow you to uncover candidates who are difficult to find because their profiles are not so precisely filled or they used different keywords than most recruiters expect.

Seeking Professionals by City or Area

You can choose a country in the search form but you are not able to choose a specific city there without typing a postal code and the range within which LinkedIn® users should be searched. It really depends on the region where you are recruiting, but sometimes it might be difficult to seek candidates in some cities other than the capital.

There are countries where it is pretty common for people to travel to find work in other cities, and people do not update their postal codes. Another confusing thing is whether a postal code is related to a work place or someone's home. There are people commuting tens and sometimes even hundreds of kilometers to work.

Sometimes it makes sense to include a whole country into a search. However, there are countries where it is not a part of the culture to commute to other cities, or maximally from minor cities to the capital. In such cases, we need to somehow target candidates only in the specific city or surrounding area.

How do you do that?

The first option is obvious from the search form. You can specify a postal code and the number of kilometers as a range around the place with the specified postal code (*see figure 6.22*).

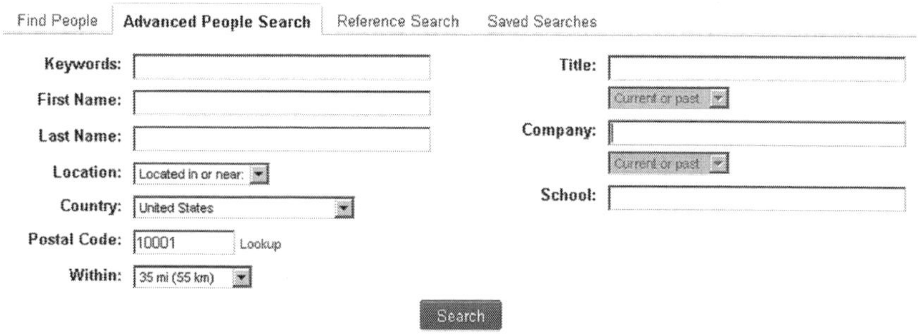

Figure 6.22: Searching candidates by location

As you probably noticed, you can only specify a country in the Country field. For example, in Europe it is not such a problem because there are many independent countries and you as a recruiter function in just one of them, usually. Each country is a separated market; but how about the United States? You are not able to specify each state of the USA precisely by name, so you need to use a postal code.

In the same way, you can target particular cities or larger areas anywhere else in the world. The problem is that the postal code is a field which users do not update on a regular basis, so it sometimes might not be up-to-date. Therefore, it is necessary to combine it with other methods to localize candidates in a specific area.

> **NOTE**
> You would not believe how many LinkedIn users do not specify their country or specify it as *Other*. Just in my network (1st + 2nd + 3rd degree connections) there are about seven thousand of them! This is again a chance for you to step out of the crowd from your competitors who are specifying a specific country. With such a search, they are excluding potential candidates who did not fill-in their country or filled it in as *Other*.

You can also use the post-search filter *Location* to target potential candidates in different cities. I will use the example with accountants in Canada from the previous sections (*see figure 6.23*).

183

Figure 6.23: Post-search filter Location

As you can see, you can easily filter candidates from the different areas of a specified country.

Another way to localize users from a specific city or area is by using the name of the city as a keyword in the search form *Keywords* field. This is not 100% reliable at all. You will not target all users from the specified city, probably not even the majority of them; but it does some work for you. Some users use the city name in the company field or also the school field. We can assume that if the user studied in that city, that he is working there as well. This varies based on country and culture differences.

Yet another way to target candidates from a specific city is to specify companies from that city where the potential candidates might be employed. Especially when you know that the city is the only city where the company has premises in a country. This is a very effective and reliable method to target potential candidates from a specific area.

In a similar way, you can also use a school. For example, if you recruit a workforce from the finance industry, you can find all economic universities and faculties from the specific city and prepare a Boolean search command. Let's say we are interested in candidates from the finance industry in Prague, Czech Republic:

"University of Economics" OR "Faculty of Finance and Accounting" OR "Faculty of Business Administration" OR "Faculty of Economics" OR

"Faculty of Economics and Management" OR "International Prague University" OR "College of information Management and Business Administration" OR "University of New York in Prague" OR "Metropolitan University Prague" OR "Banking Institute" OR "University of Finance and Administration" OR "University of Economics and Management" OR "Jan Amos Komensky University Prague"

Plus, I would add the universities' and faculties' name in the local language – Czech, in this example. So to cover a larger audience and include those who state the university or faculty name in Czech, modify the search as follows:

"University of Economics" OR "Faculty of Finance and Accounting" OR "Faculty of Business Administration" OR "Faculty of Economics" OR "Faculty of Economics and Management" OR "International Prague University" OR "College of information Management and Business Administration" OR "University of New York in Prague" OR "Metropolitan University Prague" OR "Banking Institute" OR "University of Finance and Administration" OR "University of Economics and Management" OR "Jan Amos Komensky University Prague" OR "Vysoka skola ekonomicka" OR "Fakulta financi a ucetnictvi" OR "Fakulta podnikohospodarska" OR "Narodohospodarska fakulta" OR "Fakulta ekonomiky a managementu" OR "Vysoka skola manazerske informatiky a ekonomiky" OR "Metropolitni univerzita Praha" OR "Bankovni institute vysoka skola" OR "Vysoka skola financni a spravni" OR "Vysoka skola ekonomie a managementu" OR "Univerzita Jana Amose Komenskeho"

This is put into the search form field *School*. In fact, it could be a little bit shorter when we would merge names which are included in other ones.

Again, take into account culture differences. The effectiveness of using the field *School* as a localization parameter is different e.g. in the USA, where people usually study in a different US state or at least city. On the other hand, it is pretty effective in Europe.

> **NOTE**
> LinkedIn tries to be proactive in its search algorithm and even if you type some term into the field *School*, it also searches across other

profile sections to some extent. The same is valid for using quotes where you would expect that LinkedIn shows only profiles with the exact term in the Education section. However, LinkedIn goes beyond that and might include other profiles not fulfilling these criteria precisely.

Sometimes you need to search for candidates based on their year of graduation. For example, audit companies such as Ernst & Young, Deloitte or PricewaterhouseCoopers are known for the fact that they recruit junior staff only when they are maximally one year from fresh graduation. With an embedded LinkedIn people search you cannot find such candidates. There is no option to do this; but it is possible to realize with a so called *X-Ray Search*. Read further.

Seeking Professionals Currently Looking for a Job

This is again a tricky one. There is no filter which would help you to filter LinkedIn users who are or might be looking for a new job at the moment. We have to think of what are the shared characteristics of these people in terms of LinkedIn profiles; based on these we can use a particular method to filter these people out.

1) **Using Keywords in Advanced People Search**

One of the shared characteristics is that these people might use some of the following strings in their profile:

seeking
seeking new
searching
actively searching
looking for
new job
open to
available for
new opportunity
new opportunities
etc.

Based on this, we can use LinkedIn Advanced People Search where we choose a location, and past title we are interested in, and we put the following search query to the field *Keywords*:

seeking OR "seeking new" OR searching OR "actively searching" OR "looking for" OR "new job" OR "open to" OR "available for" OR "new opportunity" OR "new opportunities"

You can modify this search query if you find some other terms which are relevant.

Of course, you get many false positives – i.e. users who mention some of these terms in their profiles, but are not looking for a new job at the moment.

One group of false positives is recruiters who have in their profiles e.g. *Seeking pharmaceutical representatives*, etc. At least this group can be easily eliminated by a slight modification of the search query (*see figure 6.24*). Apart from the keywords in the search query, you need to put the following into the *Title* field:

-(recruitment OR recruiter OR sourcer OR headhunter)

Figure 6.24: Excluding HR personnel from the search results

2) Using Current Title in Advanced People Search

Some people put the active job seeker phrase into the *Title* field. Based on this, you can use the same search query from the previous examples but put it into the *Title* field in Advanced People Search (*see figure 6.25*).

seeking OR "seeking new" OR searching OR "actively searching" OR "looking for" OR "new job" OR "open to" OR "available for" OR "new opportunity" OR "new opportunities"

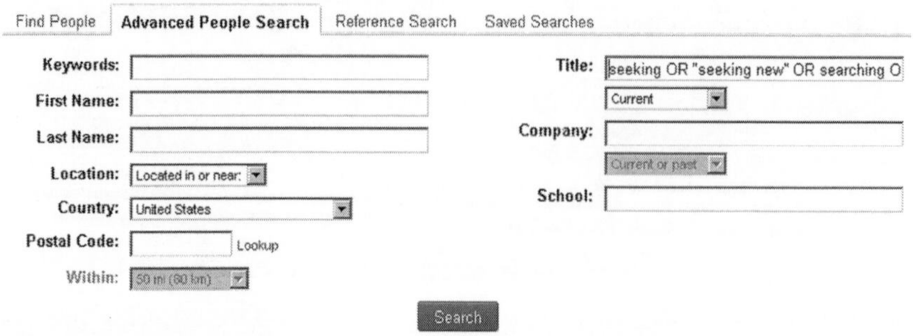

Figure 6.25: Searching people currently looking for a job using the Title field

This example will provide you with fewer results but on the other hand, it will be more targeted with a minimum of false positives.

Notice that once you see the search results, LinkedIn will suggest companies, locations and industries to you, sorted by the largest number of results (*see figure 6.26*). Based on this, you can determine which company has the most unsatisfied employees or which location has the most available employees.

Figure 6.26: Current Companies filter suggesting important companies to you

Do not forget that not all users stating that they are looking for new opportunities are unemployed at the moment. Often they are still working for their employer.

3) Using Dates in X-Ray Search

One common characteristic of unemployed people is that their present job usually ends with some recent date. LinkedIn® does not provide us with a method of filtering this aspect; but we can help ourselves with a so called X-Ray Search which is thoroughly explained in the section *X-Ray Search*. It is basically a method where you search LinkedIn users from the outside using search engines such as Google.

Let's say we want to filter potential candidates who finished at their last job in the past three months, based on data published under each engagement on LinkedIn® (*see figure 6.27*). If today is March 2013, we want to search for users who finished their last job in March 2013, February 2013 or January 2013.

 EXPERIENCE

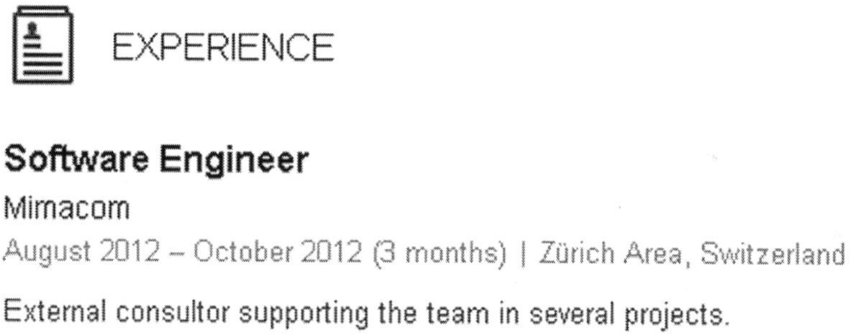

Software Engineer
Mimacom
August 2012 – October 2012 (3 months) | Zürich Area, Switzerland

External consultor supporting the team in several projects.

Figure 6.27: Time period of a particular job engagement

The X-Ray query would look as follows:

site:linkedin.com "Java software engineer" Zurich OR Swiss OR Switzerland **("January 2013" OR "February 2013" OR "March 2013") -present**

Do not bother now with the parts which are not bold. They basically mean that we are looking for Java software engineers from Switzerland.

Users who work somewhere have the word *present* in their profiles. Therefore, with the option *-present* we can exclude these users from our search. Plus, we include users whose profile contains one of the recent three months. You can easily modify it to the last five months, if you wish.

4)   Using X-Ray Search to Target Users without a Current Title

This method basically follows the previous one. We are looking for LinkedIn profiles which have no current title set up. This most probably means that such a person is not employed at that moment.

They can be found easily by excluding the keyword *present*.

site:linkedin.com "Java software engineer" Zurich OR Swiss OR Switzerland **-present**

You will get some false positives, especially LinkedIn users who set their privacy setting where they avoided visibility of current positions.

5)   Using LinkedIn® Groups

There are groups on LinkedIn created for people who are looking for a job. I will describe how to operate with groups in the chapter *08, Plunder at Your Own Will: Utilizing Groups and Companies for Recruitment.*

Examples of such groups are:

Job Openings, Job Leads and Job Connections! – over 1,114,000 members

Global Jobs Network – over 129,000 members

Job Postings and Job Boards! – over 93,000 members

Personally, I am not big fan of this method because people usually join these groups but do not leave them when they find a job. Also, there are a limited amount of groups you can join. So I'd rather join other groups which I can more easily take advantage of.

How to Store Boolean Searches Using LinkedIn® Advanced Operators

You need to store your searches done over Advanced People Search to be able to use them again in the future or for searches you do repeatedly. One way to do this is to save each particular field *Company, Title*, etc. into a text file. Then you can share it with your peers if you are used to working in a team. This is called 'crowdsourcing'.

Not so many people are aware of advanced LinkedIn® operators or even their existence. These operators can be used in basic LinkedIn searches as a substitute for advanced people searches. To cut a long story short, instead of filling in each search field such as *Company, Title, Keywords*, etc., you merge all fields into one command using advanced LinkedIn operators. Basically you can bypass the LinkedIn search interface.

> ### NOTE
> Support for advanced LinkedIn operators is rather erratic. Sometimes it is available, sometimes it isn´t. Therefore, it might not be available when you read this book.

Further in this section, you can see the list of advanced operators and how they were stated at the *LinkedIn Center Page*. The table is actually not available anymore.

There was a period of time when these operators did not work. They work again now, but LinkedIn fixed one issue which basically had the effect that even non-premium users could access search filters which were only available to premium users. This is not possible anymore; but it's no big deal. As I said, the vast majority of such filters are not beneficial for recruitment purposes.

Let's say you want to locate managers currently working for Boeing in the United States, Washington D.C. area, within a radius of 25 miles.

The standard way, as you already know, would be by using Advanced People Search (*see figure 6.28*).

This is pretty awkward to store in a text file; but with LinkedIn advanced operators, you can transform this search into a single command:

ccompany:Boeing ctitle:manager country:"united states" zip:20001 radius:25

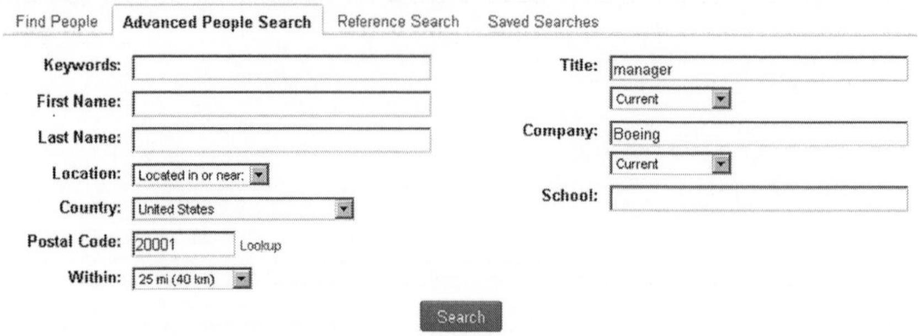

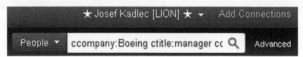

Figure 6.28: Using Advanced People Search in a standard way

You will simply just type this command into a basic people search (*see figure 6.29*).

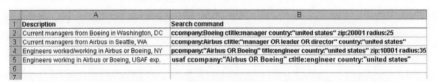

Figure 6.29: Using advanced LinkedIn operators

This command is easily stored in a spreadsheet (*see figure 6.31*).

	A	B
1	Description	Search command
2	Current managers from Boeing in Washington, DC	ccompany:Boeing ctitle:manager country:"united states" zip:20001 radius:25
3	Current managers from Airbus in Seattle, WA	ccompany:Airbus ctitle:"manager OR leader OR director" country:"united states"
4	Engineers worked/working in Airbus or Boeing, NY	pcompany:"Airbus OR Boeing" title:engineer country:"united states" zip:10001 radius:35
5	Engineers working in Airbus or Boeing, USAF exp.	usaf ccompany:"Airbus OR Boeing" ctitle:engineer country:"united states"
6		
7		

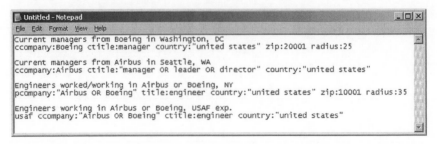

Figure 6.30: Storing advanced LinkedIn operators in a spreadsheet

Or also in a text file for repeated searches and sharing with your colleagues (*see figure 6.32*).

Untitled - Notepad

File Edit Format View Help

Current managers from Boeing in Washington, DC
ccompany:Boeing ctitle:manager country:"united states" zip:20001 radius:25

Current managers from Airbus in Seattle, WA
ccompany:Airbus ctitle:"manager OR leader OR director" country:"united states"

Engineers worked/working in Airbus or Boeing, NY
pcompany:"Airbus OR Boeing" title:engineer country:"united states" zip:10001 radius:35

Engineers working in Airbus or Boeing, USAF exp.
usaf ccompany:"Airbus OR Boeing" ctitle:engineer country:"united states"

Figure 6.31: Storing advanced LinkedIn operators in a text editor

Description	Operator Name	Dependency	Possible Values
First Name	fname:	n/a	<keyword>
Last Name	lname:	n/a	<keyword>
Current Title	ctitle:	n/a	<keyword>
Past Title	ptitle:	n/a	<keyword>
Title	title:	n/a	<keyword>
Current Company	ccompany:	n/a	<keyword>
Past Company	pcompany:	n/a	<keyword>
Company	company:	n/a	<keyword>
School	school:	n/a	<keyword>
Country	country:	n/a	<valid country>
Zip Code	zip:	country:	<valid zip code>
Radius	radius:	country: and zip:	<10, 25, 35, 50, 75, 100>
Industry	industry:	n/a	<valid industry>
Interested In	interest:	n/a	<p:potential employees, c:consultants/contractors, e:entrepreneurs, h:hiring managers, i:industry experts, d:deal-making contacts>
Joined LinkedIn	joined:	n/a	<login:since last login, d:in the last day, w:in the last week, 2w:in the last 2 weeks, m:in the last month, 3m:in the last 3 months>

You will discover its benefit especially for more complicated searches containing longer Boolean searches with the operators OR, AND, etc. You and your team will be able to create a large database full of different searches which are immediately available for use.

However, beware, as you can see in the examples, there is a little bit different syntax when using the Boolean operator OR. You have to use quotes instead of parentheses. For example:

usaf ccompany: "Airbus OR Boeing"

If you type *usaf ccompany:(Airbus OR Boeing),* you can easily check your search in the search form which appears on the left-hand side of the screen, next to the search results (*see figure 6.32*). Incidentally, *usaf* is supposed to be a keyword which you would normally fill in the *Keywords* field in the Advanced People Search, but in this case, it is nonsense, obviously.

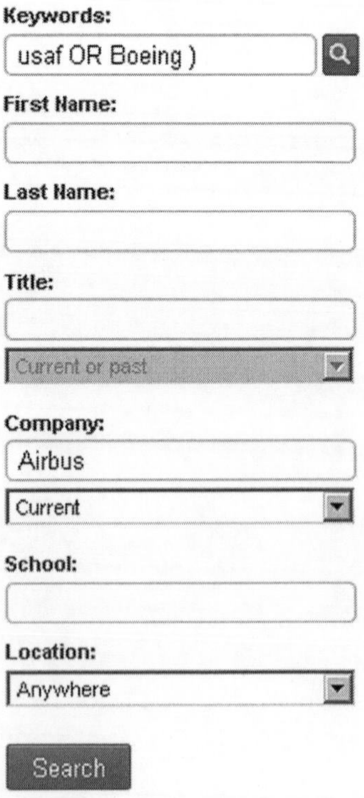

Figure 6.32: Incorrect syntax of advanced LinkedIn operator

Once you use quotes *usaf ccompany: "Airbus OR Boeing"*, you will get the right results (*see figure 6.33*).

There is an option to save your search in LinkedIn; **but as a basic user you are limited to only three saved searches**. With a premium account you can extend this limitation to some extent, precisely up to fifteen when using a Talent Pro account. However, with advanced LinkedIn® operators and your own database of searches, you are able to completely override this limitation and save your search on your own without any barriers.

Keywords:

usaf 🔍

First Name:

Last Name:

Title:

Current or past ▾

Company:

Airbus OR Boeing

Current ▾

School:

Location:

Anywhere ▾

Search

Figure 6.33: Verification of the correct advanced LinkedIn operator syntax

On top of this, it is also possible to effectively substitute the *LinkedIn Saved Search Alerts* service with search automation which I will describe in detail in the section *Candidate Search Automation*. Linkedin Saved Search Alerts notifies you about new LinkedIn® users fulfilling the saved search criteria.

Let's say somebody changes their job or expertise and he/she is currently in alignment with one of your saved searches. You are immediately (daily or weekly as you wish) informed about this fact and you can contact such a person right away, before your competition. I will get back to this in a moment.

X-Ray Search

X-Ray search is a special search which uses general search engines such as Google, Yahoo or Bing, for localization of potential candidates. It is very powerful and as a recruiter you should definitely use it because **it can substantially increase the amount of job candidates you can access as a basic LinkedIn user**. You can access even more than premium LinkedIn users because premium LinkedIn accounts also have a limit of displayable results; they are just higher than a basic account. With X-Ray search you have no limitation whatsoever.

It basically works in the same way as when you put a Boolean search command into Google and get results with links to the public profiles of your potential candidates. You can also get some non-relevant links such as links to LinkedIn job advertisements and discussions which are technically part of search results; but I will show you how to eliminate these unwanted results later.

The advantages of such searches are that you are not limited by the number of displayed candidates (to be precise, the limit is very high, a thousand users) in comparison to embedded LinkedIn searches where you are limited to one hundred LinkedIn users for the basic account. To be able to see a thousand candidates on LinkedIn (i.e. one hundred pages), it would cost a serious amount of money.

Secondly, Google and other search engines offer more sophisticated options in terms of searches. You can use more complex operators including asterisks. Even more, you can filter candidates based on factors which you are not able to do with LinkedIn Advanced People Search – e.g. seeking people based on the date of their graduation or based on the number of their connections.

The minor disadvantage is that LinkedIn® users with a private profile will be excluded from such searches. Another con is that you cannot search based on particular parts of user profiles such as *Title, Company, School,* but you are searching based on keywords through the whole profile.

How many targeted results you get depends just on your skills and knowledge of Google searching; or other search engines like Bing or

Yahoo if you prefer them. They are all very similar but you have to expect some deviation in the syntax of each search engine. I will focus on Google primarily.

Because you are searching LinkedIn® from the outside, you can do this without being logged in to your LinkedIn account. This means you can face one quite paradoxical situation. When you are logged to LinkedIn and open the profile of a LinkedIn user who is a 3rd degree connection to you, you are not able to see their full profile and read where they work worked, etc.

However, when you are signed out of LinkedIn and access such a profile, you can see their full profile. Of course, without the option of contacting them, but that's another story. Firstly, you need to screen their records and profile, and for 3rd degree connections it is better to do this without being logged into LinkedIn.

Let's dive into it. Open your internet browser and open www.Google.com or any of your regional versions – www.Google.ca, www.Google.co.uk, www.Google.ua, etc.

Firstly, set the results per page to one hundred in Google preferences:

http://www.google.com/preferences?hl=en

To be able to do this you will probably need to turn off *Google Instant Results* as well (*see figure 6.34*).

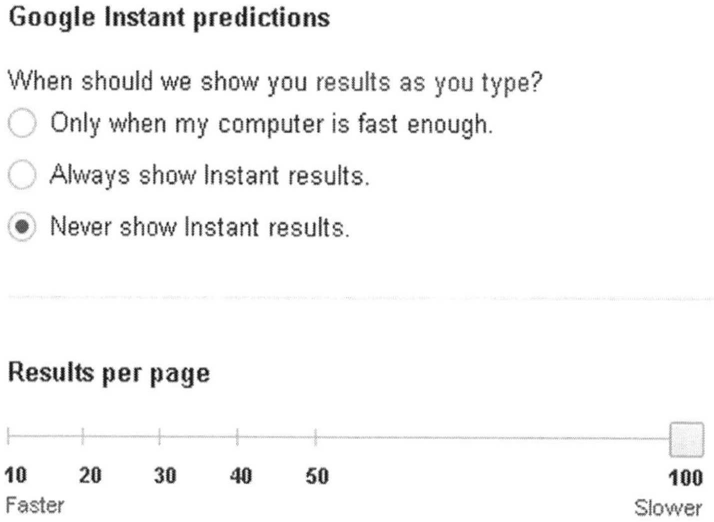

Google Instant predictions

When should we show you results as you type?

○ Only when my computer is fast enough.

○ Always show Instant results.

◉ Never show Instant results.

Results per page

10	20	30	40	50		100
Faster						Slower

Figure 6.34: Adjusting Google search parameters

You do not need to have a Google account to do this by the way. Such a simple example of X-Ray Search might be the following one:

site:linkedin.com "Java software engineer" "Zurich"

You simply put this command into the Google search bar to get the results (*see figure 6.35*).

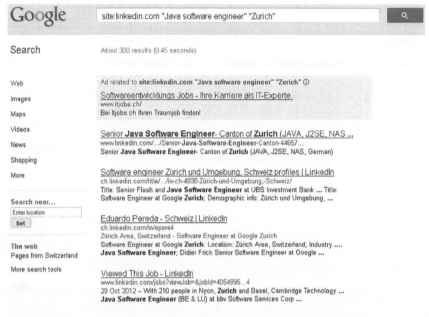

Figure 6.35: Example of an X-Ray Search query

NOTE
Don't be fooled by the number of results Google shows you, check how many pages are really available. The previous example says that you should have three hundred and eighty eight results, but the reality might be a bit different.

With such a command you seek, obviously, Java software engineers from Zurich. Typing just Zurich might be too specific because few users state the actual city, so we can upgrade it a little bit:

site:linkedin.com "Java software engineer" **Zurich OR Swiss OR Switzerland**

Google does not require parentheses, but you can use them to visually improve your search command. It will have no impact on the results whatsoever.

site:linkedin.com *"Java software engineer"* **(Zurich OR Swiss OR Switzerland)**
For the USA you should use e.g.:

site:linkedin.com *"Java software engineer"* **Columbus Ohio OR OH**

Instead of OR you can also use the character "|".

site:linkedin.com *"Java software engineer"* **Columbus Ohio | OH**

> ### NOTE
> There is a limit to the number of keywords you can use when searching via Google. That limit is thirty two keywords and operators themselves are not included in this limit. Maybe it sounds too little but recently the limit was only ten so we can be glad with what we have. With this limit you are able to do pretty powerful searches containing e.g. a list of targeted companies.

You can also target your search to a specific country by using a regional version of the LinkedIn website address (so called URL), e.g.:

*site:**ch.linkedin.com*** *"Java software engineer"* Zurich OR Swiss OR Switzerland

We can get even more results by using a slightly different operator than the operator *site:*

*inurl:**ch.linkedin.com*** *"Java software engineer"* Zurich OR Swiss OR Switzerland

These commands narrow your search to just the Swiss LinkedIn.

Here you can find a complete list of LinkedIn® country prefixes:

Afghanistan	af.linkedin.com	Jordan	jo.linkedin.com
Albania	al.linkedin.com	Kazakhstan	kz.linkedin.com
Algeria	dz.linkedin.com	Kenya	ke.linkedin.com
Argentina	ar.linkedin.com	Korea	kr.linkedin.com
Australia	au.linkedin.com	Kuwait	kw.linkedin.com
Austria	at.linkedin.com	Latvia	lv.linkedin.com
Bahrain	bh.linkedin.com	Lebanon	lb.linkedin.com
Bangladesh	bd.linkedin.com	Lithuania	lt.linkedin.com
Belgium	be.linkedin.com	Luxembourg	lu.linkedin.com
Bolivia	bo.linkedin.com	Macedonia	mk.linkedin.com
Bosnia and			
Herzegovina	ba.linkedin.com	Malaysia	my.linkedin.com
Brazil	br.linkedin.com	Malta	mt.linkedin.com
Bulgaria	bg.linkedin.com	Mauritius	mu.linkedin.com
Canada	ca.linkedin.com	Mexico	mx.linkedin.com
Chile	cl.linkedin.com	Morocco	ma.linkedin.com
China	cn.linkedin.com	Nepal	np.linkedin.com
Colombia	co.linkedin.com	Netherlands	nl.linkedin.com
Costa Rica	cr.linkedin.com	New Zealand	nz.linkedin.com
Croatia	hr.linkedin.com	Nigeria	ng.linkedin.com
Cyprus	cy.linkedin.com	Norway	no.linkedin.com
Czech			
Republic	cz.linkedin.com	Oman	om.linkedin.com
Denmark	dk.linkedin.com	Pakistan	pk.linkedin.com
Dominican			
Republic	do.linkedin.com	Panama	pa.linkedin.com
Ecuador	ec.linkedin.com	Peru	pe.linkedin.com
Egypt	eg.linkedin.com	Philippines	ph.linkedin.com
El Salvador	sv.linkedin.com	Poland	pl.linkedin.com
Estonia	ee.linkedin.com	Portugal	pt.linkedin.com
Finland	fi.linkedin.com	Puerto Rico	pr.linkedin.com
France	fr.linkedin.com	Qatar	qa.linkedin.com
Germany	de.linkedin.com	Romania	ro.linkedin.com
Ghana	gh.linkedin.com	Russian Federation	ru.linkedin.com
Greece	gr.linkedin.com	Saudi Arabia	sa.linkedin.com
Guatemala	gt.linkedin.com	Singapore	sg.linkedin.com
Hong Kong	hk.linkedin.com	Slovak Republic	sk.linkedin.com
Hungary	hu.linkedin.com	Slovenia	si.linkedin.com
Iceland	is.linkedin.com	South Africa	za.linkedin.com
India	in.linkedin.com	Spain	es.linkedin.com
Indonesia	id.linkedin.com	Sri Lanka	lk.linkedin.com
Iran	ir.linkedin.com	Sweden	se.linkedin.com
Ireland	ie.linkedin.com	Switzerland	ch.linkedin.com
Israel	il.linkedin.com	Taiwan	tw.linkedin.com
Italy	it.linkedin.com	Tanzania	tz.linkedin.com
Jamaica	jm.linkedin.com	Thailand	th.linkedin.com

Japan	jp.linkedin.com	Trinidad and Tobago	tt.linkedin.com
Tunisia	tn.linkedin.com	United States	www.linkedin.com
Turkey	tr.linkedin.com	Uruguay	uy.linkedin.com
Uganda	ug.linkedin.com	Venezuela	ve.linkedin.com
Ukraine	ua.linkedin.com	Vietnam	vn.linkedin.com
United Arab Emirates	ae.linkedin.com	Zimbabwe	zw.linkedin.com
United Kingdom	uk.linkedin.com		

If you want to exclude terms, you can use the operator dash or minus (-) in the same way as in an embedded LinkedIn search:

*site:ch.linkedin.com "Java software engineer" Zurich OR Swiss OR Switzerland **-agile***

This command excludes profiles containing the term agile. You would use it when you seek candidates who most probably do not use agile development methods.

When we go deeper, making our results as relevant as possible, we have to eliminate unwanted links from our results such as job advertisements, discussions and links to LinkedIn directory pages which are simply lists of LinkedIn users. To eliminate these irrelevant results, modify the command as follows:

*site:ch.linkedin.com "Java software engineer" Zurich OR Swiss OR Switzerland -agile **-inurl:dir -inurl:directory -inurl:jobs -inurl:groups -inurl:title -inurl:updates -inurl:viewjob -inurl:companies***

With this filtering, you will avoid a vast amount of irrelevant results and you will now get only links to actual LinkedIn® user profiles (*see figure 6.36*).

If you already tried an X-Ray search, you might notice that URLs to LinkedIn user profiles usually have the term *in* or *pub*. For example:

http://www.linkedin.com/in/marcfreydefont
http://www.linkedin.com/pub/boris-baldinger/51/667/164

Knowing this, we can make our results even clearer by using *in* or *pub* in our searches. For example:

*site:ch.linkedin.com "Java software engineer" Zurich OR Swiss OR Switzerland -agile -inurl:dir -inurl:jobs -inurl:groups -inurl:title **inurl:in OR inurl:pub***

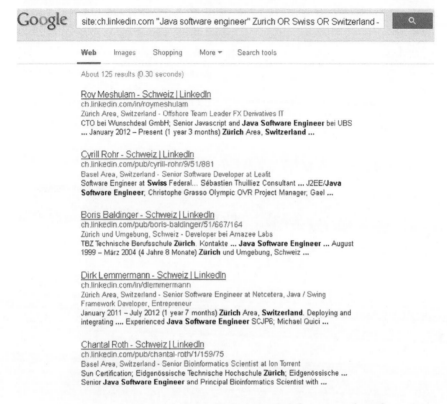

Figure 6.36: Cleaning X-Ray Search results of unwanted results

We already know how to use the OR operator from the embedded LinkedIn search, so I will not be explaining this again. I would just add that as in LinkedIn® searches, all Google search operators are case-sensitive, so use them in upper-case. Keywords are not case-sensitive.

As you can see from the previous section, to master recruiting also means playing around with synonyms and related terms. Google offers a nice feature using tilde (~). If you use this character before a keyword, Google will produce results with your original keyword plus words associated with that keyword. For example, if you type *~developer* in Google, it shows results with the words software, develop, dev, development, programming, design, etc:

site:ch.linkedin.com **~developer** *Zurich OR Swiss OR Switzerland -agile -inurl:dir -inurl:jobs -inurl:groups -inurl:title inurl:in OR inurl:pub*

Similarly you can eliminate people with managerial job posts, recruiters and, for instance, also contractors:

site:ch.linkedin.com ~developer Zurich OR Swiss OR Switzerland -agile -inurl:dir -inurl:jobs -inurl:groups -inurl:title inurl:in OR inurl:pub **-recruitment -manager -leader –contractor -sales**

I am giving examples from Switzerland because it is a well known financial center:

site:ch.linkedin.com ("fund accountant" | "fund accounting" | ("account manager" (funds | fund))) -inurl:dir -inurl:jobs -inurl:groups -inurl:title inurl:in | inurl:pub **-recruitment -director -vp -manager –head -cfo -founder -vice**

Take into account that parentheses are not mandatory. Not using them will provide you with the very same results.

Google also supports wildcards; specifically, the asterisk character, which can substitute any word. For example, let's say you are looking for a chief officer regardless of their field of expertise:

*"Chief * Officer"*

The complete command would look as follows:

site:ch.linkedin.com **"Chief * Officer"** *Zurich OR Swiss OR Switzerland -inurl:dir -inurl:jobs -inurl:groups -inurl:title inurl:in OR inurl:pub*

You can use more asterisks, so e.g. *"Chief * * Officer"* (you have to type quotes to get correct results) means that you get results where there are two words between the terms *Chief* and *Officer* – e.g. *Chief Information Security Officer*. You can use more of them if you need to. Just be aware that there have to be spaces between asterisks.

For similar purposes, the operator AROUND can be used. Let's say you are not sure how many words might be between the term *Chief* and *Officer*. It might be one like in *Chief Executive Officer*, it might be two like *Chief Information Security Officer* or it might be three like *Chief Marketing & Customer Satisfaction Officer*. To cover all options you could use the following command which makes sure that you only get results with less than three words included between typed terms:

site:ch.linkedin.com **"Chief"** *AROUND(3)* **"Officer"** *Zurich OR Swiss OR Switzerland -inurl:dir -inurl:jobs -inurl:groups -inurl:title inurl:in OR inurl:pub*

You can use a similar operator in Bing called NEAR.

There is also a search technique called **stemming**. Google does stemming for you automatically. When you search for the expression *security consult* for example, it will include results containing the terms *security* and *consult, consultant, consultancy,* etc. This does not work when you type only a one-word term into Google.

> **NOTE**
>
> Maybe you are wondering where the operator AND is and why I have not used it yet. Basically each space between terms means AND if there is no other operator like OR. It's similar to a LinkedIn embedded search. You can use the AND operator implicitly (sometimes called implicit AND) to make sure that all terms connected with this operator will be included in search results. Google is the same as LinkedIn. Try to be smart. If you do not use AND between terms, you will also get results containing not only the typed terms, but probably they will not appear in the first positions.

We can use an X-Ray search to find LinkedIn® users who typed their e-mail address into their profile:

*site:www.linkedin.com (inurl:in OR inurl:pub) "Sales * Consultant" New York* **(gmail.com OR yahoo.com OR aol.com)** *-inurl:dir -inurl:directory -inurl:jobs -inurl:groups -inurl:title -inurl:updates -inurl:viewjob -inurl:companies*

With this command you can uncover LinkedIn profiles which contain an e-mail address; *Sales Consultants* from the New York area in our case. You can use company e-mails as well even if it does not make much sense because you can determine company e-mail based on the first and last name of any LinkedIn user. I will come back to this problem in the next chapter.

*site:www.linkedin.com (inurl:in OR inurl:pub) "Sales * Consultant" New York (pg.com OR kimberly-clark.com OR unilever.com OR jnj. com) -inurl:dir -inurl:directory -inurl:jobs -inurl:groups -inurl:title -inurl:updates -inurl:viewjob -inurl:companies*

E-mail addresses can be gathered manually or using software – e.g. *Contact Capture* by Broadlook (*www.broadlook.com*). I will discuss how to work with this tool in the next chapter *07, Shoot to Kill: How to Reach Candidates with LinkedIn® Every Time*, section *A Company E-mail Address*. There are also Firefox extensions which do the same job.

Especially when looking for salespeople, it might be beneficial to search by adjectives to get people who are above standard in their field. For example:

inurl:us.linkedin.com ("business development" OR "sales manager" OR "sales rep") (sales | "sales representative") (~increased | ~lead | ~top | ~first | ~ highest | ~most | ~exceed | ~quota) -title -jobs

You can also filter people who might be interested in new job offers:

site:linkedin.com "software engineer" Beijing "interested in new job" – "not interested" -inurl:dir -inurl:directory -inurl:jobs -inurl:groups -inurl:title -inurl:updates -inurl:viewjob -inurl:companies

As you will notice, firstly we filter profiles including the expression *"interested in new job"* and secondly, exclude users who state *"not interested"* in their profiles. Some users explicitly state that they are not interested in any job offer at the moment.

Another great example of effective X-Ray usage is seeking candidates based on the year of their university graduation. This is not something you would be able to do with an embedded LinkedIn® people search.

With the following example, you will get LinkedIn users who studied at King's College in London between 2008 and 2011:

site:linkedin.com **"King's college London"** *("2008 * 2011") -inurl:dir -inurl:directory -inurl:jobs -inurl:groups -inurl:title -inurl:updates -inurl:viewjob -inurl:companies*

Another trick using X-Ray search is seeking candidates based on their number of connections. This is again not possible to realize with LinkedIn itself. You can only sort by number of connections in LinkedIn.

Let's say you want to target software engineers having five hundred or more connections, from which we can assume that they maintain their profile well and are active users:

site:linkedin.com **"connections * 500"** *"software engineer" -inurl:dir -inurl:directory -inurl:jobs -inurl:groups -inurl:title -inurl:updates -inurl:viewjob -inurl:companies*

If you go for users having between one hundred and two hundred connections, you might use the following command:

site:linkedin.com **connections AROUND(0) 100..200** *"software engineer" (Spain OR France) -inurl:dir -inurl:directory -inurl:jobs -inurl:groups -inurl:title -inurl:updates -inurl:viewjob -inurl:companies*

This command is not 100% precise though. You can expect some users to be out of this range in your results.

So far we have used X-Ray search without being logged into our LinkedIn account because it is better for displaying the full profiles of our potential candidates. Now I will describe a different approach.

In this case, we have to be logged into LinkedIn® to be able to take advantage of this approach. So far, we were excluding sites containing the string *pub/dir* in their URL to avoid user's directories in our results. Now I am going to do vice versa and show you how to take advantage of LinkedIn people directories.

Let's do a search where we explicitly state that we want to see only people directories:

site:linkedin.com *"Current * software engineer" "San Francisco"* **profiles directory** *-inurl:jobs -inurl:groups -inurl:updates -inurl:viewjob -inurl:companies*

With such searches you get different Google results than you are used to. Instead of links to individual LinkedIn user profiles, you get links to sets of LinkedIn users from the same professions and geographical area (*see figure 6.37*).

Figure 6.37: Using X-Ray Search while being logged into LinkedIn

Let's open, for example, the second link (*see figure 6.38*).

If you click on a different link in our Google results, you will get another set of LinkedIn® users. With this approach you are able to expand your base of potential candidates even more.

Figure 6.38: Using X-Ray Search while being logged into LinkedIn

In addition, as you can see, there is the full name of a 3rd degree connection on the list.

What does this mean?

It means that LinkedIn assumes that you know the user's full name, therefore you are able to access their full profile. On the other hand, if you do an embedded search as you are used to, you cannot see the full surname of your 3rd degree connections and therefore, even their profiles are prohibited to you. I will show you a procedure to uncover full names of private profiles and 3rd degree connections in the next chapter.

There are also further operators in Google, but the mentioned one will be most useful to you. The possibilities are even wider. It is just a question of how you can manage Google Boolean searching and implement it with the purpose of seeking LinkedIn users. For a complete list of Google search operators and how to use them, please refer to:

http://www.GoogleGuide.com

As a recruiter, you should use this on a regular basis, creating pretty complex Boolean searches. Some of them can target just a group of companies. Instead of making them from scratch every time which is pretty time consuming and awkward, I recommend to save your search commands in a spreadsheet (Google Spreadsheet or simply MS Excel) for LinkedIn embedded searches with advanced LinkedIn® modifiers, which I described in the previous section.

In the first column, put your description, in the second, the Boolean search command and the third column can be allocated for potential comments (*see figure 6.39*).

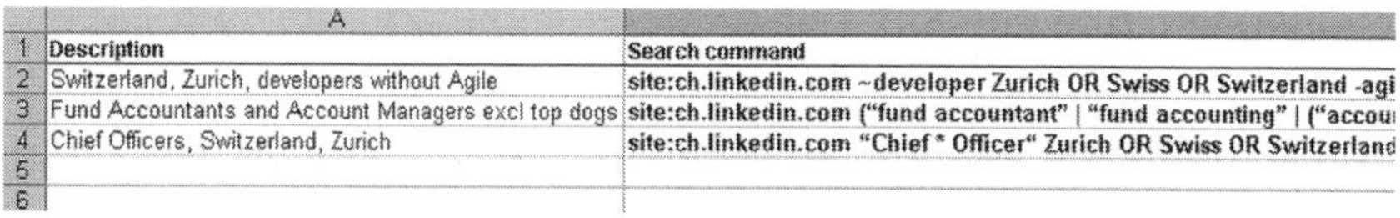

	A	
1	Description	Search command
2	Switzerland, Zurich, developers without Agile	site:ch.linkedin.com ~developer Zurich OR Swiss OR Switzerland -agi
3	Fund Accountants and Account Managers excl top dogs	site:ch.linkedin.com ("fund accountant"	"fund accounting"	("accou
4	Chief Officers, Switzerland, Zurich	site:ch.linkedin.com "Chief * Officer" Zurich OR Swiss OR Switzerland
5		
6		

Figure 6.39: Storing X-Ray Search queries in a spreadsheet

You can use any other system which suits you – e.g. using text files or a database (*see figure 6.40*).

Do not use MS Word for saving search queries because it can modify your strings, and your search queries will then probably not work properly.

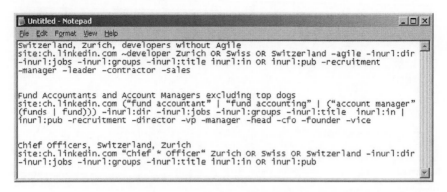

Figure 6.40: Storing X-Ray Search queries in a text editor

Candidate Search Automation

Daily recruitment duty is often routine work where you need to repeat most of the steps on a regular basis. One day you run a search and the second day you have to run it again because more people are needed and you also expect that some LinkedIn® users changed their profile, so they might fulfill your criteria at that moment.

One LinkedIn functionality which helps you with these regular tasks is the *Saved Search* feature. You are basically able to save every search you do with LinkedIn People Search. You can do this with a small button called *Save Search* (currently in the top right area of your search results).

You just name your search and save it. Then you can run your search again easily with just one click. You can access the list of your saved searches when you click Advanced next to the main search input field and click *Saved Searches* in the last tab (*see figure 6.41*).

So the first great advantage is that you can automate your searches; but there is one even more important feature, alerts. You can be notified by LinkedIn when there are new LinkedIn users fulfilling your criteria. Imagine that somebody just became a C/C++ developer or maybe just updated their profile reflecting this fact or somebody just created a new LinkedIn account.

LinkedIn runs your search in the background on a regular basis and when there is somebody like that, you are alerted to it (*see figure 6.42*). Then, you can be the very first recruiter who contacts such a potential candidate.

Figure 6.41: LinkedIn Saved Searches

LINKEDIN SAVED SEARCH UPDATE

We found **10 new results** that match your saved search "Linux QA Engineers Beijing":

Saved Search Results
- View all new results

- Ronald Vazquez
  Senior Network Engineer (Unix/Linux) [RHCE] at TerpSys®

- Wesley Dillingham
  Linux Administrator / Engineer.

- Brad Simonin, RHCE, RHCSA, Security+
  Red Hat Enterprise Linux System Administrator/Engineer

- Jefferson C.
  Linux Systems Administrator at NYC Department of Correction

- James Adeyemi Fowe
  Research Scientist and Telecoms Solution Architect

View more new results »

Figure 6.42: LinkedIn Saved Search Alerts

LinkedIn® lets you set these alerts to monthly, weekly or, when you have a premium account, to a daily basis. Of course the daily alerts are the best because they create a regular daily pipeline of candidates where you can expect that they have not yet been contacted by any other recruiter (mind you, they could have been contacted according to their role or expertise). However, it does not necessarily mean they have not been contacted at all.

Another significant disadvantage of this feature is that you can manage only three searches in the basic LinkedIn account. With a premium account, you can reach up to fifteen saved searches. This is still a very limited number.

But do not worry. I will show you how to completely substitute the LinkedIn Saved Search Alerts features with your own. We will use X-Ray search as a base platform for this.

I recommend you to automate searches only when:

- You recruit the same profiles regularly or often

- Your search is effectively targeted - at least 75% relevant candidates

- Your search has not more than one hundred results.

Using Bing

The first method of automation when using Bing is RSS (Rich Site Summary), a sort of Bing trick. Let's open the Bing search engine at Bing.com and do a search (*see figure 6.43*), e.g.:

site:linkedin.com java oracle unix "senior software engineer" "Greensboro" -profiles -inurl:dir -inurl:directory -inurl:jobs -inurl:groups -inurl:title -inurl:updates -inurl:viewjob -inurl:companies

Now we need to convert the site(s) we want to RSS. Bing supports a great thing which provides you with the possibility of transforming any URL to RSS. You simply connect string *&format=rss* to the URL (*see figure 6.44*).

When you hit enter, the site you selected will be transferred to RSS which you can save as a bookmark in Mozilla Firefox (choose *Live Bookmarks* and hit *Subscribe Now* – see *figure 6.45*) or in any other internet browser in a similar fashion. You can also import it to your RSS reader (select *Choose Application* and hit *Subscribe Now*).
Alternatively, you can use an online RSS reader such as *Bloglines, MyYahoo, Newsgator*.

Once you have your RSS search saved in your bookmarks, you can easily access potential candidates and separate those you have already checked and those who are new (*see figure 6.46*).

Then you just check these bookmarks on a regular basis, daily is best, and you have knowledge of new potential candidates in each search. Every time there is a new LinkedIn user fitting your criteria, they will appear at the top of the list.

WEB   IMAGES   VIDEOS   NEWS   MORE

bing   site:linkedin.com java oracle unix "senior software engineer" "Greenst   🔍

61 RESULTS

Firas Farah | LinkedIn
www.**linkedin.com**/in/firasif ▾
Senior Software Engineer at Quoin · Computer Software · 98 connections
Senior Software Engineer Location **Greensboro**/Winston-Salem, ... **Java Unix** C#
Firas Farah's ... **Java**, **Oracle**, WebSphere, SAP, ...

Andy Allred | LinkedIn
www.**linkedin.com**/pub/andy-allred/29/149/871 ▾
Independent Consultant - **Senior** ... · Computer Software · 3 recommendations
... **Senior Software Engineer** at ... **(Java** (Eclipse), **Unix** Shell Scripting ... HTML,
XML/SOAP, Proprietary CX Web Server, Microsoft IIS, Apache, **Oracle** 8i ...

Yaochun Zhang | LinkedIn
www.**linkedin.com**/pub/yaochun-zhang/4/814/a6 ▾
Oracle Applications Developer at ... · Information Technology and Services
Greensboro/Winston-Salem, North Carolina Area ... **Java Oracle** SQL Linux Data
Modeling **Unix** Data Warehousing XML VB.NET Application Development ETL SDLC

Michael Tyler | LinkedIn
www.**linkedin.com**/pub/michael-tyler/19/7a6/88a ▾
Development Operations Manager at ... · Information Technology and Services
Senior Software Engineer ... University of North Carolina at **Greensboro** ... ibm
websphere, iis, **java**, j2ee, javascript, linux, microsoft windows, mysql, **oracle** ...

Bob Dudash | LinkedIn
www.**linkedin.com**/pub/bob-dudash/14/94a/94b ▾
Senior Software Engineer at Sonus ... · Information Technology and Services
Senior Software Engineer ... Architected/designed/coded large databases and complex
client/server applications using **Oracle**/C/C++/Tuxedo/**Unix** ... **Greensboro**
/Winston-Salem ...

Figure 6.43: X-Ray Search using the Bing search engine

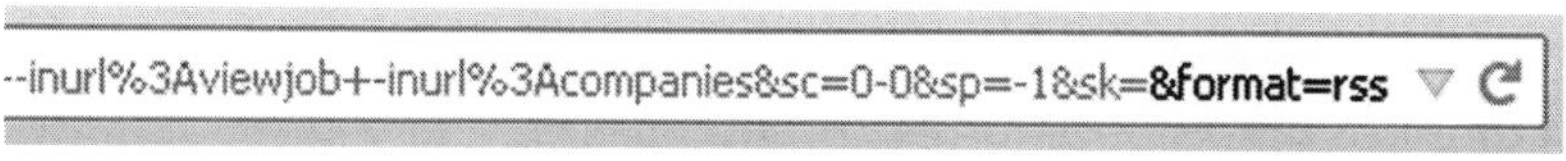

--inurl%3Aviewjob+-inurl%3Acompanies&sc=0-0&sp=-1&sk=**&format=rss** ▽ C

Figure 6.44: Converting URL to RSS using Bing

Figure 6.45: Saving an RSS page into bookmarks

Using Google with RSS Converter

Because I prefer Google to perform X-Ray searches, I was looking for a solution where I could use Google search. I am not aware if Google has a similar RSS feature to Bing and as far as I know, you need a different tool which creates RSS feeds from URLs. I use the Feed43 service (*www.feed43.com*) which offers free and also paid plans. With the free plan you have to take into account that your RSS will be updated every six hours and that you can have up to twenty items in the feed.

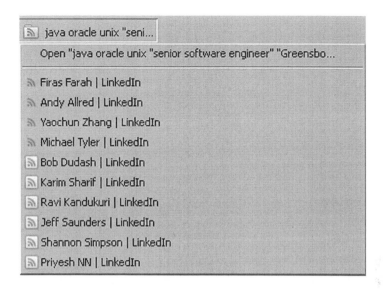

Figure 6.46: Accessing an automatically updated list of users via RSS

When you have your RSS feed ready, you just import it into your RSS reader or save it like an RSS bookmark in your Mozilla Firefox browser as you saw in the previous section.

So how do you convert Google search URLs into an RSS feed?

Let's assume that the following search is the one we want to follow and be alerted about when new results fitting our criteria pop-up:

site:fr.linkedin.com ("corporate recovery" | insolvency) accountant -head -consultant -principle -manager -director -partner -owner (inurl:in | inurl:pub) -inurl:dir -inurl:companies

Put this search command into Google and copy the URL, which should look as follows:

https://www.google.com/search?hl=en&tbo=d&noj=1&q=site%3Afr.linkedin.com+%28%22corporate+recovery%22+|+insolvency%29+accountant+-head+-consultant+-principle+-manager+-director+-partner+-owner+%28inurl%3Ain+|+inurl%3Apub%29+-inurl%3Adir+-inurl%3Acompanies&oq=site%3Afr.linkedin.com+%28%22corporate+recovery%22+|+insolvency%29+accounta

*nt+-head+-consultant+-principle+-manager+-director+-partner+-
owner+%28inurl%3Ain+|+inurl%3Apub%29+-inurl%3Adir+-
inurl%3Acompanies&gs_l=serp.3...0.0.0.4104212.0.0.0.0.0.0.0.0..0.0.
les%3B..0.0...1c.DZ1M02I20UA*

You can strip the URL string by removing the 's' from 'https' and
also everything after the last ampersand '&'.

So you get:

*http://www.google.com/search?hl=en&tbo=d&noj=1&q=site%3
Afr.linkedin.com+%28%22corporate+recovery%22+|+insolven
cy%29+accountant+-head+-consultant+-principle+-manager+-
director+-partner+-owner+%28inurl%3Ain+|+inurl%3Apub%29+-
inurl%3Adir+-inurl%3Acompanies&oq=site%3Afr.linkedin.com
+%28%22corporate+recovery%22+|+insolvency%29+accounta
nt+-head+-consultant+-principle+-manager+-director+-partner+-
owner+%28inurl%3Ain+|+inurl%3Apub%29+-inurl%3Adir+-
inurl%3Acompanies*

Now open www.feed43.com in your browser and hit *http://www.
feed43.com/feed.html?action=new.* Paste your URL into the field and
click *Reload* (*see figure 6.47*).

On the next page, fill-in *Step 2. Define extraction rules*, in the form.
Including the field *Item (repeatable) Search Pattern* with the following
regular command:

<h3 class="r"><a href="{%}">{%}</a></h3>

And hit *Extract* (*see figure 6.48*).

You should see the confirmation *OK (10 items found)* (or any other
number) in green color.

Scroll down to the section *Step 3. Define output format* and fill-in
the form according to *figure 6.49* (*RSS item properties* especially).

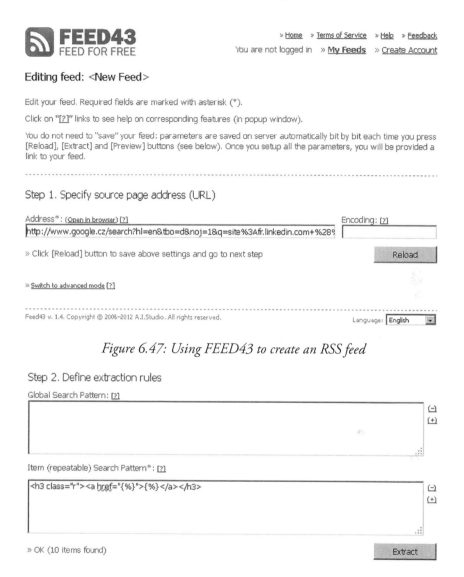

Figure 6.47: Using FEED43 to create an RSS feed

Figure 6.48: Using FEED43 to create an RSS feed

Fill-in the field *Feed Title* according to the actual search you want to follow. Hit *Preview* which should be followed by an *OK* confirmation and you are done.

Finally, just open your RSS in a new browser tab. The link can be found at the very bottom of the Feed43 page in the section *Step 4. Get your RSS feed*, field *Feed URL is* (*see figure 6.50*).

Step 3. Define output format

RSS feed properties

Feed Title*: [?]

| corporate recovery insolvency accountant France |

Feed Link*: [?]

| http://www.google.cz/search?hl=en&tbo=d&noj=1&q=site%3Afr.linkedin.com+%28%22corporate+recovery%22 |

Feed Description*: [?]

| site:fr.linkedin.com ("corporate recovery" | insolvency) accountant -head -consultant -principle -manager -director -partner -owner (inurl:in | inurl:pub) -inurl:dir -inurl:companies - Google Search |

RSS item properties

Item Title Template*: [?]

| {%2} |

Item Link Template*: [?]

| {%1} |

Item Content Template*: [?]

| {%2} |

☐ Merge all items into single one, optionally applying global template: [?]

» OK (Preview mode)   Preview

Figure 6.49: Using FEED43 to create a RSS feed

Step 4. Get your RSS feed

» Feed URL is: 🔊 /2232716432556515.xml [?]

Point your news aggregator to this URL or test this feed in browser.

» Edit URL is: /feed.html?name=2232716432556515 [?]

Please save this link for future use.

Figure 6.50: Using FEED43 to create a RSS feed

Now you can save it as a bookmark in Mozilla Firefox (choose *Live Bookmarks* and hit *Subscribe Now*) or you can save in any other internet browser similarly.

You can also import the link to your RSS reader, I prefer Google Reader. You need just a Google account to access Google Reader (*www.google.com/reader*). Then you just hit *SUBSCRIBE* where you paste the RSS link you created with Feed43.com.

Using Google Alerts

Google Alerts is a great service which is usually used so you wil be automatically informed about news based on set keywords. For example, when you want to be informed about new internet posts mentioning the company Honeywell, you can create a Google alert for this. You can watch what is new about this company or how their clients review them. You can do the same with your company as well.

This feature can also be used as a substitution for LinkedIn® Saved Search Alerts. You just simply put your X-Ray search command into the field *Search query* in Google Alerts. You choose *Everything* for *Result type* and *All results* for *How many* (*see figure 6.51*). You should choose daily (option *Once a day* for the field *How often*) receiving of alerts.

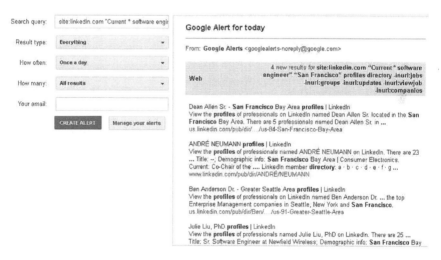

Figure 6.51: Google Alerts setup

When you set the alert up, you will be notified about new results by e-mail. The advantage of Google Alerts is that you can create as many alerts as you want.

Using Google Custom Search Engine

CSE (Custom Search Engine) can be used for simplifying your routine searches.

Let's take the example:

site:ch.linkedin.com "Java software engineer" Zurich OR Swiss OR Switzerland -agile -inurl:dir -inurl:directory -inurl:jobs -inurl:groups -inurl:title -inurl:updates -inurl:viewjob -inurl:companies

Instead of typing 80% of a search query each and every time, we can set up our own search engine which has 80% of a search queries embedded in it and you need only set variable parts like:

"Java software engineer"

Firstly, you need to have a Google account. Then open the CSE dashboard:

http://www.google.com/cse/manage/all

Next, click *New search engine…* and fill-in the sites which should be searched (*see figure 6.52*). Wildcards are also allowed.

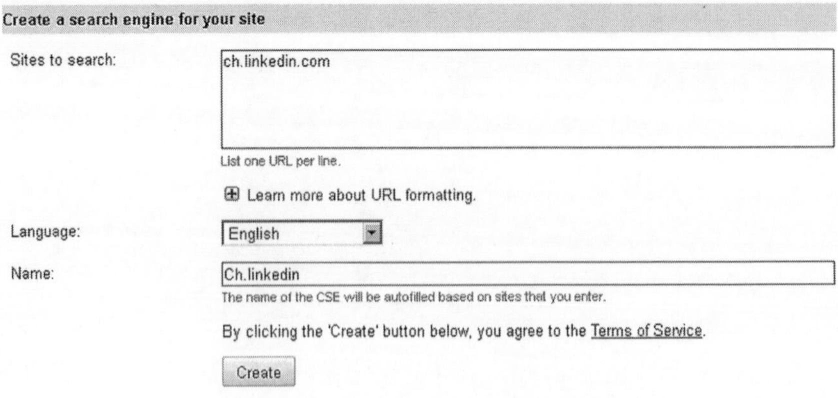

Figure 6.52: Custom Search Engine setup

When you hit *Create*, you can verify if it works properly. You are also provided with code to embed your new search engine into your website, for example.

When you open *Basics* or *Edit*, you can tweak your search engine with other routine parameters (*see figure 6.53*):

-agile -inurl:dir -inurl:directory -inurl:jobs -inurl:groups -inurl:title -inurl:updates -inurl:viewjob -inurl:companies

Basic information

Your search engine's name and description will be shown on its Google homepage.

Search engine name: Ch.linkedin

Search engine description:

Keywords describe the content or subject of your search engine. These keywords are used to tune your search engine results.

Search engine keywords: -agile -inurl.dir -inurl.directory -inurl:jobs -inurl.groups -inurl:title -inurl:t
e.g. climate "global warming" "greenhouse gases"

Search engine unique ID: **017891884574377032430:ke5es_2fwq0**

Save Changes | Cancel

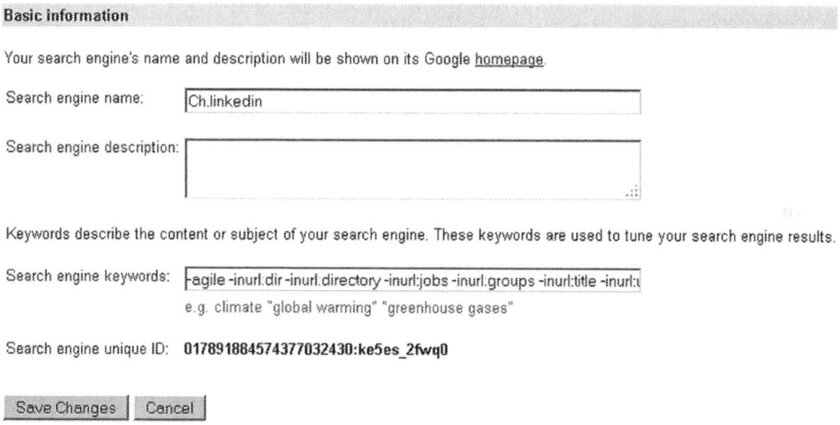

Figure 6.53: Custom Search Engine setup

When you open your search engine, you can type just (*see figure 6.54*):

"Java software engineer" Zurich

…or easily change it to:

"Python software engineer" Geneva

It is significantly easier than using the whole search query:

site:ch.linkedin.com "Java software engineer" Zurich OR Swiss OR Switzerland -agile -inurl:dir -inurl:directory -inurl:jobs -inurl:groups -inurl:title -inurl:updates -inurl:viewjob -inurl:companies

You can make it even simpler by defining tabs where each will represent one city or location. I focused on Switzerland so my refinements will be Swiss cities.

Ch.linkedin

| "Java software engineer" Zurich | | Search |

Search engine details [Edit this search engine]

searches sites including: ch.linkedin.com

Keywords: -agile -inurl:dir -inurl:directory -inurl:jobs -inurl:groups -inurl:title -inurl:updates -inurl:view

Last updated: January 21, 2013

Add this search engine to your Google homepage: [+ Google]
Add this search engine to your blog or webpage »

Figure 6.54: Using Custom Search Engine

In the edit of your search engine, click on *Refinements* and click *Add Refinement* (*see figure 6.55*).

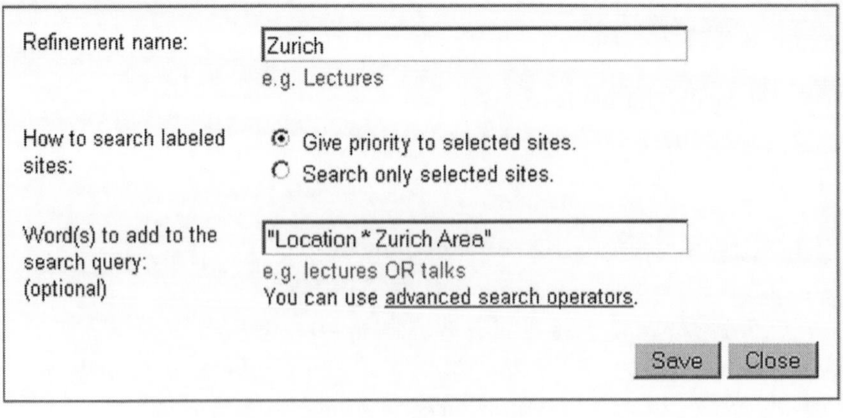

Refinement name:	Zurich
	e.g. Lectures
How to search labeled sites:	⦿ Give priority to selected sites.
	○ Search only selected sites.
Word(s) to add to the search query: (optional)	"Location * Zurich Area"
	e.g. lectures OR talks
	You can use advanced search operators.
	Save Close

Figure 6.55: Custom Search Engine setup

Instead of *"Location * Zurich Area"* you can use just Zurich if you figured out that it is sufficient. Then you can just type the basic keyword such as the name of a sought after position and click through different locations in the predefined tabs (*see figure 6.56*).

There are no limits to what you can define with a Custom Search Engine. When you use X-Ray search on a daily basis, it will save you a lot of time and effort. With one click you can change, for instance, the location or whatever else you predefine.

Figure 6.56: Using Custom Search Engine with refinements

See LINREA.com where you can find such a predefined embedded custom search engine which you can use on a daily basis to make your searches as effective as possible.

Chapter Summary

- The value of LinkedIn® paid services is not as significant as it is marketed. A lot of paid functions are useless or can be substituted with free options

- You cannot avoid Boolean searches when you want to be successful at hiring people

- One of the most effective ways to target potential candidates is to use a search engine such as Google

- LinkedIn Saved Search Alerts is a very beneficial function which can be substituted with Google Alerts or RSS

- Targeting candidates is about diversity based on their level of competency, geographical area, past company engagements, average or top achievers in terms of skills, etc.

07

Shoot to Kill: How to Reach Candidates with LinkedIn® Every Time

Shoot to Kill: How to Reach Candidates with LinkedIn® Every Time

---

What you will learn in this chapter

- Which contact methods are the most effective and how to measure their efficiency

- How to uncover the hidden LinkedIn® profiles of your potential candidates without upgrading to premium

- How to observe your competitors´ activity on LinkedIn®

Once you know how to target, locate and filter your potential candidates, it is time to learn how to effectively contact them. There are several methods you can use to reach LinkedIn® users. Basically you have the following choices:

- **Invitation** (option *Connect*)

- **Introduction** (option *Get introduced*)

- **Message** (option *Message* or *Send a message*)

- **InMail®** (option *Send InMail*)

- **E-mail**

- **Telephone and VoIP.**

Each option has its own pros and cons, so I will go through each of them thoroughly. After which, I will describe the three main strategies you can use to contact your potential candidates based on a recruiter's approach – aggressive, conservative and super conservative.

LinkedIn® Invitation

In my experience, **invitations are next to e-mails** (not counting telephone contact where it really depends on the target group) **as one of the most effective ways to reach your potential candidates.** However, you have to take time and effort and compose the text of the invitation properly.

A great side effect of using invitations is that you naturally expand your LinkedIn network with new connections. So you not only get your message through, but you also get new connections which potentially increases your chances of contacting further potential candidates.

The second thing is that you are not able to contact a single LinkedIn® user twice via invitation without knowing their e-mail address, which you normally do not. So basically you need them to accept your invitation or at least reply to the invitation without accepting it to be able to make contact in the future.

There is also the aspect of declined invitations, which can cause you to be suspended from sending more invitations; you will be forced to solve this with LinkedIn support, which blocks you from sending invitations for a week or two. With proper and customized invitations you can avoid this easily.

As I already described in the chapter *05, Cultivate Your Hunting Ground: LinkedIn Networking Strategy for Recruiters*, in the section *Dealing with a Limited Amount of Invitations*, you have a limited amount of invitations – **three thousand**. Even if it sounds like a lot and even if I described ways to get around this limitation, you have to consider every sent invitation carefully. Do not waste them.

You can send invitations to your 2nd degree connections without any problems. The option *Connect* is at your disposal for this group of users. You are able to do so also with 3rd degree connections, even if you cannot see the *Connect* button. But you need to uncover their full name firstly, which I am going to explain in the section *How to Uncover any Full Profile View without Upgrading to Premium*. A positive side effect of this is that the *Connect* button appears.

So finally, there are no obstacles to sending an invitation to anybody.

In the *LinkedIn Inbox* you can check who accepted your invitation and who did not. See the *Inbox -> Invitations -> Sent.*

Let's say you are seeking candidates for some vacancy. You do your search, with LinkedIn® People Search or X-Ray search, and you get the search results. To speed up the process of screening and contacting potential candidates, I recommend you to open about twenty LinkedIn profiles in separate browser tabs and go through them one by one. When you are done with those, open another twenty and so on; it is better than doing them one by one.

Then compose the text of an invitation and save it for future use. You can use any kind of word processor - MS Notepad, MS Word, Apple TextEdit, etc.

You have to take into account that space is very limited for text in invitations so you have to be brief and persuasive. So think minimalist and avoid useless words.

I celebrated success with the following composition:

<candidate's name>,

Your profile is very interesting - your experience with <experience> especially. Currently I am seeking <vacancy> in <city, country>.

Unfortunately, space is limited here so for more information please accept this invitation.

<your firstname>

The only thing you have to change every time is the candidate's first name. I swear to you that it is worth the effort. It takes a few more seconds but it increases your chances of getting rapid feedback. From a personal point of view, it is a tiny ice breaker.

The second rule when composing invitations is flattery. Everybody likes to be flattered about their knowledge or experience. Again, you are getting deeper under the candidate's skin.

Next, you need to specify who you are looking for and for which region – city or country.

At the very end, you just proclaim that there is not enough space to specify more information and add your signature.

Based on the actual number of characters you used on name, name of the job post, etc. you might face the characters limit. If so, you need to shorten your message a little bit. On the other hand, if you have a few more extra characters, you can utilize them on a nicer farewell – e.g. *Take care, Best wishes, Best regards.*

See the example template in practice in *figure 7.1.*

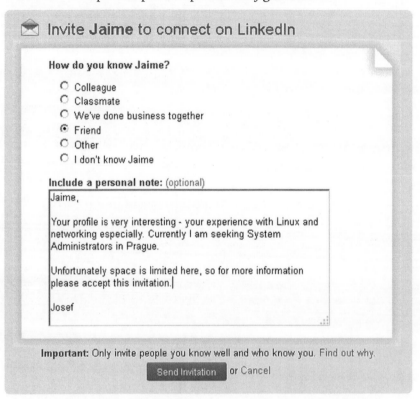

Figure 7.1: Sending a customized LinkedIn invitation

As you can see, you can choose from several options of how you get to know a particular LinkedIn user. You can choose the option *Friend* which is newly available without the necessity of adding the user's e-mail address.

Another option, which I prefer, is: *We've done business together.* Here you can choose the job role which you consider the most appealing to the specific candidate. In the majority of cases it would be your current role as a recruiter.

You can also choose the option *Colleague*, and choose another engagement from the past. Sometimes I take advantage of my past history when I worked as a software engineer. A contacted software engineer most probably will not decline an invitation from someone from the same field.

Sometimes you might have a chance to choose the option *Classmate*. LinkedIn will show you if you studied at the same school as the addressed LinkedIn user.

The last option is to choose *Groups,* but I do not recommend this for recruitment purposes. The relations among LinkedIn® groups are not as tight as for the other mentioned options.

Weblinks are not allowed, but of course you can help yourself, modifying the link to be permitted. For example:

www.jobsconsulting.org/bulgarian-it-talents-needed/

...could be converted to the permitted format:

jobsconsulting(org)/bulgarian-it-talents-needed/

In addition, you can use a service for shortening URLs to save more characters. I have a Google account, so I prefer the service called *goo.gl* available via *http://goo.gl.* It can convert your original URL to the format as follows:

http://goo.gl/YT1cS

Which you can convert to the allowed format in a LinkedIn introduction as:

goo(gl)/YT1cS

or

goo(dot)gl/YT1cS

NOTE

For shortening URLs you can also use any of the following services:

TinyURL.com
Bitly.com
ShortURL.com
Ow.ly

After much testing experience, I **do not recommend pasting links in introductions.** At least when using the strategy I described above. The reason is that it will rapidly increase the number of unaccepted invitations because of the people who open the pasted URL and decide that they will not reply to you.

Even if my recruitment agency is one of the first or maybe the very first which started to advertise job vacancies with company names (i.e. no hidden company names), I recommend not putting all information in the invitation. The space for words is limited so you are not able to properly explain what it is all about. And just pasting the URL is too vague, which causes the ratio of accepted invitations to drop. **Your goal is not only to reach the candidate, but also grow your network,** so you have to have a reason for the candidate to accept your invitation. And the reason is simply that they will get more information without any further obligation.

Once the candidate accepts your invitation you should react immediately and send them the promised information. In the vast majority of cases, I recommend to do this via an e-mail address, which is not hidden for 1st degree connections.

How to structure a proper e-mail to your potential candidate is covered in the *E-mail* section of this chapter.

LinkedIn® Introduction

Introduction is one way to approach 2nd or 3rd degree connections. It works on the basis that you compose a message which will be forwarded to the desirable user by one of your 1st degree connections based on your choice. LinkedIn offers you a list of 1st degree connections which are directly connected with the desirable user (*see figure 7.2*).

Figure 7.2: Sending a LinkedIn introduction

The addressee will get your introduction once the person in the middle approves it. Introduction does not mean creating a connection between you and the addressed people. It is basically just a message which can be replied to or declined.

NOTE
There is a practice called *tollboothing* where a LinkedIn user would like to charge you for forwarding the introduction. If you meet this, just ignore it.

Overall, I found it ineffective and also very limited for a basic LinkedIn account where you have only five available introductions. You are obviously very dependent on the person who is forwarding your introduction, which is usually the critical part.

LinkedIn® Message

Message is the standard way to contact other users on LinkedIn. The pros are that you are not limited by the number of characters you can type or web links you can send.

The cons are that you can contact only your 1st degree connections and also group members; however, there is one small hidden trick.

Let's say you want to contact someone who is not one of your 1st degree connections with a LinkedIn® message. It is possible in cases when you are member of the same group as the targeted potential candidate.

Firstly, you have to find out if there are some groups you share with the user. In the LinkedIn search results you are able to recognize this only for 3rd degree connections and *out of network* connections without opening a targeted profile, they have group tags next to their name. You are not able to recognize this for 1st and 2nd level connections because the tags of 2nd degree connections have priority.

When using LinkedIn people search, you can filter group members with the *Relationship* filter. With this option you filter only LinkedIn users which share some group with you (*see figure 7.3*).

Figure 7.3: Filtering LinkedIn users sharing at least one group with you

You do not know which specific groups you share with the user. Therefore, you need to open each profile anyway regardless of which tag they have next to their name. Once you open a user's profile, you can see which groups you share with the user in the *Groups you share with <user's name>* table. As you will notice, it looks like you are not able to connect to the user using a message. There is no such option as *Send message*.

To send a message to such a user you have to copy his/her full name to your clipboard or remember it, enter one of the shared groups, enter the tab *Members* and paste the full name into the table *Search members* (*see figure 7.4*).

Be aware that you are not able to see the full name of 3rd degree connections and users which are out of your network. There is one trick you can use to do this though; see the section *How to Uncover Any Full Profile View without Upgrading to Premium* in this chapter where I provide a step-by-step guide about how to uncover full names and profiles for 3rd degree connections and out-of-network users.

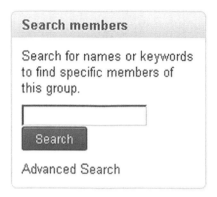

Figure 7.4: Sending a message to a member of the same group you are member of

If the group is not large, sometimes only a combination of first name and the user's photo might be sufficient to locate them via *Search members*.

Once you see the person in the results and move the mouse cursor over the user, option *Send message* appears.

The structure of the message is basically the same as for e-mail. You have a subject and main body of the message. Attachments are not allowed but I do not recommend using attachments, even for e-mails. Not for the very first message to a potential candidate.

Overall, I value the effectiveness of messages as average. If you do not have the chance to use e-mail, you will most probably use a message.

Also your first contact with an invitation will probably turn out to be a LinkedIn messages conversation. Sometimes there is also an e-mail address included in messages from other users. If so you do not need to access the LinkedIn website to reply, you can just reply directly to the message notification which arrives to your e-mail inbox.

InMail®

InMail® is a version of message for premium members. If you have a premium LinkedIn account, you are able to send a limited amount of so called InMails. As a premium user you can send this type of message to 2nd degree connections only. You are not able to send it to 3rd degree connections and out of network users.

Also, as a premium user, you can adjust your account so that other users, basic LinkedIn® users included, are able to send InMails to you.

So you ultimately pay for the privilege to be contacted by other non-premium users.

With a premium account, you can have up to fifty InMails sent at a time, which is really not much for an active recruiter. If you don't get a response to an InMail within seven days, LinkedIn will return the number of InMails to your account. Unused InMails roll over and accumulate for up to ninety days while you are a subscriber.

Despite this, I do not consider InMails as beneficial. I would say that they are even less effective than common LinkedIn® messages. One study showed that the approximate response time for InMails is two and a half weeks, while a professional e-mail contact with a person you barely known is around two days, and I completely agree. Use them if you have a premium account and you have no other option but InMail.

E-mail

Sending a proper e-mail is probably the most effective way to approach a candidate. I am not counting phone contact because it really depends which industry your candidates are in.

When I worked as a techie for one international software house, it was pretty awkward picking up the phone and finding out that there was a recruiter on the line calling to offer me some job. I resented it. Not because there was a chance my employer might be listening but just because of my listening colleagues around me and the situation did not seem appropriate. I think it shows **zero empathy** from recruiters who call during working hours.

However, back to e-mails; e-mails are the best non-invasive way to reach a potential candidate. Research shows that the average e-mail responses are:

- **7 hours for close friends**
- **11 hours for professional contacts**
- **50 hours for people you barely know or e-mail you when you're not expecting it.**

When you compare this with LinkedIn InMails where the average response is around two weeks, it is worth sending e-mails. There are several types of e-mails you face on LinkedIn, each of them has its own specifics which you have to modify your behavior to.

An E-mail Address Connected with LinkedIn® Account

You can see e-mail addresses of your 1st degree connections in the *Contact Information* section, usually on the right side of a profile. So your 1st degree connection might be easily connected via e-mail. If you have some 2nd degree connections, you need to send them an invitation which is accepted, hopefully, to be able to contact them over that e-mail address.

This is one of the natural flows where you contact candidates who accepted your invitation over this type of e-mail.

The problem with such an e-mail is that LinkedIn users often use a separate e-mail address for their LinkedIn account and they do not have forwarding set up. In this case you might face delays in their replies.

An E-mail Address Published on a LinkedIn® Profile

LinkedIn users often put their e-mail address directly on their LinkedIn profile. It might be in various places, including *Summary* or *Personal Information*. Such an e-mail address is usually the primary private e-mail address of a LinkedIn user, so you can expect a quick reply.

While screening a particular profile, take this into account and watch out for their e-mails. It is a waste of an invitation if LinkedIn® users have their e-mail published on their profile.

To be sure that there is no e-mail address on the profile, you can simply use a fulltext search (*Ctrl+F* usually) and look for the character @. This is not 100% reliable for sure, but it does the job. LinkedIn users can use the @ character for other purposes. On the other hand, some users do not use @ to avoid spam and they substitute it with strings such as *(at)*, *[at]*, etc.

There is also a method to systematically locate only profiles with e-mail published on their websites which I already described in the previous chapter. You need to know which domain you are seeking the e-mail in though.

*site:www.linkedin.com (inurl:in OR inurl:pub) "Sales * Consultant" New York* (**pg.com OR kimberly-clark.com OR unilever.com OR jnj.com**) *-inurl:dir -inurl:directory -inurl:jobs -inurl:groups -inurl:title -inurl:updates -inurl:viewjob -inurl:companies*

Using such an X-Ray search command will mostly provide you with

LinkedIn profiles containing *pg.com, kimberly-clark.com, unilever.com* or *jnj.com* on their profile. It does not need to be an e-mail address, but it usually is, in practice.

An E-mail Address Published on the Internet

Sometimes it is worth doing a little research about the potential candidate on the Internet. Simply put the user's name into Google or your favorite search engine. If there are a lot of irrelevant results, you can add some specific keyword from the candidate's expertise or field of work such as *SAP, Linux, Java*.

Sometimes they have their personal website published on their LinkedIn profiles. This is obviously typical for IT guys and online marketing experts as they often publish their work, projects, etc there. Next to this, they usually publish their e-mail address so you can contact them right away.

A Company E-mail Address

A very powerful way of contacting your potential candidates is to reach them on their company e-mail. They are available there all the time.

But how to get a candidate's company e-mail?

They rarely have such an e-mail address published on their profiles or connected with their LinkedIn account. But when you know the candidate's full name and the name of the company where the candidate is working at the moment, you are able to determine the company e-mail address in 99% of cases.

Firstly, you need to locate the e-mail domain name of the company. It is usually on the company's website. You can locate it easily by putting the company's name into Google or any other search engine. Or using LinkedIn®, where you simply move the mouse cursor over the company name (*see figure 7.5*).

Manager Division Maritime

TOS - Transport & Offshore Services
January 2002 – Present (11 years 1 month

TOS (Transport & Offshore Services) is an
head office in Rotterdam and a strong forei
dredging and inland shipping. Our division
based jobs. Besides recruiting TOS also p
www.tos.nl

TOS - Transport & Offshore Services

TOS (Transport & Offshore Services) offers employment in the maritime, offshore, oil & gas and renewables industry for new and seasoned professionals and students. TOS is also the right address for ... More »

Co. Size: 501-1000 employees
Website: http://www.tos.nl
HQ: Rotterdam Area, Netherlands
Industry: Staffing and Recruiting

Follow company

Figure 7.5: Figuring out a company domain name with LinkedIn

Next you need to find out what is the correct e-mail format of the company. There are several options. Let's say that the name of our desirable candidate is *John Deen* and he is working for a company called *Firm* which has the domain *Firm.com*.

The format might be one of the following:

john.deen@firm.com
john_deen@firm.com
jdeen@firm.com
deen@firm.com
deenj@firm.com
john.deen@ca.firm.com
john.deen@firm.ca

Some companies might combine one or more formats together. Usually large corporations do this because they sometimes face the problem where there is more than one person with the same name, so they have to differentiate them.

The way to determine the correct e-mail format is using a search engine such as Google again. In Google you can use the following search command:

*+firm.com

Where *firm.com* is the company website of company you are looking for. You are looking for some results where you can see someone's e-mail in highlights. The answer does not need to be right on the first page, so check further pages to locate real e-mail addresses.

For example, the company called Logica. As you can see here there is an e-mail address of a real employee in the third result which tells us the e-mail format of this company (*see figure 7.6*)

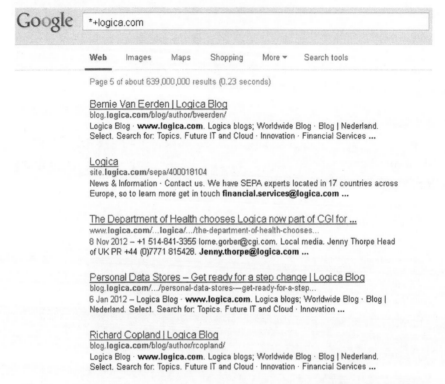

Figure 7.6: Determining the format of a company e-mail address using Google

However, I know that some employees of this company also have a different format using just the first letter of the first name instead of the full name.

Because it is not 100% reliable, we can test the e-mail address before trying to send an email there. We would recognize that the e-mail address is not reachable after sending an e-mail anyway; the mail server would return such an e-mail back to us.

If you want, you can test the e-mail address in advance using the service at *www.MailTester.com*.

You just type in the full e-mail address and verify it (*see figure 7.7*).

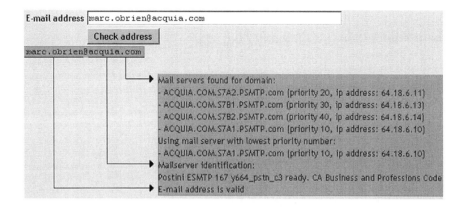

Figure 7.7: Verifying the existence of an e-mail address using
www.MailTester.com

Sometimes you might end up with a message saying that the mail server does not allow e-mail address verification (*see figure 7.8*).

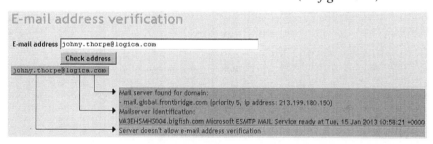

Figure 7.8: Mail server does not allow e-mail address verification

In such a case, you have only the domain name verified and you need to take a chance on sending an e-mail to such an address. In the worst case scenario this e-mail returns to you with the error message from the mail server. So you know that the format is incorrect, and you can try another one.

Sometimes the e-mail format can be found from the contact information on the company website. This is usually not the case with international corporations. But some corporations, e.g. IBM, have a people finder on their company website. So you can easily find the desirable person by their name.

Another trick to verify an e-mail address is to use a *Gmail* account (*www.gmail.com*) with the browser extension called *Rapportive* (*www.rapportive.com*). This extension will upgrade your Gmail interface with an informative window which can be used for searching information connected to a specific e-mail address.

For instance, I can put there the e-mail address of social media expert Lewis Howes, to see what happens (*see figure 7.9*).

Figure 7.9: Using Rapportive to determine a candidate's e-mail address

As you can see, this e-mail address obviously exists and is connected with some internet services. If you cannot see any information there, the e-mail address most probably does not exist (*see figure 7.10*).

Figure 7.10: Using Rapportive to determine a candidate's e-mail address

This of course works for any kind of e-mail address, including private and company ones. Instead of trying different formats of e-mail addresses, you can use an e-mail address permutator. Into this permutator, which is just a predefined spreadsheet form, you will fill the first and last name and also a domain name. This creates a list of all the possible kinds of e-mail addresses *(see figure 7.11)*.

	A	B	C	D	E
1				**Possible e-mail addreses**	
2	First name:	Jozef		jozef.chudy@logica.com	
3	Middle name:			chudy.jozef@logica.com	
4	Last name:	Chudy		jozefchudy@logica.com	
5	Domain name:	logica.com		jozef@logica.com	
6				jozef_chudy@logica.com	
7				chudy@logica.com	
8				jchudy@logica.com	
9				chudyj@logica.com	
10				j.chudy@logica.com	
11				chudy.j@logica.com	
12				jc@logica.com	
13				j.c@logica.com	
14					

Figure 7.11: Using a permutator to generate all possible e-mail formats

You can use the permutator which is for download at LINREA. com.

Then you just copy and paste all the e-mail addresses into Gmail and move the cursor over each address and look for the one which displays information indicating that you found the right one *(see figure 7.12)*.

Figure 7.12: Using Rapportive to determine a candidate's e-mail address

As you can see, the cursor is moved to *j.chudy@logica.com,* which shows some information. I know that Jozef is a manager at Logica, so we have the right one. Notice that even though we verified that someone working at this company has the e-mail format *name.surname@company.com* using MailTester, we found out using Rapportive that there are also employees at this company who have a completely different e-mail format or alias.

Another way to verify the e-mail address without calling the company and asking, is to use a *Jigsaw.com* database. But it is not that effective for every day recruitment purposes. However, if you have no other chance, this is your backup.

Not every name has just a simple first name and last name. There are countries where it is normal to have a middle name or more complicated names such as *Robert Van Scheers, Anupam Kumar Singh, Lawrence Lars Cosh-Ishii,* etc. Or women publish their maiden name rather than their married name. In this case, your situation is a bit more complicated and you have to try and find out which combination is the right one – hopefully it is just divided by dots in most cases or a middle name is not used in the e-mail address. However, you can use the e-mail address permutator with Rapportive to solve this issue.

Another name issue is when a LinkedIn® user does not type their precise name but uses the colloquial form – e.g. Joe instead of Joseph. In this case, you have to watch out and use the right form of such a name.

To automate the process of gathering company e-mail addresses, you can use grabber software like *Contact Capture* by Broadlook (*www.BroadLook.com*) which is for free. It works simply. Install and start Contact Capture software, use LinkedIn to search potential candidates currently working for one specific company. Once you see the first page of the LinkedIn results, select all text by pressing *Ctrl+A.* Then press *Ctrl+CC* (i.e. *C* twice). The results will appear in the Contact Capture (*see figure 7.13*).

Switch to the *Append* option in Contact Capture and go to the second page of the LinkedIn results and repeat the whole process. You will face some invalid items but do not worry about it. Once you gather the maximum possible employees of a particular company, you can export the shortlist and based on the proper e-mail address format, prepare an e-mail list which you can use for automatic (using software for mass e-mailing) or semi-automatic (sending one by one) bulk e-mails.

Do not forget that your **e-mail should be customized, at least in terms of using the personalized greetings**; especially when you send job offers to a company e-mail address, which is more sensitive than using a private one.

Here are a few more tips on software you can use. For grabbing contacts you can also use *AddressGrabber* from eGrabber (*www.eGrabber.com*). This software is not for free but, as with the Contact Capture, it can be used for capturing e-mail addresses from your e-mail-like X-Ray search.

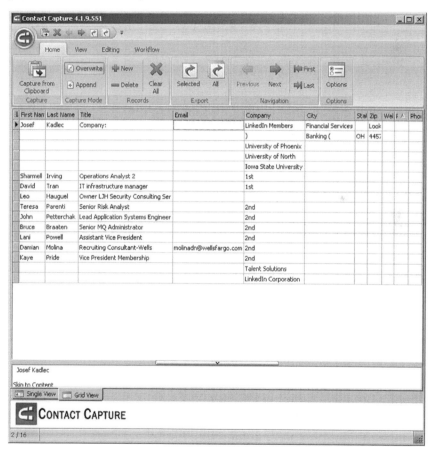

Figure 7.13: Using Contact Capture to automate users' names from LinkedIn results

For sending bulk e-mails, I recommend *GroupMail* (*www.GroupMail.net*), but you will find many other similar applications.

You may disagree with me and think that it is not right, and maybe also not legal, to send e-mails to a candidate's company e-mail; but if recruiters call candidates on their company number, they consider it all right. Legally, it might be different based on the specific legal jurisdiction, but common sense says there is no difference.

In terms of spam issues, it might be considered as spam, but sending e-mails to a private e-mail might be considered in the same way. My personal approach is that an e-mail address is a utility for communication, so sending one e-mail causes no harm. As a recruiter, you must get used to balancing on the brink a little and taking risks. So get used to it.

From time to time, you get a reply like "*Do not contact me on my company e-mail.*", and usually you will receive a reply from the private e-mail address of the same person. Therefore, I structure such an e-mail starting:

"Firstly, I am sorry to contact you on your company e-mail but I have found your professional profile very interesting – especially ..."

And end the e-mail stating:

"If you provide me with your private e-mail, we can continue our conversation over there."

I do not recommend contacting employees of one company in bulk using their company e-mail addresses. It is not reliable among addressed people because they will speak about the offer and it makes your offer ultimately unattractive. And secondly, some of their managers might discover that someone is pressuring their employees in bulk and they might complain.

I did such a mass contacting of employees at one IT corporation once, and even though it led to a few successful hirings, it also led to complaints from the management. Such complaints were not only addressed to my agency, but also to my client where contacted employees were recommended to. So I had to extinguish a fire. These companies did not want an open battle for employees. So keep the battle under the radar.

Avoidance of such a scenario is simple. Do not contact lots of employees of one company at the same time; spread the e-mails over a longer time period.

The bottom line of what I'm explaining here is that sometimes we do not have time to spend thirty minutes finding a candidate's e-mail address. As a recruiter you have to be go, go, go. So firstly, you should deal with candidates who are easy to reach – your 1st degree connections who have their e-mail address published for you, users with the e-mail address in their LinkedIn profiles and users whose company e-mail can be easily determined - if contacting candidates via their company e-mail is an option for you.

Beyond these candidates, there will also be a bunch of candidates who are more difficult to reach; not only for you, but for other recruiters as well. So to make the difference, you have to spend time finding the right contact information for these users. The reward is the fact that nobody has contacted such a user, which increases your chances of a successful hiring.

Example of a Proper First Contact E-mail

There are some rules which you should keep to when contacting a potential candidate with a first e-mail. Keep in mind that they have to feel that it took you some effort to make them a proposal. If you let them know that they are just one of many or that they are part of your bulk e-mailing, the chances are that such a conversation will end unsuccessfully.

What follows is an example of a job proposal for a managerial opening at the company called Acision.

Re: Acision - Operations Team Manager - new management offer

Dear Mrs. Wilson,

I would like to inform you that the company Acision is seeking a suitable candidate for a managerial role at their support center in Brno, which matches your interesting professional profile – especially your team leader experience in the Unix environment.

Operations Team Manager (Unix-oriented)
http://www.jobsconsulting.org/Acision/operations-team-manager/

The Acision support center in Brno has about 300 employees and is supporting over 300 clients (mobile operators) worldwide. It has about 1,200 installations in total.

The company itself has high standards for its employees and its owner, Atlantic Bridge Ventures, provides excellent financial backing. Standard terms include an annual financial bonus, 5 weeks of vacation, sick-days, lunch vouchers and Sodexho Flexi Passes, insurance contribution, interest-free loans, technical and language certifications, etc.

Interview information, support during the hiring process and a Jobs Consulting loyalty bonus to the value of 10,000 czk for the purchase of electronic devices and e-books is included.

Do you think that this role could be interesting for you?

As reference, I can mention some of my clients whom you probably know as your colleagues from IBM and who were recruited to other companies including Acision, by me. For instance, Viden Dimitrov or Pavel Krumnikl can provide you with references.

With friendly regards,

Josef Kadlec
IT Career Advocate

Jobs Consulting - prestige IT jobs
Tel: +420 602 757 435
Email: josef.kadlec@jobsconsulting.org
LinkedIn: http://www.linkedin.com/in/josefkadlec
WWW: www.JobsConsulting.org

Unix techies choose Jobs Consulting. Find out why...
http://www.jobsconsulting.org/reference/

Let's analyze each part of this example.

Greeting

Dear Mrs. Wilson,

If you contact people from management, you should probably be more formal and use "*Dear Mr. Diamond*". The general rule is to try and turn the conversation to a more informal tone. When contacting non-managerial candidates, I strictly use their first name, e.g. "*Hello Peter*" or just "*Peter*".

Be aware that this is also country sensitive. Some languages are used to using the 'polite form' of address more often than others. However, even in such cases, it is often beneficial to take a risk and use an informal greeting. I calibrated success with this because candidates were not used to receiving anything other than formal greetings like "*Good morning Mr. Diamond*" or "*Dear Mr. Diamond*". Once they received something like "*Hi Peter*" they were surprised, and it usually turned the conversation to a more informal one.

Subject

Re: Acision - Operations Team Manager - new management offer

Because this type of e-mail is often done as a reply to an accepted invitation, do not be afraid to use "*Re:*" before the subject. It works pretty well and it helps to speed up the candidate's response time. If there was no communication prior to this, do not use it. It does not look reliable.

Introduction

I would like to inform you that the company Acision is seeking a suitable candidate for a managerial role at their support center in Brno, which matches your interesting professional profile – especially your team leader experience in the Unix environment.

In the very first e-mail to a potential candidate, I recommend focusing the job proposal on a single company and avoid sending a list of vacancies from different companies. When you promote just one company, it is easier to explain advantages and it is not confusing for the potential candidate. Anyone can get a list of vacancies anywhere on the Internet. You have to bring added value to the table.

So, the first part of the introduction should contain who you are seeking, for which company and in which city or location.

The second part of the introduction should be flattering and be about the potential candidate's relevant experience. Everybody likes to hear that they are exceptional and needed.

Another powerful part of the introduction is to **mention something you have in common with the potential candidate**. For example, you worked for the same company or studied at the same university. It makes your message much more personal and it increases the chances of successful communication. LinkedIn® can help you with this with their new feature *In common with user* which you can find on user profiles (*see figure 7.14*).

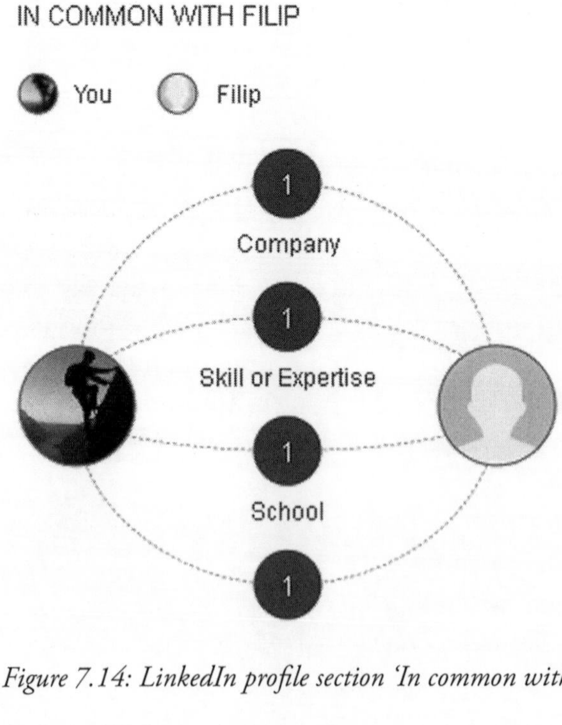

IN COMMON WITH FILIP

Figure 7.14: LinkedIn profile section 'In common with'

This feature will help you to immediately recognize which companies (in terms of your experience), groups, schools and skills & expertise you share with a user. You can move over the number to see the names of common links (*see figure 7.15*).

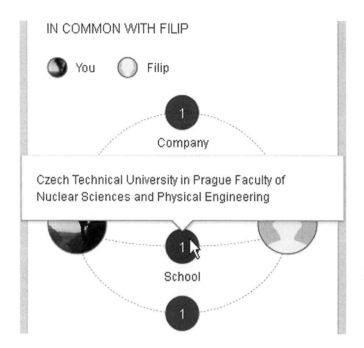

Figure 7.15: LinkedIn profile section 'In common with'

As you can see, the link between Filip and I, is the fact that we studied at the same faculty *Nuclear Sciences and Physical Engineering* apart from other common things. This can be immediately utilized in your favor by mentioning this in the e-mail. Being a schoolmate, even if not from the same class, means significantly more than being just a stranger.

Link to the web proposal

Operations Team Manager (Unix-oriented)
http://www.jobsconsulting.org/Acision/operations-team-manager/

On a separate line publish the name of the vacancy with a link to the proposal on the web – preferably on your home recruitment agency website for sure. In brackets next to the name of the job post, you can put some information which makes the vacancy more definite.

Company teaser

Acision support center in Brno has about 300 employees and is supporting over 300 clients (mobile operators) worldwide. It has about 1,200 installations in total.

The goal of this part of the e-mail is to make the targeted company as attractive as possible. Who would like to join a company which has nothing interesting about it at all? So see the references on the Internet, i.e. the company website and figure out why that particular company could be interesting for potential candidates.

There are various reasons which make a company attractive to employees, such as:

- Interesting clients and publicly known projects

- Access to enterprise technologies

- Awards such as Best Employer of the Year

- The possibility to travel world-wide

- Challenging goals

- Outstanding company premises

- Salary and company benefits (see the next point).

Salary and company benefits

The company itself has high standards for its employees and its owner, Atlantic Bridge Ventures, provides excellent financial backing. Standard terms include an annual financial bonus, 5 weeks of vacation, sick-days, lunch vouchers and Sodexho Flexi Passes, insurance contribution, interest-free loans, technical and language certifications, etc.

In this section you should publish the salary range and benefits which might be expected. If you do not want to divulge numbers, you can get around this with a sentence like the one I used. On the other hand, stating specific numbers is very powerful and if the numbers are rational and reasonable, it increases the response rate.

Loyalty bonus

Interview information, support during the hiring process and a Jobs Consulting loyalty bonus to the value of 10,000 czk for the purchase of electronic devices and e-books is included.

If you can, offer your potential candidates a bonus which is covered from your potential commission. The goal is to strengthen the relationship between you and the addressed candidate which makes them choose you instead of another recruiter. The second reason is that you can easily get a text or video testimonial from such a user.

Final question

Do you think that this role could be interesting for you?

Finalize your e-mail with a question every time. If you do not use a question, nothing is psychologically forcing your prospective candidate to reply. I found out that when I use a question, I receive a reply more often.

References

As reference, I can mention some of my clients whom you probably know as your colleagues from IBM and who were recruited to other companies including Acision, by me. For instance, Viden Dimitrov or Pavel Krumnikl can provide you with references.

If it is possible, attach some names of former successful candidates who your prospective candidate might know. It forms a very strong argument for your prospective candidate.

Farewell

With friendly regards,

Josef Kadlec
IT Career Advocate

Jobs Consulting - prestige IT jobs
Tel: +420 602 757 435
Email: josef.kadlec@jobsconsulting.org
LinkedIn: http://www.linkedin.com/in/josefkadlec
WWW: www.JobsConsulting.org

Unix techies choose Jobs Consulting. Find out why...
http://www.jobsconsulting.org/reference/

If you used the formal greeting at the beginning, use the informal at the end. Basically, an informal farewell can be used in every case.

When you have the chance, do not title yourself as *Recruiter, Senior Recruiter* or any other common title. Think out of the box and try to differentiate yourself whenever you can.

Do not forget to attach an e-mail address, telephone number and link to your LinkedIn profile as well.

Finally attach a link to your agency references to support the quality of your recruitment services.

The overall structure of such an e-mail has to be clear, with attractive and proper formatting.

Telephone and VoIP

Some users publish their telephone number, Skype or GTalk nickname in their profiles. If you have the candidate's name and the name of the company, you will have no problem reaching such a candidate on his/her company phone via the company reception. Prepare a nice story for the receptionist because you can be sure that if you introduce yourself as a recruiter, you will be cut off in a second.

I recommend thinking out of the box and finding friends in the companies which you hire candidates from. Such a person might provide you with direct telephone numbers, company ongoings and other insightful information. As an active recruiter, you are in contact with many people and you should be able to turn most conversations to an informal form. Then it is much easier to find such a person who will be cooperating with you.

Consider the industry you are recruiting in. Try to imagine yourself in your candidate's position and consider if you would want to be contacted by phone as a first contact from a recruiter. I bet that, for example, an employee working for a technological company in an open office space might have a problem with that. On the other hand, people from sales and managers, for example, are mostly fine with that.

The rule is to use the same language and communication methods which your potential candidates prefer. For example, if you are an extrovert forcing your style on an introvert, you will most probably not have good communication.

There are techniques which recommend picking up the phone and calling with the premise that if you want to hire the best, you need to be first, which you can do only by using the telephone. There are companies for good and average candidates as well. So using other means of communication are satisfactory for those candidates.

Apart from all the mentioned contact options, you might find a few others which are not so direct. Some users might publish some other contact information like a Twitter account, for example.

How to Measure the Efficiency of Your Job Proposals

You cannot manage what you cannot measure. Imagine that you are seeking a *Senior Financial Analyst* and you send two hundred e-mails to potential candidates. Some of them will reply with a positive or even negative answer.

But what happened with the rest?
Have they read the email or invitation?
Are they not attracted by the content of the proposal?
Or did they click on the proposal link and then lose interest?

For us as recruiters, this is a very important ratio which should tell us that we need to improve our proposal or change the job proposal on the website.

This can be done easily if you use some website statistics counter. I prefer *Google Analytics (www.google.com/analytics/)*. There are plenty of features, and it is for free.

Firstly, you need to have your company or recruitment agency website integrated with Google Analytics so that you are able to measure various parameters, including:

- The unique number of visitors

- Where those visitors came from

- Which keywords they used to find your website

- From which geographical location your visitors are from

I will not be describing how to set Google Analytics itself on your webpage as this is not the purpose of this section and the process is pretty straightforward. So if your website is not set up with Google Analytics, go to their website.

Once your website is working with Google Analytics, you are able to measure how many visitors came and which web page of your website they looked at. Let's say I take an example from the previous section where I used the following link for a job proposal:

http://www.jobsconsulting.org/Acision/operations-team-manager/

Without doing anything, we can check how many page views and unique visitors are visiting this web page (*see figure 7.16*).

Google Analytics -> your domain -> Content -> Site Content -> All pages:

Pageviews	Unique Pageviews	Avg. Time on Page	Entrances	Bounce Rate
285	**234**	**00:02:01**	**106**	**51.89%**
% of Total: 0.46% (62,100)	% of Total: 0.47% (50,025)	Site Avg: 00:04:24 (-54.19%)	% of Total: 0.38% (27,973)	Site Avg: 60.08% (-13.63%)

Primary Dimension: **Page**   Other ▾

Plot Rows | Secondary dimension ▾ | Sort Type: | Default ▾ | |

	Page		Pageviews ↓	Unique Pageviews	Avg. Time on Page	Entrances
☐ 1.	/Acision/operations-team-manager/	⬚	285	234	00:02:01	106

Figure 7.16: Using Google Analytics to measure your recruitment efficiency

We can see that two hundred and thirty four unique visitors spent some time on this web page looking at the *Operations Team Manager* position. What we do not know is how many of these visitors came because of our e-mail proposal.

We are going to tweak the link we are pasting into e-mails a little bit. Open Google Analytics URL Builder:

http://support.google.com/analytics/bin/answer.py?hl=en&answer=1033867

...and fill-in the form. As a Website URL you will put there the web page you want to measure. In our case we will put:

http://www.jobsconsulting.org/Acision/operations-team-manager/

Campaign Source is just the name of the source and how it will be displayed in Google Analytics.

Campaign Medium is again just a label for Google Analytics which can then be used to filter this traffic.

And *Campaign Name* is the name of your job proposal campaign (*see figure 7.17*).

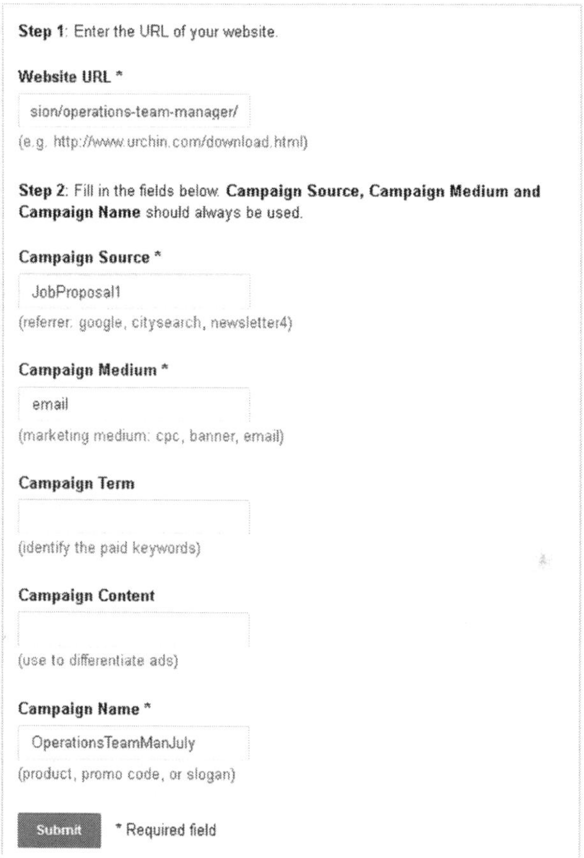

Figure 7.17: Using Google Analytics URL Builder

Once you hit *Generate URL*, you will get a longer URL with more URL variables.

http://www.jobsconsulting.org/Acision/operations-team-manager/?utm_source=JobProposal1&utm_medium=email&utm_campaign=OperationsTeamManJuly

259

You will use this URL instead of the original one in your proposals. The down side of this is that the URL is significantly longer which makes the job proposal not so user friendly. To fix this you can use one of the URL shortening services I described in the *Invitation* section.

After this, you are able to easily distinguish traffic which comes from your job proposal from traffic which came from elsewhere on the Internet or from any other proposals you sent before. You can run several different proposals for the very same job and be able to track each of these campaigns separately.

Next, login to Google Analytics and click on *Other -> Traffic Sources -> Campaign* (*see figure 7.18*).

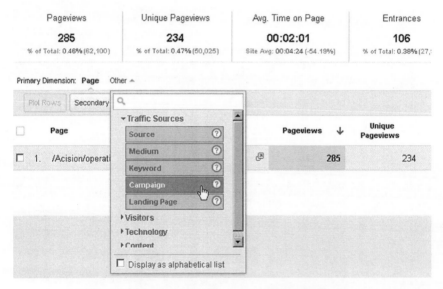

Figure 7.18: Create campaign using Google Analytics

Here you can see how many potential candidates click through the link you pasted to the e-mail with a job proposal for this particular campaign (*see figure 7.19*).

In our case, the campaign is called *OperationsTeamManJuly* and fifteen visitors clicked through.

Main Contacting Strategies

Now you are aware of several different ways of contacting any LinkedIn user. But how do you form these techniques into some sort of systematic contact strategy? If you send an invitation to a candidate and they do

Pageviews	Unique Pageviews	Avg. Time on Page	Entrances
285	**234**	**00:02:01**	**106**
% of Total: 0.46% (62,100)	% of Total: 0.47% (50,025)	Site Avg: 00:04:24 (-54.19%)	% of Total: 0.38% (27,9

Primary Dimension: Page Campaign ▾

Plot Rows Secondary dimension ▾ Sort Type: Default ▾

	Campaign	Pageviews ↓	Unique Pageviews
☐ 1.	(not set)	270	229
☐ 2.	OperationsTeamManJuly	15	5

Figure 7.19: Measuring of candidates click through rate in Google Analytics

not reply, would you be able to track that he/she *really* did not reply to your invitation? Should you use another contact channel to reach them?

Based on these questions, I will define three basic strategies for contacting potential candidates on LinkedIn. Which one you choose depends on several factors.

Culture Habits of a Particular Country

Some countries might not like the use of aggressive styles of making contact, which might include reaching a candidate on their company phone or e-mail. Some nationalities, such as Americans, are often too diplomatic/polite so that candidates are afraid to answer with a negative decision like *"No, I am not interested in the proposed vacancy at the moment."*

In such cases you cannot know if your message was read but not replied to or if the message was not delivered. Based on this, you have to use a telephone and verify what happened which slows the whole process down.

Industry Specific Habits

As I already described, some professionals are used to using a telephone more often than e-mail and vice versa. If you recruit managers and directors, do not be afraid to use a telephone as a primary contact channel. If you recruit IT professionals, use any other channel than a company or private telephone during working hours at first.

Your Personal Habits

The contact strategy should be chosen in alignment with your style. Nobody says that you have to use one strategy all the time. Sometimes you can afford to be more aggressive. Sometimes you have to be conservative based on the particular candidate or, more specifically, the company he/she is working for at that moment.

It also depends if you are in a hurry for those recruits (i.e. you need to choose a more aggressive strategy) or you are proceeding just with a regular recruitment for permanent openings (i.e. you would choose a more conservative strategy).

Based on these things, I have defined three basic strategies:

- **Aggressive**
- **Conservative**
- **Super conservative**

For those of you who do not know how flow charts work, I will explain. You simply start at the *Start* and follow the arrows. Based on decision boxes (diamonds in the following examples) you follow the arrows until you get to an *End*.

The flow chart does not reflect the fact that you have a premium account or a basic one. So if you meet the step *LI InMail* while you have just a basic account, you kindly skip it.

The actual time gaps between each step on the flow charts vary based on the strategy. They will be quite short or converging on zero for an aggressive strategy. For conservative strategies you should set time gaps in a matter of days; around two days for conservative and five days for super conservative.

Aggressive Strategy

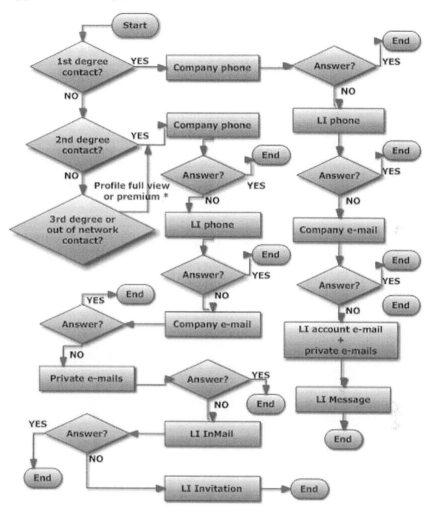

Figure 7.20: Aggressive Strategy

* This operation means that you have to uncover the full profile view of a candidate. A procedure to do this is described in the next section.

Conservative Strategy

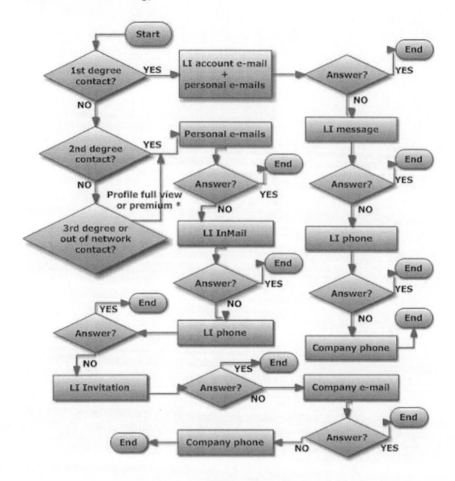

Figure 7.21: Conservative Strategy

* This operation means that you have to uncover the full profile view of a candidate. A procedure to do this is described in the next section.

Super Conservative Strategy

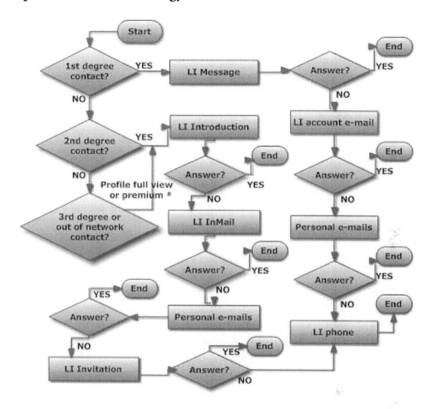

Figure 7.22: Super Conservative Strategy

* This operation means that you have to uncover the full profile view of a candidate. A procedure to do this is described in the next section.

How to Uncover Any Full Profile View without Upgrading to Premium

Depending on how well established your LinkedIn profile is in terms of the number and quality of your connections, you will face a percentage of profiles which you cannot display fully.

The first case is 3rd degree connections. For such connections you can see only the capital letter of a user's last name and a very limited view of his/her profile (*see figure 7.23*).

Figure 7.23: Hidden LinkedIn profile of a 3rd degree connection

The second case is users who are out of your network – i.e. those users who do not have one connection whom could connect them with you. For such connections, you are not able to see their name at all and the profile is limited to the very minimum information containing just the current title and geographical location (*see figure 7.24*).

As you might notice from the warning message, one option to uncover such profiles is to upgrade to a premium account.

This chapter could easily be called 'Exploiting LinkedIn for Fun and Profit'. There are two very quick tricks to uncover the full view of such a user's profile.

In addition, there are a few other ways to reach the same goal but they are more complicated. It seems that LinkedIn is not able to fix these shortcuts.

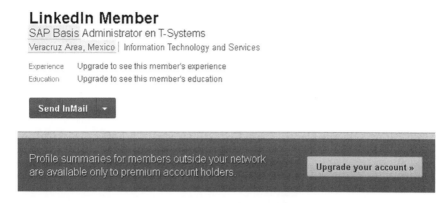

Figure 7.24: Hidden LinkedIn profile of an out of-network-connection

1) ID Variable Trick

This trick can be used regardless of whether a user is a 3rd degree connection of yours or they are out of your network. It presumes that you are logged into LinkedIn®, which you probably are, already.

Firstly, you need to figure out the user's ID. This ID can be determined from the URL of the user whose profile you are not able to see fully.

Let's use the example of Anabel's profile. The URL (do not mix it with her public profile URL, which we do not know yet) of her profile that we can see is:

*http://www.linkedin.com/profile/view?id=**45034321**&authType=OUT_OF_NETWORK&authToken=jp_t&locale=en_US&srchid=88b43d4a-aa27-4863-9436-256673f6612b-0&srchindex=1&srchtotal=2&goba ck=.fps_PBCK_Anabel+SAP+Senior+Consultant+_*1_*1_*1_*1_*1_* 1_*2_*1_Y_*1_*1_*1_false_1_R_*1_*51_*1_*51_true_*2_*2_*2_*2 _*2_*2_*2_*2_*2_*2_*2_*2_*2_*2_*2_*2_*2&pvs=ps &trk=pp_profile_name_link*

We can see her ID in bold. It is the string following "*id=*".

Now we will open a new browser tab and type there the following URL, where **45034321** is the ID of the user you are looking for:

http://www.linkedin.com/pymk/pcard?mid=45034321

You should see the following output containing not only Anabel's full name, but also an option to *Send Invitation*, which you can immediately use (*see figure 7.25*).

Figure 7.25: Using the ID variable trick to uncover a restricted profile

When you click on her name, you will see the full view of her profile. In the very same way you would proceed for out-of-network users, where you only see *LinkedIn Member* instead of their name.

2) Share Profile Trick

This workaround can be used only for 3rd degree connections. Whilst logged into LinkedIn®, you simply use the *Share profile* functionality and share the hidden profile with anybody (*see figure 7.26*).

Figure 7.26: Using the LinkedIn share functionality to uncover a restricted profile

Put yourself into copy - option *Send me a copy* (*see figure 7.27*).

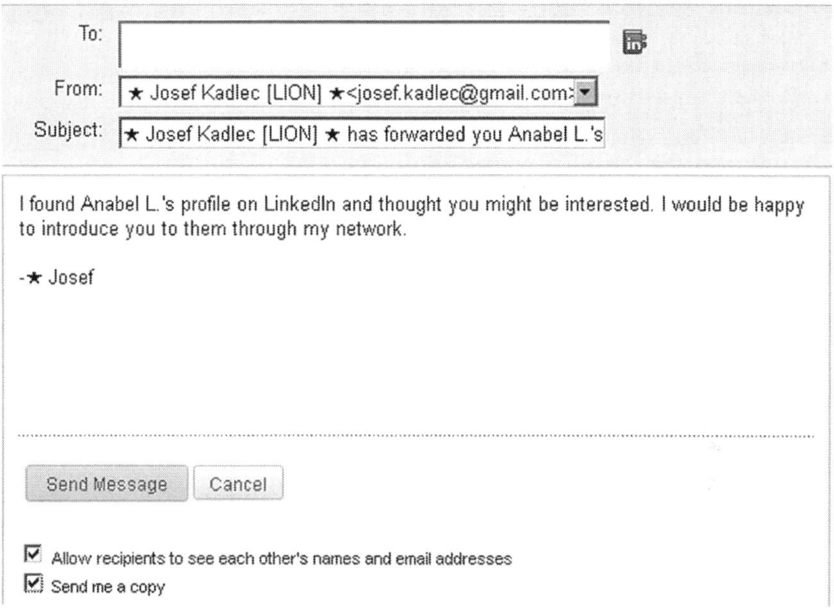

To: ▢

From: ★ Josef Kadlec [LION] ★ <josef.kadlec@gmail.com> ▾

Subject: ★ Josef Kadlec [LION] ★ has forwarded you Anabel L.'s

I found Anabel L.'s profile on LinkedIn and thought you might be interested. I would be happy to introduce you to them through my network.

-★ Josef

[Send Message] [Cancel]

☑ Allow recipients to see each other's names and email addresses
☑ Send me a copy

Figure 7.27: Using LinkedIn share functionality to uncover a restricted profile

By doing this, you will receive an e-mail with a direct link to the user's profile which can be displayed in the full version. Just click on *View profile on LinkedIn* which can be found in the e-mail message, or use the fully expanded link from the bottom part of the e-mail message (*see figure 7.28*).

Awesome right?

The only thing is that we don't know how long such shortcuts will be working. Of course LinkedIn® developers should be looking to close these loopholes, but the reality is different. These vulnerabilities have been there for years. Will this book change it finally? We will see.

Perhaps these loopholes will soon be closed? So I will now show methods which lead to the same results but they should remain for a longer period of time.

They basically include two steps. Firstly, determining the full name of such a user or his/her public profile URL. Secondly, uncovering the complete profile using their full name.

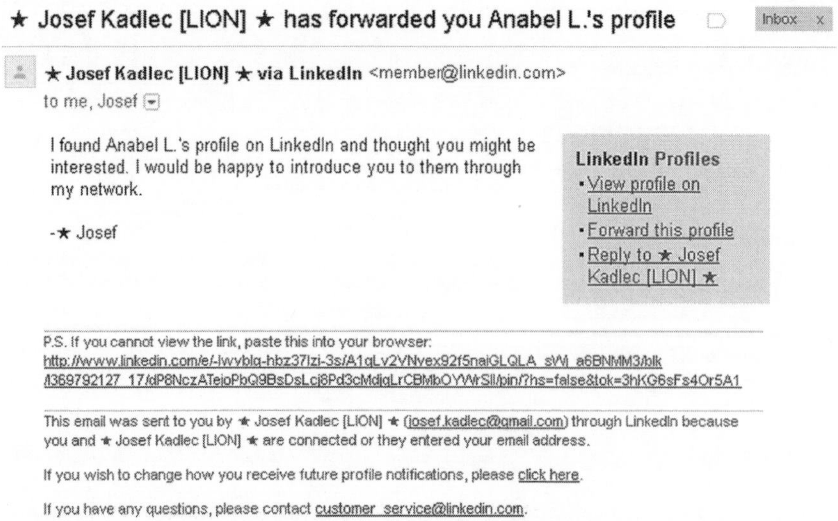

★ Josef Kadlec [LION] ★ has forwarded you Anabel L.'s profile   Inbox   x

★ **Josef Kadlec [LION]** ★ **via LinkedIn** <member@linkedin.com>
to me, Josef

I found Anabel L.'s profile on LinkedIn and thought you might be
interested. I would be happy to introduce you to them through
my network.

-★ Josef

LinkedIn Profiles
- View profile on LinkedIn
- Forward this profile
- Reply to ★ Josef Kadlec [LION] ★

P.S. If you cannot view the link, paste this into your browser:
http://www.linkedin.com/e/-lwvblq-hbz37lzi-3s/A1qLv2VNvex92f5naiGLQLA_sWj_a6BNMM3/blk
/1369792127_17/dP8NczATeioPbQ9BsDsLcj6Pd3cMdjqLrCBMbOYWrSll/pin/?hs=false&tok=3hKG6sFs4Or5A1

This email was sent to you by ★ Josef Kadlec [LION] ★ (josef.kadlec@gmail.com) through LinkedIn because
you and ★ Josef Kadlec [LION] ★ are connected or they entered your email address.

If you wish to change how you receive future profile notifications, please click here.

If you have any questions, please contact customer_service@linkedin.com.

Figure 7.28: Using LinkedIn share functionality to uncover a restricted profile

3) X-Ray Search to Determine a Full Name

One reliable method to figure out the full name of such users and
display it is using an X-Ray search.

Let's analyze the first example with the user *Anabel L.* Based on the
information we can see, we should be able to find her full profile using
Google or another search engine.

We know that her first name is *Anabel* and her title is *SAP Senior
Consultant*. Both of these strings are the exact strings which exist on her
LinkedIn profile. On top of this, we can see her picture which can be
used as proof that we have found the right LinkedIn profile.

The following X-Ray search command should be sufficient to locate
Anabel's profile (*see figure 7.29*):

site:linkedin.com "SAP Senior Consultant" "Anabel"

As we can see from the results, the very first item is a link to a
candidate's profile, *Anabel Lugue* which matches our results. If we open
the link, we can make sure it is the right profile we wanted to uncover
(*see figure 7.30*).

The difference is that now **we can see Anabel's full name and public
profile URL. In addition, the *Connect* button is now available.**

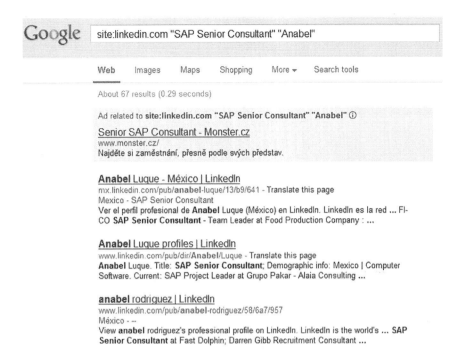

Figure 7.29: Using X-Ray Search to uncover hidden LinkedIn profiles

So you are able to send Anabel a LinkedIn® invitation without any obstacles. Firstly, you should screen her full profile which is still hidden from you.

Figure 7.30: Using X-Ray search to uncover hidden LinkedIn profiles

> **NOTE**
>
> If you see a result like this where you can see the full name, public profile URL but you cannot see the full profile, it means you are logged into your LinkedIn account. If you see another view containing a full profile but missing buttons such as *Connect*, you are probably signed out of your LinkedIn account.

4) Using a Public Profile URL Trick

Once we know the public profile URL, we are able to see the complete profile of any user. The only thing we have to do is to log out of LinkedIn or use a separate internet browser where no LinkedIn user is logged in, to avoid logging in and out, back and forth. You can use private browsing, which is the option I described in the section *Using the X-Ray Search While Logged-out of LinkedIn®* well.

In our case, we simply open the following URL to see the complete profile:

mx.linkedin.com/pub/anabel-luque/13/b9/641

If you use an internet browser where you are not logged in or use private browsing, you should see the complete user's profile (*see figure 7.31*).

Do not bother with the *View Full Profile* button. We are able to see her full profile including information about her career but, of course, as a logged-out user, we are not able to see her connections, contact buttons, etc. LinkedIn has the *View Full Profile* button because it wants to force you to sign up or log in to LinkedIn.

Anabel Luque

SAP Senior Consultant

Mexico | Computer Software

Join LinkedIn and access Anabel Luque's full profile.

As a LinkedIn member, you'll join 175 million other professionals who are sharing connections, ideas, and opportunities. And it's free! You'll also be able to:

- See who you and **Anabel Luque** know in common
- Get introduced to **Anabel Luque**
- Contact **Anabel Luque** directly

> **View Full Profile**

Anabel Luque's Overview

Current	**SAP Project Leader at Grupo Pakar - Alaia Consulting**
Past	SAP Project Leader (Contractor) at Queseria Dos Lagunas
	SAP Senior Consultant at Queseria Dos Lagunas
	MM-SD SAP Senior Consultant (Contractor) at Loreal
	see all ˅
Education	Language Center Universidad Buenos Aires
	Particular course
	Related coursework
	see all ˅
Recommendations	**2 people have recommended Anabel**
Connections	**291 connections**

Anabel Luque's Experience

SAP Project Leader
Grupo Pakar - Alaia Consulting

Figure 7.31: Using the LinkedIn public profile URL trick

5) Using a Full Name Trick

There are basically three ways to uncover a complete profile using the full name:

- **Using LinkedIn® People Search while logged in to LinkedIn®**
- **Using X-Ray search while logged-out of LinkedIn®**
- **Using LinkedIn® search while logged-out of LinkedIn®**

Using LinkedIn® People Search While Logged in to LinkedIn®

With this method, we assume you are logged into LinkedIn, you see the user's full name, and public profile URL, but you cannot see their complete profile. One way to display the full profile of such a user is to put the user's name into LinkedIn People Search.

Let's consider our example, open advanced People Search and put Anabel's information there – first name, last name, title (with option *Current or past*) and country (*see figure 7.32*).

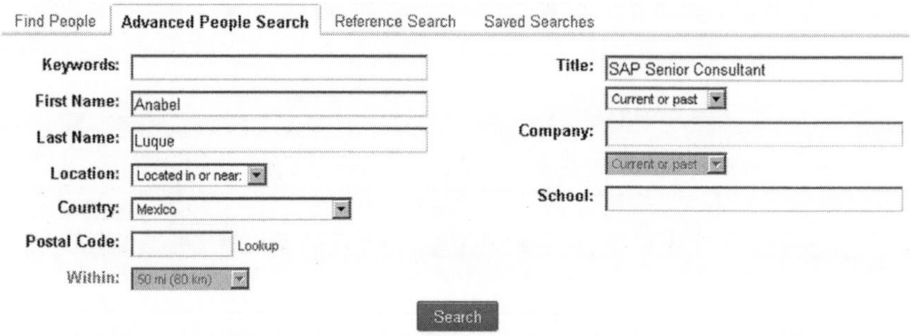

Figure 7.32: Uncovering a hidden profile while logged in to LinkedIn

With such a search our results should be precise and limited to a single user, who is hopefully our desired potential candidate (*see figure 7.33*).

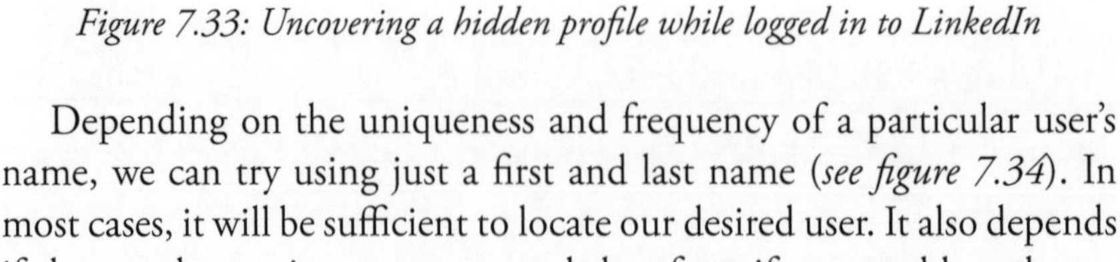

1 result		Sort by: Relevance
	Anabel Luque (3rd) **SAP Senior Consultant** Mexico · Computer Software Similar	Connect

Figure 7.33: Uncovering a hidden profile while logged in to LinkedIn

Depending on the uniqueness and frequency of a particular user's name, we can try using just a first and last name (*see figure 7.34*). In most cases, it will be sufficient to locate our desired user. It also depends if the user has a picture or not, and therefore, if we are able to locate him/her easily in people search results or not. As our time as recruiters is very valuable and we need to get volume, we should prefer this.

Figure 7.34: Uncovering a hidden profile while logged in to LinkedIn

Of course, if you are getting plenty of results and you cannot locate the person you are seeking, then you need to narrow your search by specifying more information, such as title or country.

We can see our desired user in the very first position (*see figure 7.35*) in our search, so we have no problems.

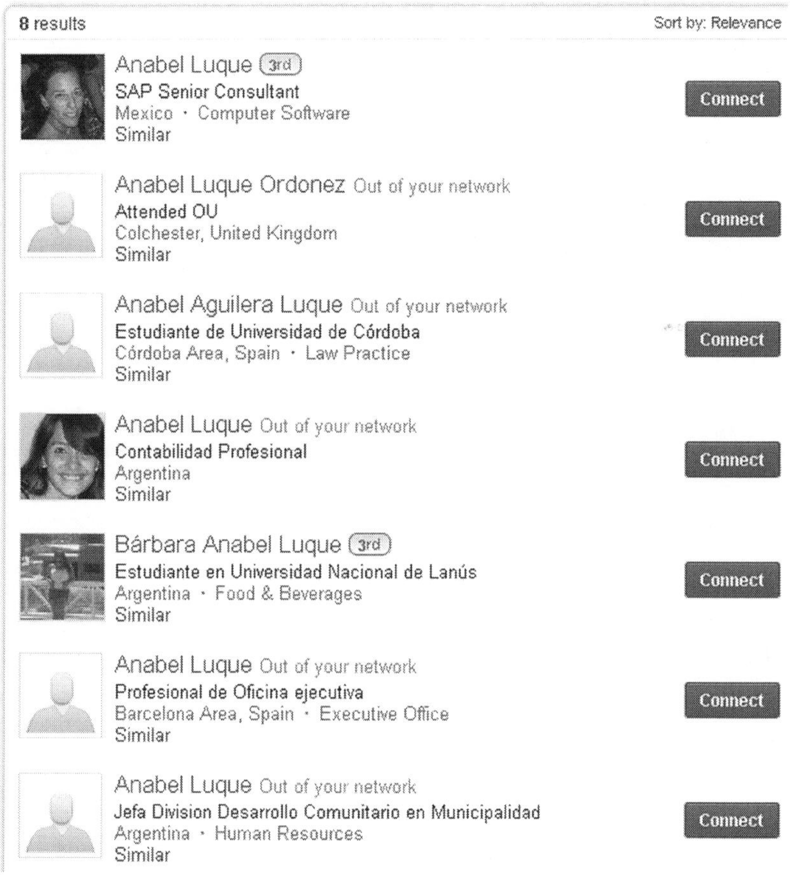

Figure 7.35: Uncovering a hidden profile while logged in to LinkedIn

Now, when you enter Anabel's profile, you will see her complete profile (*see figure 7.36*).

Experience

SAP Project Leader
Grupo Pakar - Alaia Consulting
January 2012 – Present (11 months)

Project Leader:
Support and Enhancement Project SAP ECC 6.0 - AFS:
Responsible for leading Project, creating Project Plan and priorities of enhancements and problems to be solved.
Responsible for leading Status meetings.
In charge of coordinating the Project team and create status documentation.
Anabel has 1 recommendation (1 co-worker) including:
(GROUP) Germán B., *Consultor .Net/SAP ABAP, Soluciones 4G*

SAP Project Leader (Contractor)
Queseria Dos Lagunas
October 2011 – April 2012 (7 months) | Mexico

Responsible for leading project, creating Project Charter, Project Plan, planning and controlling

Figure 7.36: Uncovering hidden profile while logged in to LinkedIn

Looks silly, right?

This is simply because of the fact that LinkedIn® assumes that if you know a user's full name and are searching with it, you are allowed to see the user's complete profile. If you would be searching just by the first name, such a user would display again without their full last name. **As long as you keep the last name in the search, you maintain access to complete profiles.**

Using the X-Ray Search While Logged-out of LinkedIn®

We repeat the same X-Ray search when looking for Anabel's full name. BUT the difference is that we do this without being logged-in to LinkedIn. Use the following Google search command again:

site:linkedin.com "SAP Senior Consultant" "Anabel"

You should see basically the same results. Open Anabel's profile from Google search results.

In contrast to the situation when we were logged into LinkedIn, we can now see Anabel's full profile in the same way as we would using her public profile URL. So now we are able to screen her capabilities, education and further information.

When we are done with this, we login to LinkedIn again, open Anabel's profile (for instance, using her public profile URL) and we can send her an invitation using the *Connect* button.

This will not work for LinkedIn® profiles which are private ones. Luckily, the vast majority of users have their profile set as public.

Logging in and out of LinkedIn whenever you want to uncover a profile might be pretty tedious. Therefore, I recommend using a separate internet browser for X-Ray searches. This means if your primary browser is Mozilla Firefox, use Google Chrome or MS Explorer for opening profiles from X-Ray searches; or you can use private browsing if your browser supports it.

Mozilla Firefox – *Start Private Browsing*
Google Chrome – *New incognito window*
MS Explorer – *Safety -> InPrivate Browsing*
Safari – *Private Browsing*

Using the LinkedIn® Search While Logged-out of LinkedIn®

Once you know the name of a desired user, you can also use people search which is available on LinkedIn's front page when you are logged out.

This search is available on www.LinkedIn.com, but also at its regional mutation mx.LinkedIn.com, ca.LinkedIn.com, etc.

We will stick with our example and type Anabel's full name in here (*see figure 7.37*).

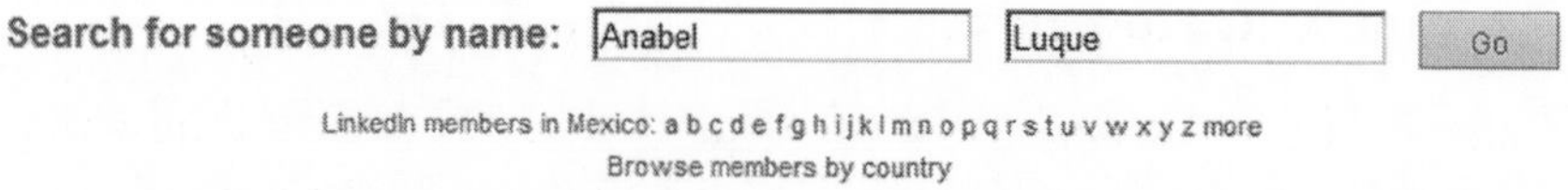

Search for someone by name: | Anabel | | Luque | | Go |

LinkedIn members in Mexico: a b c d e f g h i j k l m n o p q r s t u v w x y z more
Browse members by country

Figure 7.37: Uncovering a hidden profile while logged-out if LinkedIn

You will get a set of results where you should be able to locate your desired potential candidate.

We can see Anabel in the very first position (*see figure 7.38*). When you open Anabel's LinkedIn profile by clicking on her name (not using the *View Full Profile* button), you will see her full profile in the same way as using X-Ray search while being logged-out of LinkedIn®.

This search can be used for any name search, when you are in the situation that you know the name of the desired person but they are a 3rd degree connection or out of your network. So as you can see, it is beneficial to use LinkedIn externally in some cases.

There are some other ways to determine the full name and complete profile of a user, such as using the *Viewers of this profile also viewed...* section or upgrading to the premium account. But none of them are as effective in terms of time and money as the ones I have described here.

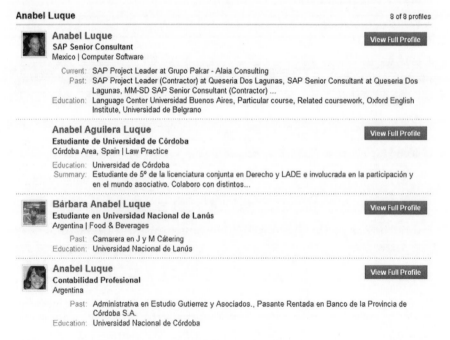

Figure 7.38: Uncovering a hidden profile while logged out of LinkedIn

The LinkedIn Honeypot

You should watch which methods your competitors use and how they structure messages. To realize this you need to create a 'honeypot'. Such a LinkedIn® honeypot is basically a fake profile from your recruitment field which you create to attract other recruiters. Such a profile starts to be bombarded by messages and invitations from recruiters which you need to analyze. You can also find new openings or hiring companies in your sector.

You can find out many facts, for example:

- What communication methods recruiters use – invitation, messages, InMail, e-mail, phone, etc.

- How many recruiters use more than one communication option

- The structure of people contacting you related to the job opportunity – headhunters, managers, colleagues from the same industry, venture capitalists, etc.

- Discover where recruiters are located

- How patiently they compose job proposals and which companies do this best

- Discover new companies and vacancies on the market you might not know about

- Companies can make sure that contracted recruiters keep to no poaching restrictions and are not contacting employees for the prohibited time period; or if they are not contacting company employees at all, which creates a conflict of interest. There is usually a fine for such behavior in recruitment contracts

- As a boss, you can check your subordinate recruiters to see if they are doing their jobs properly.

This method is useful also for the recruitment of HR personnel themselves. You can find talented niche recruiters with unorthodox methods.

Because creating a LinkedIn account for a non-existing person might be considered as an action against the LinkedIn User Agreement, leading to suspension of such an account and potentially also other accounts, I recommend using a TOR Browser or a proxy server which I described in the chapter *05, Cultivate Your Hunting Ground: LinkedIn® Networking Strategy for Recruiters*, section *Dealing with a Limited Amount of Invitations.*

Chapter Summary

- LinkedIn® Invitation and company e-mail are the most effective ways to contact your potential candidates

- Personalize messages to your candidates every time

- Measure the efficiency of sent messages and e-mails

- Profiles of 3rd degree connections and users out of your network can be uncovered using several methods

- Use the LinkedIn® honeypot to observe job offers of your competitors

08

Plunder at
Your Own Will:
Utilizing Groups
and Companies for
Recruitment

Plunder at Your Own Will: Utilizing Groups and Companies for Recruitment

---

What you will learn in this chapter

- What are the limitations of LinkedIn® Groups and Companies

- How to penetrate foreign LinkedIn® Groups and create your own

- How to utilize LinkedIn® Companies

Taking advantage of LinkedIn groups for recruitment is an advanced school for any human resources professional. On the other hand, if you allocate time to it, you can gain an advantage against your competition.

Firstly, we need to learn some theory. There are two types of LinkedIn groups – private and public. Public groups can be observed without joining them. Private groups, on the other hand, require joining a group to see its content. Joining a LinkedIn® group has to be approved by the owner of the group or one of the group moderators. Each group can have subgroups as well.

Each group has an owner and, optionally, can have managers and moderators. LinkedIn sets relatively strict rules for different parameters related to groups.

Group limits for members:

1. How many parent (main) groups can I own and/or manage at one time? **10 (total).**
2. How many subgroups can I own at one time? **20.**
3. How many groups can I be a member of at one time? **50.** (Once you reach 50, you would need to withdraw from one before you would be able to request to join a new group).
4. How many subgroups can I be a member of at one time? **50.**
5. How many groups can I be a moderator of at one time? **50.**
6. How many people can I follow at one time? **20,000.**

Group limits per main (parent) group:

1. How many owners can a group have? **1.**
2. How many managers can a group have? **10.**
3. How many moderators can be in a given group? **50.**
4. How many members can be in a given group? **20,000** (maximum default). Once your group reaches 20,000 members, you will be notified by LinkedIn that you cannot grow your group further without undertaking their procedure.

Group limits per subgroup:

1. How many subgroups can be created under a given parent group? **20.**
2. How many owners can a subgroup have? **1.**
3. How many managers can a given subgroup have? **10.**
4. How many moderators can a given subgroup have? **50.**

There are two approaches to exploit LinkedIn® groups for recruitment:

- Penetrating foreign groups
- Creation of your own groups.

Penetrating Foreign Groups

As you can see from the group limitations, you can join up to fifty groups at maximum. No matter how big this number sounds to you, it is not. You have to think of which groups you will join. You can join a group temporarily because there is also an option that allows you to leave a group (group menu: *More... -> Your Settings -> Leave Group*).

The main reasons you should join groups are:

- To create another resource for your potential candidates
- To reach them more easily.

Joining Niche Groups

For example, let's say you recruit SAP professionals. In this case, you are interested in joining groups with SAP as a topic. You can locate such groups by typing the term SAP into the group search field, which will provide you with suggestions (*see figure 8.1*).

As you can see, there are several strong groups with tens of thousands and hundred of thousands of members, including:

SAP Community (182,630 members)
SAP Career Opportunities Group (45,491 members)
SAP Professionals (Globally) (45,444 members)
SAP People (9000+ Member) (23,710 members)
SAP Functional Consultants (30,041 members)

And this is just the tip of the iceberg.

Do not be driven only by the overall number of group members. Of course, 182,630 members sounds attractive. However, some niche groups can have just hundreds of members when they are limited by some region and can be as effective as the listed 'monster' groups.

Let's say you are interested in SAP professionals from Belgium. You type *SAP Belgium* into the group search field and, once you exclude global groups, get the following shortlist:

SAP Belgium (1,311 members)
Belgium SAP Community – Hosted by www.eursap.eu (859 members)
Benelux SAP Community - Hosted by www.eursap.eu (5,060 members)
SAP Opportunities in Belgium (298 members)
New SAP Freelancers Belgium (237 members)

Figure 8.1: Seeking LinkedIn groups by keywords

Utilizing these groups for recruitment purposes is usually even more effective because your audience is better targeted, also in terms of geographical location, than mainstream groups which are usually global.

Other examples of global industry specific groups are:

Electronic Entertainment Industry Network (9,720 members)
TopLinked IT (Information Technology) Professionals (6,730 members)
Java Developers (144,840 members)
.NET Developers (155,910 members)
eMarketing Association Network (499,930 members)
Social Media Marketing (539,260 members)
The Project Manager Network - #1 Group for Project Managers

(401,120 members)
Project Manager Community – Best Group for Project Management
(162,270 members)
CXO (CEO, COO, CKO, CFO, CMO, CAO, CVO, CDO, CRO, CLO, CSO & CTO) Community (92,340 members)
Digital Marketing (296,170 members)
Retail Industry Professionals Group (240,990 members)
Oil and Gas People (225,920 members)
Banking Careers (225,560 members)
Information Security Community (155,530 members)
Telecom Executives Business Network (152,350 members)
Biotech & Pharma Professionals Network (97,410 members)
Etc.

Joining Company Groups

One way to locate and approach employees of the companies you are used to sourcing, might be via their company groups.

For instance:

IBM Official Alumni Group: The Greater IBM Connection
(79,000 members)
IBM co/ex workers independent group (31,420 members)
PepsiCo Alumni & Employees (3,000+ members) (18,100 members)
PepsiCo Employees and Alumni (7,240 members)
PepsiCo Türkiye (2,750 members)
Dell Alumni (19,900 members)
Shell Network (8,200 members)

Sometimes you might have a problem to join these alumni groups if you have not worked for the particular company. It is up to your moral standards if you want to cheat this. However, technically it is not a problem to add a relevant title to your LinkedIn profile history until your request to join is accepted. Then you can erase such a title from your LinkedIn profile.

Company groups are a powerful way to contact employees of a particular company if you do not like other methods, such as using their company e-mail.

As you already know, you are allowed to send a LinkedIn message to any other member of a group you are a member of, regardless if these people are your 2nd or even 3rd degree connections. How to do this was described in the chapter *07, Shoot to Kill: How to Reach Candidates with LinkedIn® Every Time.*

This is why it is beneficial to join LinkedIn groups where you can expect to find your target group, rather than join various HR and recruitment groups where you can expect to find your colleagues or competition. This way, you have a great chance to contact a significant amount of potential candidates who are group members. You can filter them easily with the *Relationship* filter in LinkedIn® Advanced People Search (*see figure 8.2*).

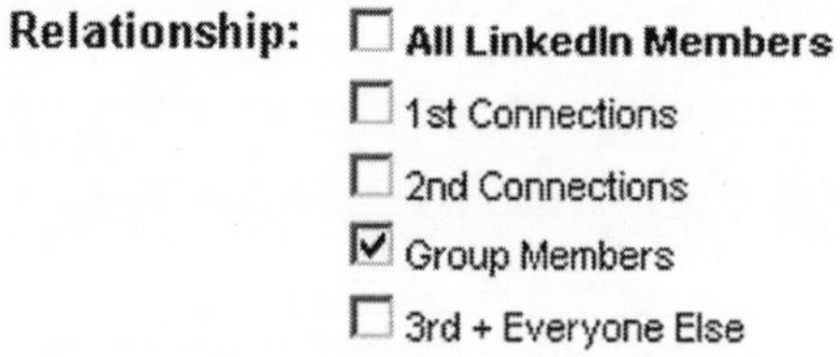

Relationship: ☐ **All LinkedIn Members**
☐ 1st Connections
☐ 2nd Connections
☑ Group Members
☐ 3rd + Everyone Else

Figure 8.2: Filtering group members from search results

Results filtered in this way can be contacted via LinkedIn message without exceptions. The more quality groups in relation to your target group you join, the more often you will be able to contact these people with a LinkedIn® message.

If your results filtered by *Group Members* reach the maximum LinkedIn users you can display (one hundred for a basic account, more for premium ones), you can break down the search by selecting only a particular group with the *Groups* filter (*see figure 8.3*). As a LinkedIn basic user you can select just one group. If you want to search across more groups, you need to upgrade to premium. In any case, this feature is not a feature you would consider purchasing a premium account for.

If you recruit Java professionals, you will join groups focused on Java. If you recruit managers, you will join groups for managers, leaders and C-level management. But do not forget to join regional specific groups which usually have a lot of members. These include groups like:

Germany Business and Professional Network (12,750 members)
Belgium Business and Professional Network (3,340 members)
Czech & Slovak Professional Community (8,720 members)

The Prague Networking Group (3,860 members)
Canada Business and Professional Network (6,160 members)
Etc.

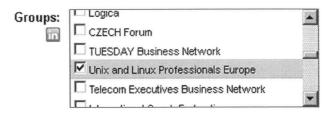

Figure 8.3: Group filter

You can also expect potential candidates in regional jobs related groups such as:

Job Openings, Job Leads and Job Connections! and its subgroups (1,177,500 members)
JOBS 2.0: Job Search Career Networking Staffing and its subgroups (170,890 members)
India Jobs Network (82,770 members)
Professionals, Jobs & Career in India (33,000 members)
Jobs in Moscow / Работа в Москве – Russia (7,700 members)
Etc.

Take into account also general groups for open networkers:

TopLinked.com (Open Networkers) (136,560 members)
LION500.com (Open Networkers) (60,000 members)
Leading International Open Networkers (LION) (25,010 members)
Singapore Open Networkers (7,000 members)
LIONs (Open Networkers) (5,720 members)
Top Connected Open Networkers – ONA (5,000 members)
ONA ~ Open Networkers Alliance (5,000 members)
OPEN NETWORKERS! (3,710 members)
Etc.

I suggest avoiding groups which are not relevant to your target groups of potential candidates. But what if you want to join groups where you could gather more information, tips and cooperate with your peers? You can give up a few groups for this purpose or you can use another LinkedIn® account for this. Consider if you need to be part of any recruitment groups at all. The reason that you are a recruiter is not justifiable in this case. You might benefit from them or you might not.

Examples of such groups are:

Linked:HR (#1 Human Resources Group) (783,780 members)
The Recruiter Network - #1 Group for Recruiters (418,080 members)
Finance and Accounting Recruiter Group (32,630 members)
HR & Talent Management Executive (178,870 members)
TopLinked Recruiting Professionals (3,870 members)
E-Recruitment (108,220 members)
EMEA Executive Search (6,860 members)
The Executive Search Group (62,360 members)
IT Recruiters (122,060 members)
Recruiters United (7,060 members)
The Recruitment Network (241,650 members)
Etc.

How to Search Through Groups You Are Not a Member of

Yes. There is a trick which helps you search through groups you are not a member of. Maybe the manager or the owner does not want to approve your request to join, or you simply do not have free slots which you could use to join any other groups.

Firstly, you need to get the ID of the group you want to search in and you are not a member of. Let's say we want to search candidates in the group *DHL Networking Group*.

We find the group via LinkedIn Search and open it. We should see the button *Join Group*. The URL of this site is:

*http://www.linkedin.com/groups?gid=***55791***&mostPopular=&trk=tyah*

The number in bold is the group ID.

Next, we proceed with the LinkedIn Advanced People Search which we would like to apply to the group (*see figure 8.4*).

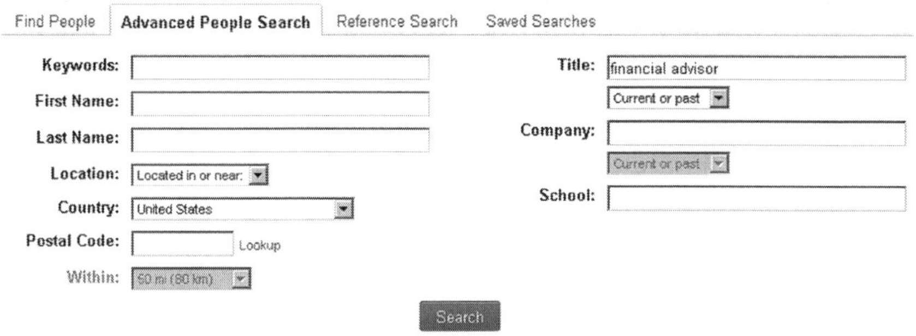

Figure 8.4: LinkedIn Advanced People Search

When you hit *Search*, you will get some results; mainly you can expand the *Groups* filter (*see figure 8.5*).

Figure 8.5: LinkedIn Group filter

In the *Groups* filter can be only groups you are a member of. Our goal is to get the group *DHL Networking Group* on this list. Firstly, click onto any of the groups. The page URL should change.

We should see a URL like the following:

http://www.linkedin.com/search/fpsearch?title=financial+advisor&current Title=CP&searchLocationType=I&countryCode=us&keepFacets=keepFac ets&page_num=1&pplSearchOrigin=ADVS&viewCriteria=2&sortCrite

293

*ria=R&redir=redir#facets=keywords%3D%26search%3DSearch%2520
Search%26fname%3D%26lname%3D%26title%3Dfinancial%2520a
dvisor%26company%3D%26school%3D%26postalCode%3D%26com
panyId%3D%26facetsOrder%3DCC%252CN%252CI%252CPC%2
52CED%252CL%252CFG%252CTE%252CFA%252CSE%252CP
%252CCS%252CF%252CDR%252CG%26inNetworkSearch%3Dfal
se%26pplSearchOrigin%3DFCTD%26currentTitle%3DCP%26search
LocationType%3DI%26countryCode%3Dus%26keepFacets%3Dtrue%
26facet_FG%3D**1976445**%26openFacets%3DCC%252CN%252CI
%252CFG*

I bolded the part you need to substitute with the group ID of *DHL
Networking Group* you gathered earlier.

Once you hit enter, you should have group *DHL Networking Group*
in the group filter (*see figure 8.6*).

☐ All LinkedIn Members
☐ Job Openings, Job... (1710)
☐ Linked:HR (#1 Human... (1321)
☐ Executive Suite (1186)
☐ The Recruiter Network... (637)
☐ TopLinked.com (Open... (629)
☐ The Project Manager... (357)
☐ The Recruitment Network (342)
☐ OpenNetworker.com (259)
☐ LION500.com (Open... (237)
☐ JOBS 2.0: Job Search... (225)
☑ **DHL Networking Group** (7)
   Show less...

[Enter group name]

Figure 8.6: A group added to a group filter using a simple trick

Now we are filtering users of a group we are not a member of.
Mission accomplished! This can be applied to any other group.

Creating Your Own Groups

Joining foreign groups is beneficial but even more powerful is to create and develop your own group. Why? Simply because you set the rules and you have the possibility of sending announcements to all group members. This is what you are not able to do in a foreign group where you can only contact members one by one. However, this is of course very time consuming.

Group announcements provide you with a great chance to supply your potential candidates with updates and offers.

Maybe you ask yourself, what kind of group should I create?

Of course it might be difficult to find some niche which is not covered yet, especially when you consider the global market. But your market is most probably local – one country, one city or one company. So you do not need to create global groups which would be useless to you.

So analyze groups in your region related to your recruitment niche and find out if there are some strong groups like that. Maybe you find some groups with just a few members. These groups you can exclude and not bother with.

If you are recruiting in the accounting industry in Chicago, USA, you could establish e.g. a group called *Accountants Professional Network – Chicago Greater Area.*

Maybe your target groups are *Unix and Linux specialists in France.* Then go ahead and create a group called *Unix & Linux Professionals France.*

You can also try to create local but general groups in terms of focus. It seems like, for example, that the United Kingdom does not have a general networking group. You have a great chance to establish a strong group which can be called, for example, *United Kingdom Professional Community.* These groups have great potential for automatic growth because they have a larger target group but they are not global. The aspect of nationality plays a role in these places.

How to do such research?

The problem with group searches is that results are not sorted by the number of members and there is no option to sort results. I will show you one little trick which can help you target significant groups in terms of the number of members.

Let's take my example with the United Kingdom professional network. Firstly, you can try and type the following expressions into the *Group search*:

United Kingdom network
United Kingdom professionals
Great Britain network
Great Britain professionals

If you do not find any relevant or strong groups on the first three pages of results, use search suggestions to figure out what are the groups with the highest number of members (*see figure 8.7*).

Figure 8.7: LinkedIn Groups suggestions

And try again all mentioned terms through group search suggestions. It is not 100% reliable, but with this method you will usually get groups sorted by members.

Another approach is to set up a group for a company from the industry you recruit in. This is usually already occupied but sometimes you can be lucky. I am, for example, the owner of the group *Acision Network* which is the group representing the international corporation Acision globally. You have to be on the alert to be first. If any world company from your industry established a branch in your region, you should create a group *Company name Country* – e.g. *Exxon Mobile France*.

You can also take advantage of different mergers and acquisitions. Companies change their names, sell divisions, etc. All of these might be utilized for establishing a strong company group.

If you are an internal HR specialist and your company does not have a company group, you'd better create one. You can do the same even if you are a recruitment agency but it does not make sense as with regular companies.

Warning! As the owner of such a group, do not allow other recruiters in! And I guarantee that they will knock on the door. **You did not sweat blood and tears for your competition.**

How to speed up the growth of your groups?

You can expect some pace of automatic growth. But do not expect that you will get hundreds or thousands of members overnight. To reach such incoming members, you need to support such growth.

People usually join groups in two ways. Firstly, they do a search where they try names of a company where they work or worked. Then they try to type in their expertise such as Java, Linux, retail, lean management, etc. and also the country or city where they work or live. The second, and I would say more probable way of joining a group, is via other profiles. For instance, a user looks through their colleague´s profile and sees a list of groups there. Some of them are appealing to them and they join the group.

So, the first factor can be influenced by choosing the right name for the group and description.

The second factor can be influenced by starting a fly wheel of joining members. The more LinkedIn® users that have your group listed in their profile, the more new members you can expect; as well as spreading the group name over updates which appear in the user's profile if any of their contacts connect to the same group.

The only way to grow your group is by sending invitations. You can send invitations by using the option *Send Invitations* in the section *Manage Group*. You can send invitations to your 1st degree connections or to anybody else by entering their e-mail (or pre-prepared list of e-mails).

Using the first method is limited by fifty 1st degree connections even if it can be done repeatedly. It can take some time till you send invitations to all of your direct connections.

The second way is more powerful. You can use output from the chapter *07, Shoot to Kill: How to Reach Candidates with LinkedIn® Every Time* and prepare an e-mail list of LinkedIn users who represent your potential candidates. The easiest way is to prepare e-mail lists by companies which you can source potential candidates from.

Imagine that sending a job offer directly to a company e-mail address might be evaluated as an illegal or at least immoral act but sending invitations to join some expert group is not that invasive. Once an employee accepts your invitation, you are able to contact them using their private e-mail address even if they are not one of your 1st degree connections.

So you can use groups as another way to attract potential candidates to your network. If somebody did not accept your regular LinkedIn invitation, maybe they will accept an invitation to join your group.

Groups will expand your circle of potential candidates. You would not believe how many people join some expert group, but do not state the keyword for their expertise in their LinkedIn profile. We can do a test with the group *.NET Developers* which has almost one hundred and sixty thousand members.

Let's prepare the following search. We are going for LinkedIn® users who are in this group which assumes that they are .NET professionals, but they do not state the keyword *.NET* anywhere in their profile (*see figure 8.8*).

You can also use X-Ray search to locate LinkedIn users based on the name of the group they are members of. There is one trick which is actually working and which takes advantage of the fact that if you are a member of some group, its name will appear in the source code as *logo • group name* for Google.

This can be utilized using the following command:

inurl:www.linkedin.com **"logo * Mobile Wireless Jobs"** *(inurl:in | inurl:pub) -inurl:dir*

This will provide us with links to LinkedIn® profiles of *Mobile Wireless Jobs* group members (*see figure 8.9*).

Figure 8.8: .NET Developers group members not stating .NET on their profiles

Filter potential candidates from your target group and you can consider and contact them right away.

LinkedIn® Companies

LinkedIn Companies was launched long after LinkedIn® groups started. It is a LinkedIn sub-site where a company can publish their company description, job vacancies and also products.

LinkedIn users can follow these companies when they are linked to such a sub-site and are informed about the latest updates on their LinkedIn homepage.

As a recruiter, you should follow your company clients and also other companies from your industry and area as you proceed with recruitment activities to stay updated about actual events, including who has been recently hired and fired. From this information, you are also able to determine what is happening on the market. There is nothing more to be gained from the *LinkedIn® Companies* you do not own.

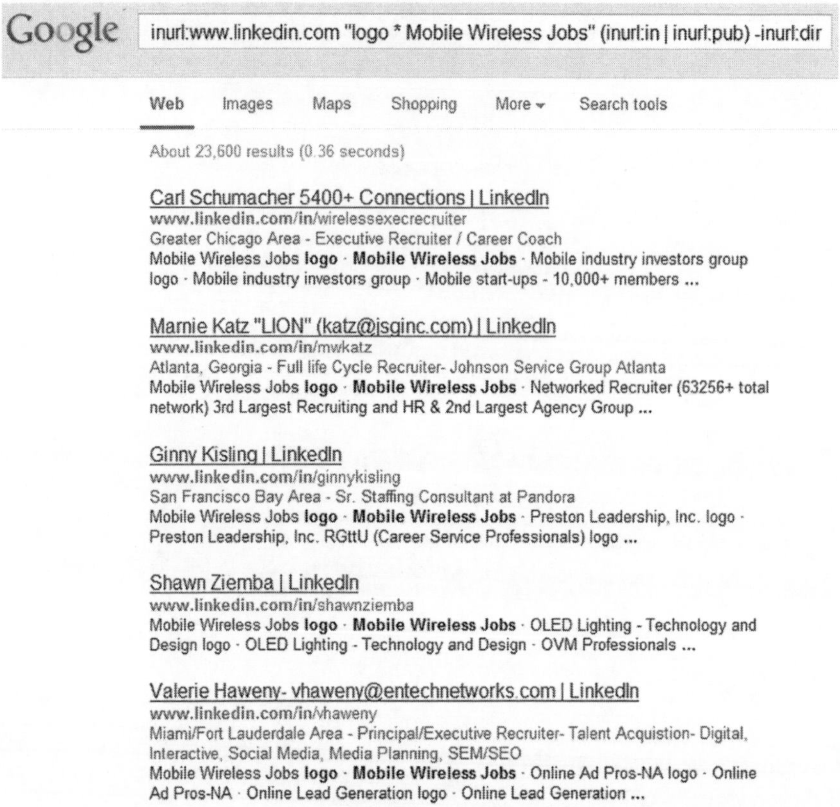

Figure 8.9: Using an X-Ray Search for targeting LinkedIn groups

You can also create your own company page. It might be the page of your recruitment agency, if you are the owner, or of your employer, if they do not have one yet. If you are an internal HR professional and your company does not have a company page, you should establish one as soon as possible; before somebody else does it.

If there are companies which you use as a resource of candidates and they do not have a LinkedIn company page, you can speculate on that and create one. You will quickly attract former and past employees of this company to follow this page and you can easily reach them with updates you compose.

The companies with the most followers include:

Hewlett-Packard – around 940,000 followers
IBM – around 870,000 followers

Google – around 760,000 followers
Microsoft – around 700,000 followers
Accenture – around 666,000 followers
Oracle – around 490,000 followers
Apple – around 473,000 followers
Deloitte – around 493,000 followers
Dell – around 383,000 followers
Cisco Systems – around 362,000 followers

Apply with LinkedIn® Button

Another useful feature connected with LinkedIn Companies is the *Apply with LinkedIn* button (*see figure 8.10*). This button can be placed on your website and creates another way for candidates to apply for a job at your company.

Figure 8.10: Apply with LinkedIn button

You can create this button from scratch and place it on your website and you will receive a candidate's CV by e-mail. Or, you can have this button integrated with the ATS you are working with at your company. Currently LinkedIn® supports:

SmartRecruiters
Bullhorn
Jobvite
PeopleFluent
JobScience

A step-by-step guide about how to set up an *Apply with LinkedIn* button can be found at:

https://developer.linkedin.com/apply-linkedin

Chapter Summary

▪ Join as many relevant groups as you can

▪ Try to establish your niche group and start the growth of its members

▪ Users who share the same group with you might be contacted via message, even if they are not one of your 1st degree connections

▪ Avoid joining recruitment groups and rather join industry-specific groups where you can meet your potential candidates

▪ You can contact all members of your groups in bulk via group announcements

----

09

Toolkit of No Effect: LinkedIn® Features You Hardly Use

09

Toolkit of No Effect: LinkedIn® Features You Hardly Use

What you will learn in this chapter

- Which LinkedIn® features are difficult to take advantage of

- LinkedIn® Applications you have to substitute with new rich media

- How to integrate LinkedIn® with corporate e-mail systems

There are some features and tools in LinkedIn® which might look useful, but from my experience, they are not so. It does not mean that there is no purpose for them, but they do not show substantial benefit for recruitment activities. It is far better to spend time on other techniques which can provide you with more results.

Maybe some of you found an effective way to produce quality results from the following features. Maybe they cannot be used in general and work just for your niche. If so, let me know and I will publish your methods on my website or in the revised edition of this book.

LinkedIn® Answers

LinkedIn Answers is a feature accessible via the *More* item in the main LinkedIn menu. It basically works on the basis of questions and answers *(see figure: 9.1).*

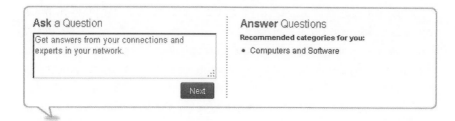

Figure 9.1: LinkedIn Answers

Based on your activity in terms of how many questions you answered, you move up and down on the scoreboard. The most active users are awarded as top experts in a specific category such as Technology, Career and Education, Finance and Accounting, Using LinkedIn, Marketing and Sales and others. The overall best contributors are listed in the *This Week's Top Expert* leaderboard (*see figure 9.2*).

This Week's Top Experts

Experts	Answers (This Week)
1. Human Resource Associate **Brijendra Chaudhary** (2nd) - see all my answers ★ Best Answers in: Using LinkedIn (345), Customer Service (14), Staffing and Recruiting (12), ...	556
2. Marketer, Social Media Marketer, Email Marketer, Marketing Coach, Marketing Trainer, Marketing Mentor, Entrepreneur **Christine Hueber** (2nd) - see all my answers ★ Best Answers in: Using LinkedIn (428), Customer Service (19), Business Development (19), ...	474
3. Facebook Marketing with 1,500,000 Fans **William T. Cooper** (2nd) - see all my answers ★ Best Answers in: Using LinkedIn (126), Customer Service (8), Advertising (5), ...	384
4. New Media Producer, i3D Programming, Acrobat i3D, Android Apps Design, Virtual World Design, GoogleTV, i3D eBooks, UI/UX **Wallace Jackson** (2nd) - see all my answers ★ Best Answers in: Using LinkedIn (176), Computers and Software (40), Web Development (25), ...	325
5. Executive Director at Rebounders United **Charles Caro** (2nd) - see all my answers ★ Best Answers in: Using LinkedIn (732), Customer Service (20), Staffing and Recruiting (20), ...	278

How do I earn expertise?   more top experts »

Figure 9.2: This Week's Top Experts leaderboard

Many sources claim that this feature is one of the best ways to boost your visibility; which is probably true in some way. But is it true for you as a recruiter? I can guarantee you that potential candidates are not interested in browsing categories on human resources, careers and recruitment.

If I were using this feature as a recruiter, I would try to be considered as an expert in the categories which are closest to my recruitment niche. In my case it would probably be Technology. There, I have a great chance to be seen by some of my potential candidates.

A similar effect can be achieved by answering questions in LinkedIn groups which you are a member of.

However, this feature is really just an additional feature where you would need to invest your time and effort. You will become more effective spending your time somewhere else.

LinkedIn® Updates

LinkedIn Updates is a great tool when you need to spread the word among your connections – 1st degree connections preferably. We assume that your connections are mostly your candidates and potential candidates. So you have a chance to let them know that you are active and recruiting. This can strengthen your name as a recruiter among your connection base.

The problem is that LinkedIn is an information-based platform, so users do not spend a significant amount of time on LinkedIn itself. They are more likely to receive messages which they are notified about at their e-mail address. Or, they check particular LinkedIn profiles of their peers and other people. However, time spent on the LinkedIn® homepage is not substantial.

LinkedIn provides you with the possibility of sending updates to your 1st degree connections only. Or you can allow the appearance of posts on the homepage of your 2nd and 3rd degree connections on the condition that a post was liked or commented on by a 1st degree connection. This post will also appear on your profile in the *Activity* section in both cases.

If you use Twitter, you can also set up the sending of such updates to a defined Twitter account (*see figure 9.3*).

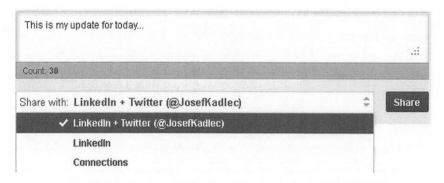

Figure 9.3: Linking a LinkedIn account updated by Twitter

If you want to earn something from this feature, I recommend to start using some social network aggregator which allows you to send updates to several social networks; and, not only to send but also to schedule future updates or uploading updates in bulk. Therefore, you can make a larger impact with minimal effort.

One of the services which enables this is *HootSuite* (*www.hootsuite.com*). Without using this kind of service you would be forced to set a weekly regime to post these updates.

LinkedIn® Applications

I already described the situation with *LinkedIn® Applications* in the chapter *04, Prepare Your Arsenal: How to Fine-Tune Your LinkedIn® Profile for Recruitment.*

However, there is also a place where you can find unofficial LinkedIn applications created by LinkedIn employees. It is called *LinkedIn Labs* and it is reachable at:

http://www.linkedinlabs.com

These applications have not been affected by the LinkedIn applications update.

There is no application which you could directly use for recruitment activities but there are a few which might be interesting for recruiters (*see figure 9.4*).

Year in Review
November 2010 Hackday Winner

The most popular email in LinkedIn history. A visual representation of everyone in your network who changed jobs in a given year.
http://www.linkedinlabs.com/yearinreview

Connection Timeline
Hackday Winner, April 2011

View your connections across the timeline of your career.
http://www.linkedinlabs.com/timeline

Resume Builder
Hackday Winner, March 2010

Build, save & share beautifully formatted resumes based on your LinkedIn profile.
http://www.linkedinlabs.com/resumebuilder

NewIn
"Pure Energy" Hackday Winner, December 2007

This application shows new members joining LinkedIn from around the world. (requires Google Earth)
http://www.linkedinlabs.com/newin

Figure 9.4: LinkedIn Labs applications

LinkedIn® Toolbar

There is also *LinkedIn® Toolbar* which you can install to your FireFox browser or Internet Explorer (*see figure 9.5*).

With this toolbar, you can quickly share websites in LinkedIn updates. It provides you with shortcuts to various LinkedIn sections including Advanced People Search, LinkedIn Jobs, Your LinkedIn profile, etc.

It is up to you if you want to be using this toolbar to make your work easier. I am used to using the LinkedIn website directly and because the toolbar does not provide me with any significant improvement, I am not motivated to use it.

If I were a job seeker, I would use *LinkedIn JobsInsider* to find vacancies based on a typed keyword.

There is also *Outlook Social Connector* which integrated LinkedIn into MS Outlook and, similarly, there is a solution for Lotus Notes called *Lotus Notes Widget.*

You can also integrate the function *Share on LinkedIn* to your browser (Google Chrome, Safari or Internet Explorer) which enables you to share content in your LinkedIn profile even if you are not logged into LinkedIn.

In addition, you can optimize your Google Toolbar by installing *Google Toolbar Assistant* which adds the LinkedIn® search button to the Google Toolbar.

Figure 9.5: LinkedIn Toolbar

Information about these extensions is available at:

http://www.linkedin.com/static?key=tools

LinkedIn® Mobile

There is an application available for your smart phone – iPhone, Android, BlackBerry and Palm. You can manage some basic operations such as posting updates, basic people searching, managing your inbox and accepting invitations.

Figure 9.6: LinkedIn mobile application

There aren't many functions which you could effectively use for regular recrutment, though it is a nice application.

Chapter Summary

- Link Twitter with your LinkedIn® account

- If you are used to using MS Outlook or Lotus Notes, install Outlook Social Connector and Lotus Notes Widget

- Substitute LinkedIn® Applications with new rich media and polish your LinkedIn® profile

----

10

Arsenal Upgrade: Pros and Cons of LinkedIn® Paid Services

Arsenal Upgrade: Pros and Cons of LinkedIn® Paid Services

What you will learn in this chapter

- How the LinkedIn® Corporation structures its paid services

- Which paid features are the most important

- When it pays to upgrade to LinkedIn® paid services

I have shown you many ways to use LinkedIn® for recruitment without paying a dime. With all these tricks and methods you are not forced to purchase any of the LinkedIn premium services. However, if you have the opportunity to purchase any of the LinkedIn paid services, they might bring you some benefits.

Upgrading to a premium account might bring you a higher level of comfort at least. And it is practically the only thing you can get from it. I have described ways to overtake limitations which you face when using the basic account e.g., number of displayable users in people search, number of saved searches, etc.

The increase in user-friendly behavior when upgrading to premium has a lower impact on your recruitment results than it looks or is presented by LinkedIn. Having user-friendly and comfortable facilities without limitations has an impact on your recruitment performance to some extent. For example, the possibility to display five hundred LinkedIn users in people search results will save you some time if you are used to getting significantly more than a thousand results. The question of ROI (Return On Investment) depends strictly on:

- **vacancies volume**
- **recruitment commission**
- **HR budget.**

It is simple math. If you have many openings to be filled, time is running against you, so saving some of it by upgrading to premium is reasonable. Next, as a recruitment agency, you are able to easily fund the overheads for premium services when you have many vacancies, which bring you more revenue.

On the other hand, when you don´t have so many openings or just occasional ones, you will probably decide not to upgrade to LinkedIn® premium.

To help you decide if or when it is reasonable for you to use any of the LinkedIn paid services for recruiters, I have described all of them from the point of view of a recruiter, focusing strictly on advantages and disadvantages. **Do not expect any marketing hype from me, as I am not affiliated with LinkedIn at all.**

LinkedIn paid services include:

- **Premium Accounts for Recruiters**

- **LinkedIn Recruiter**

- **LinkedIn Career Pages**

- **LinkedIn Talent Brand Index**

- **LinkedIn Jobs**

- **LinkedIn Ads, Recruitment Ads and Work with Us**

- **LinkedIn Talent Direct.**

Premium Accounts for Recruiters

As a basic (i.e. non-paid) LinkedIn account you have the possibility to upgrade to a premium (i.e. paid) account. Determining which account type you currently have is clear from the information in the top left corner of your screen (*see figure 10.1*).

Linked in ® Account Type: Basic | Upgrade

Figure 10.1: Account Type indicator

There are three categories of premium accounts, including:

- For Recruiters

- For Job Seekers

- For Sales Professionals.

We are interested in the first one obviously. At the time of writing this book there are three levels of account: *Talent Basic, Talent Finder* and *Talent Pro*. These accounts vary based on specific parameters (number of InMails, number of candidates you can search, the names of 3rd degree connections you can see, etc.).

These parameters might be different when you are reading this book, as well as their pricing. Therefore, I will briefly describe each of the parameters and state if it makes sense to upgrade or not.

Contact anyone directly with InMail®

This feature allows you to send a number of InMails. Currently the number varies from ten to fifty based on the specific profile. Anyway, this feature is not a good reason to upgrade to any of the premium accounts. As I described in the chapter *07, Shoot to Kill: How to Reach Candidates with LinkedIn® Every Time*, InMails are pretty ineffective for recruitment purposes.

Pinpoint candidates with advanced search filters

This feature allows you to access the premium filters available in Advanced People Search. With a basic non-paid LinkedIn® account you can see these filters shadowed and not available to you. They include filters like *Seniority, Company Size, Function, Interests,* etc. Based on the specific premium account, it will allow you a different number of filters. This feature itself isn't a good reason to upgrade either. You will not utilize these filters to improve your recruitment results.

See more candidates when you search

This feature will increase the number of users in results from one hundred to a higher number. At the moment to five hundred, six hundred or one thousand based on the specific premium account.

This feature is one of a few **good reasons** to upgrade to premium. When you use LinkedIn People search and get loads of results breaking the one hundred user limitation, you have to make your searches less general or use X-Ray Search to override this limitation. Or you can upgrade and get up to one thousand results which brings you to a higher level of comfort. Even seven hundred is enough, so it is not necessary to upgrade to a *Talent Pro* premium account, which is the most expensive.

Search for top talent within your groups

This feature allows you to filter candidates who are members of defined groups. With a non-paid account you are able to only filter candidates belonging to a single group. By upgrading you can define more than one group. This feature is not a good reason to upgrade. Even if you use filtration by groups, doing it one group at a time is not that big a handicap.

Manage your candidates with Profile Organizer

LinkedIn allows you to save candidates' LinkedIn profiles and organize them into a number of folders which you can define on your own. This number currently varies from twenty five to seventy five, based on the specific premium account.

The problem is that when you start using this system, you are dependent on LinkedIn forever because downgrading to a non-paid account will disable this functionality. So it is better to arrange another system to organize your candidates, such as ATS or at least a database or spreadsheet you are comfortable with.

See full profiles of anyone in your network

This feature allows you to display the full profile of anyone in your network. As I showed you how to easily uncover the full profile of anyone in your network, you should not upgrade just because of this. The benefit of upgrading depends on how established your LinkedIn®

profile is.

If you do not have enough high quality connections and there are still many candidates as 3rd degree connections and out of your network, you will benefit more from such an upgrade than someone with a well-rounded LinkedIn profile.

Take into account that with the premium account *Talent Basic,* you can see the full profile of anyone in your network, excluding the full name for 3rd degree connections and group members.

Open up to active candidates – allow people outside your network to contact you free with OpenLink

This feature allows anyone on LinkedIn® to contact you via InMail® without being a premium user. This is useless for you as a recruiter because you will be contacting LinkedIn users, not your candidates contacting you.

On top of this, if your LinkedIn profile becomes well penetrated into the LinkedIn network and you have many contacts, including power users such as other open networkers, you can state contact information in your profile which allows anybody to contact you without any problems.

See names of your 3rd degree and Group connections

This feature allows you to see the full name of your 3rd degree connections and group connections (i.e. connections sharing the same LinkedIn groups as you).

I showed you a few ways to easily uncover these hidden names, so this feature brings you just an insignificant conformity. Take into account that currently the full name visibility is available only for *Talent Finder* and *Talent Pro*, not for *Talent Basic.*

Who's Viewed Your Profile: Get the full list

This will allow you to see the complete list of who has viewed your profile. For a recruiter this is not an interesting feature you should go for.

Let us bring you candidates with saved search alerts

This feature increases the number of *LinkedIn® Saved Searches* from three, up to fifteen, when you upgrade to the highest premium account. I would say that this feature is, with the number of candidates you can display in search results, one of the most important reasons which could force you to upgrade to one of the premium accounts.

I described Saved Search Alerts in the chapter *06, Chase Down Your Targets: How to Target Candidates with LinkedIn®* and other ways to substitute this LinkedIn feature. Using this genuine LinkedIn Saves Search Alerts is the most user-friendly way.

Take into account that to receive alerts on a daily basis, you need to upgrade at least to a *Talent Finder* premium account. With *Talent Basic* you will get only weekly alerts, which are less effective.

Get the real story of any candidate with Reference Search

This feature allows you to see all the connections you share in common with any candidate. Based on this, you can be provided with feedback about specific candidates from people who are connected with you. It depends how you really operate and if such feedback is important to you and if you are not able to gather such feedback from a different source – e.g. searching for a LinkedIn member's coworkers on your own.

Get Priority Customer Service

There is usually nothing you would need to discuss with customer service. Therefore, this is nothing you would benefit from.

Apart from the mentioned features, you can also see the full network statistics of who viewed your profile from which industry, location, etc. This is not an important feature, though.

As you can see, there are only a few features which make premium accounts for recruiters worth considering. They are primarily:

- See more candidates when you search

- Let us bring you candidates with saved search alerts

…and secondly:

- See full profiles of anyone in your network

- See names of your 3rd degree and Group connections.

This does not mean that these features would not be replaceable, but using them will provide you with more comfort and time savings. They make the most sense for recruiters. The other ones are more or less useless.

If you consider upgrading to a recruitment premium account, choose at least a *Talent Finder* account. *Talent Basic* will not provide you with 3rd degree connections' full name visibility and Saved Search Alerts are provided only on a weekly basis.

On the other hand *Talent Pro* might be needlessly expensive for what you get. If you do not need more Saved Search Alerts and the number of displayable candidates in the results, which you usually do not, it is useless to upgrade to *Talent Pro*.

Premium account type	Price (billed annually)
LinkedIn Talent Basic	EUR 29.95
LinkedIn Talent Finder	EUR 59.95
LinkedIn Talent Pro	EUR 299.95

Prices valid for 2013

LinkedIn® Recruiter

LinkedIn Recruiter can be called a VIP interface which will provide you or your team especially with access to all potential candidates which can be found on LinkedIn **regardless of how many connections your personal account has.** *LinkedIn Recruiter* is meant as a service for a company or simply a team where you can add or delete team members from the system.

LinkedIn Recruiter is designed to work with teams. It means that none of the recruiters put into this system can go away with your know-how – i.e. candidates. This system provides them with the possibility to contact any potential candidate on LinkedIn® without any limitations, such as 3rd degree and out of network connections, hidden profiles or not having the possibility to send InMails.

You can also observe the activity and statistics of your team in the *LinkedIn Recruiter* dashboard (*see figure 10.2*).

Once you release any recruiter from your team and ultimately from *LinkedIn Recruiter*, any notes and messages will be preserved in your system. Team members get visibility into their colleagues' projects, notes and communication history. This should avoid any duplication of effort.

This system also offers you fifty Saved Searches Alerts, full name visibility, one thousand profiles per search, Project Folders, tagging candidates and all types of search filters. There are also filters which should boost your team efficiency enabling you to filter candidates who your team members have not InMailed yet.

The best one is also a filter providing you with the possibility of seeking only candidates who follow your company on LinkedIn®. You can expect that the percentage of replies from such candidates will be significantly higher.

LinkedIn Corporation is constantly improving its services so there are new and upgraded features coming all the time.

The price for one license is around 1,600 Euros per month. For three licenses it goes down to 950 Euros per license per month.

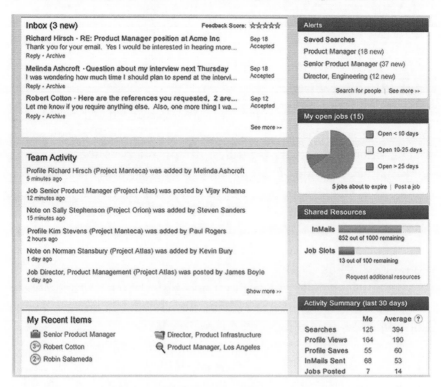

Figure 10.2: LinkedIn Recruiter dashboard

LinkedIn® Career Pages

LinkedIn Career Pages is an upgraded version of *LinkedIn Company Pages.* There are three customizable modules, employee spotlights and job postings targeted to viewer for relevance. You can also add a company culture video, employee benefits, links to additional content and users can contact your recruiters who are published on your website.

This is literally a must have for all corporations and important employers. It emphasizes your brand exceptionally. See the partial screenshot of Google Career Pages (*see figure 10.3*).

Figure 10.3: LinkedIn Career Pages of Google

There are three tiers of *LinkedIn Career Pages – Silver, Gold* and *Platinum.* The main difference among these accounts is in the number of impressions for job ads and number of visitors you can target a page to. On top of this, the Silver account does not guarantee you that only your ads will be displayed on your career page.

The cost of this service is 8,200 to 56,000 Euros annually, based on the particular package.

Career Page type	Price (billed annually)
Silver	EUR 8,200
Gold	EUR 24,000
Platinum	EUR 56,000

Prices valid for 2013

327

LinkedIn® Talent Brand Index

As I already emphasized, recruiters should start to behave more like marketers and company brand ambassadors. Now there is a tool which can help you measure the strength of your brand on LinkedIn.

Find the page of Talent Brand Index at:

http://talent.linkedin.com/talentbrandindex/

LinkedIn® measures several different parameters which you as a user have no access to, and based on this, calculates an index (*see figure 10.4*).

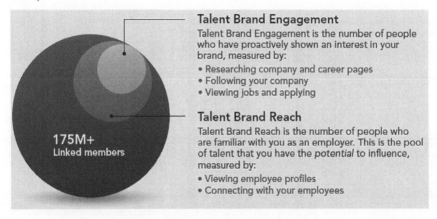

Talent Brand Engagement

Talent Brand Engagement is the number of people who have proactively shown an interest in your brand, measured by:

• Researching company and career pages
• Following your company
• Viewing jobs and applying

Talent Brand Reach

Talent Brand Reach is the number of people who are familiar with you as an employer. This is the pool of talent that you have the *potential* to influence, measured by:

• Viewing employee profiles
• Connecting with your employees

175M+
Linked members

Figure 10.4: LinkedIn Brand Index

The index score is a division of these two variables – *Talent Brand Engagement* and *Talent Brand Reach* (*see figure 10.5*).

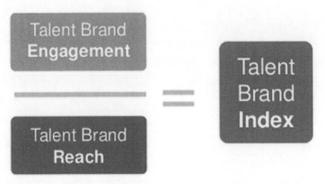

Talent Brand **Engagement**

Talent Brand **Reach**

= **Talent Brand Index**

Figure 10.5: LinkedIn Brand Index

The higher the number is, the higher impact your brand has. This service will allow you to compare this index with your competition or observe the index over certain time periods (*see figure 10.6*).

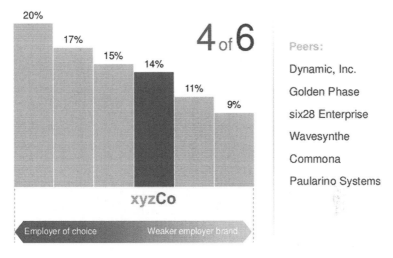

Figure 10.6: LinkedIn Brand Index comparison

LinkedIn® Jobs and Job Slots

Even as a basic LinkedIn user, you have the chance to post jobs. You can find the Jobs section on the LinkedIn main menu (*see figure 10.7*).

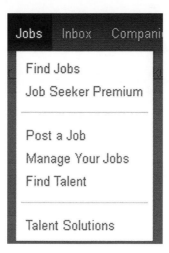

Figure 10.7: Post a LinkedIn Job

This paid service provides you with a possibility to post a job targeted to your region. The problem is that LinkedIn, unlike Facebook, is an information-based service. People do not spend so much time on it. This means that your advertisement is not seen by the necessary amount of users. On the other hand, when you proceed with an active search, users get the job proposal e-mailed to their inbox and have a chance to react to it immediately.

This can change once candidates are used to using LinkedIn jobs as an advertisement job site, like Monster.com. I do not see that happening at the moment, but I believe that it is a potential trend. And with the increasing power of LinkedIn® worldwide, there will be a time when LinkedIn is taken as one of the common job sites which you can open when looking for a job.

Of course, this fact is a little bit volatile based on region and industry. There is a higher chance that people from IT will use this service more often, and also people from countries where there is no strong authority in the job site business.

The price of posting one vacancy for thirty days is around 140 Euros not using discount packages, so you should consider if it is worth using it for your purposes rather than an active search. With a 10-Job Pack you can get it down to 89.50 Euros per job post.

With *Job Slots,* you can renew and change your job posting as you like. LinkedIn job post can also be linked with your internal job site or directly with your ATS. Jobs can also be pulled out of your career website and notifications sent to Twitter automatically.

With *Sponsored Jobs,* you can promote your job posts and get them a higher priority (*see figure 10.8*).

Figure 10.8: Post a LinkedIn Job

LinkedIn® Ads, Recruitment Ads and Work with Us

Like Google, LinkedIn allows you to set up advertisement campaigns. These campaigns are set as pay per click (CPC), or pay per impressions (CPM), which means you pay a set amount for a single click through, or for one thousand impressions (i.e. displays). You can see the ads on the right-hand side of your currently browsed LinkedIn content.

A LinkedIn *Recruitment Ad* can look as a banner placed (usually) on the right-hand side of the LinkedIn® site (*see figure 10.9*). With this ad you can drive candidates directly to your job posts or *LinkedIn Career Page.*

Targeting works on the basis of choosing from a complex filter containing Location, Company, Job Title, School, Skills, Group, Gender and Age. It sounds pretty appealing right?

Figure 10.9: Example LinkedIn recruitment ad

In comparison with the Google advertisement system, which is content related, and you have almost no chance to target based on gender, age or company, *Recruitment Ad* does these things.

With such options, you are able to target even employees of a single company which you are interested in. Or, you can set the advertisement campaign so it is shown only to a certain group of professionals based on their job title. If you want to promote your recruitment services, you can target only HR Managers, HR Directors, etc. Or, if you are a company, you might target employees of your competitor.

Now there is also the chance to set up video ads which are another trendy format you can use to promote yourself (*see figure 10.10*).

Regardless of how attractive it sounds, the problem is the same as with LinkedIn Jobs. LinkedIn® users, your potential candidates, just do not spend enough time on LinkedIn, so they are slightly influenced by these ads.

With these features, we are going deeper into the online marketing area, which is not the primary focus of this book. I focus just on recruitment, so I would conclude this by saying that for recruitment purposes, this is not an effective function at the moment. It is better for sales and general marketing purposes.

Work with Us is a special recruitment ad which will appear on all of your employees' profiles.

Figure 10.10: LinkedIn video ad

LinkedIn® Talent Direct

Talent Direct is a LinkedIn paid service which works on an InMail campaign basis. You select criteria to target your potential candidates based on title, seniority, region, etc. Then you craft a message which is sent to your audience as an InMail and appears on the top of their homepage. Based on this, you will acquire a talent pipeline which you can use for current or future job opportunities.

Chapter Summary

- *See more candidates when you search* and *Saved Search Alerts* are the most powerful features of LinkedIn® premium accounts

- Consider the cost of each LinkedIn® paid service according to your recruitment volume and solvency

- You can be a top LinkedIn® recruiter even without paying a penny

----

11

Where to Go for Further, Up-to-Date Information

Where to Go for Further, Up-to-Date Information

I described the personnel industry as a bit of a nasty business. Some of the explained techniques are in alignment with that, but I believe that it is not in our nature to be nasty. Of course, we need to be forceful sometimes but **helping other people is above business, everytime**. Otherwise, I would not be writing this book, nor donating to cancer research.

I crafted this book with the intention to make it popular and make loads of money. No questions about it. But the main reason I am doing this is to imagine the happy faces of you, my readers, while **reading through your feedback and success stories**.

That is why I want to share all my information and experience with social recruitment, LinkedIn especially, which I have been gathering for years. It is not because I have lost my competitiveness and shared my success formula so that anybody can read it. Not at all! On the contrary, revealing all information is my new weapon to stay on top.

Because some information unleashed in this book might be outdated to some extent, as time goes by, I have established **a LinkedIn® recruitment academy, LINREA.com**, where all readers can stay up-to-date. What's more, there you will find many helpful tools referenced in this book, a forum to connect with the social recruitment community and also a blog to see what is happening.

Therefore, do not hesitate and subscribe directly at:

www.PeopleAsMerchandise.com

or

www.LINREA.com

Visit *www.LINREA.com*, use the code *People as Merchandise* and obtain your bonus now!

About the Author

Josef Kadlec MSc, belongs among the first LinkedIn recruiters in Europe, the very first in the Czech Republic. His career path is logical but unexpected. He studied *Software Engineering* at the *Faculty of Nuclear Sciences and Physical Engineering* in Prague, and also earned his masters degree in Information Management. Right after his university studies he started to work for an international IT corporation as a software engineer.

That was also the moment of realization, his 'aha moment'. Why was such a corporation not able to hire to full capacity even though they had contracts with tens of staffing agencies? Why was he able to find those people and recruit them in a similar way, like he was hired by a regular personnel agency? He thought that he was capable, so he accepted the challenge and founded his own personnel agency, Jobs Consulting.

His analytical approach was completely different to all of the other personnel agencies, and was a great success. What's more, the competitive recruitment agencies adopted his progressive procedures to support their own success. His years of experience with direct recruitment have promoted him to the role of a leading world expert on LinkedIn recruitment.

His current life avenue is helping other recruiters and companies take advantage of LinkedIn and other social marketing tools. For this purpose, he established a LinkedIn® recruitment academy, LINREA.com. It is important to mention that he has never worked for the LinkedIn Corporation and he is not affiliated with them in any manner. He is also the founder and CEO of the training agency Trump Executives, which provides blue chip companies with management, business and communication training of top-notch quality.

Josef can be easily reached via his LinkedIn® profile:

www.linkedin.com/in/josefkadlec